Torn Out by the Roots

The Recollections of a Former Communist

By Hilda Vitzthum

Translated & with an introduction & notes

By Paul Schach

University of Nebraska Press: Lincoln & London

© 1993 by the
    University of Nebraska Press
All rights reserved
    Manufactured in the United
States of America
    Originally published by Ernst
Vögel, Munich,
    as *Mit der Wurzel ausrotten:
Erinnerungen einer
    ehemaligen Kommunistin*,
copyright © 1984 by
    Forschungsinstitut für sowjet-
ische Gegenwart

    Library of Congress Catalog-
ing in Publication Data
    Vitzthum, Hilda, 1902–
[Mit der Wurzel ausrotten. English]
    Torn out by the roots:
the recollections of a former Com-
    munist / by Hilda
Vitzthum; translated and with an
    introduction
and notes by Paul Schach.   p. cm.
    ISBN 0-8032-4660-9 (cloth:
acid-free paper)
    1. Vitzthum, Hilda, 1902–.
2. Women communists – Austria –
    Biography. 3. Women
political prisoners – Soviet Union –
    Biography.
I. Schach, Paul. II. Title.
    HX254.7.V58A313 1993
    324.2436′075′092—dc20 [B]
    92-23837 CIP

Contents

Born in the subalpine district of Hausruck near the city of Salzburg in 1902, Hilda Vitzthum experienced the repercussions of the military collapse and the consequent dissolution of the Austro-Hungarian empire following World War I. It was a time, as Hilda characterized it so pregnantly in the first sentence of her autobiography, "that was fraught with the coming convulsions of the century." The Dual or Hapsburg Monarchy had consisted of the Austrian Empire and the Kingdom of Hungary with a common sovereign. Of 51,000,000 inhabitants, 8,000,000 fell to the Republic of Hungary and 7,000,000 to the Republic of Austria, which was reduced to 26 percent of the area of imperial Austria; half of the former empire was divided between Poland and the newly created multinational state of Czechoslovakia, and the remainder among Romania, Italy, and the polylingual Kingdom of Serbs, Croats, and Slovenes, known after 1929 as Yugoslavia. Exhausted by the war and cut off from raw materials and markets, Austria, like Germany, suffered crippling economic and social disruption, with rampant unemployment and hunger strikes, all of which led to desperate attempts at political solution. Formerly the proud cultural and economic center of a venerable empire, Vienna was now the impoverished capital of an insignificant state rich in beautiful architecture and natural scenery. The collapse of the Austrian Creditanstalt in 1931 contributed to the world depression. The tension between extreme leftist and rightist groups—the latter abetted first by Mussolini and then by Hitler—soon erupted into civil war (through a putsch in July 1934 the Nazis would seize power in Austria). In the naive belief that Communism provided the only defense against fascist terror, Hilda had become an active member of the Communist party of Austria. Eventually her party sent her to Moscow, where she married a Russian engineer, Georgi Shcherbatov, who played a major role in the construction of a mammoth metallurgical complex at Kuznetsk (now Novokuznetsk) in Siberia.

After centuries of czarist despotism, the plight of the Russian people was even more dire than that of the Austrians. The first revolution was precipitated by the military disaster inflicted upon Russia by Japan in 1904–5, when Russia suffered the loss of two major fleets and the defeat of her army at the massive Battle of Mukden. World War I brought still more trials. In February 1917 a combination of military incompetence and domestic unrest forced the abdication of Czar Nicholas II. Army mutinies, peasant revolts, and urban strikes soon engulfed the country, contributing to the Bolshevik seizure of power later that year (in October by the calendar then used in Russia but in November by the Gregorian calendar, which replaced it). As envisioned by Lenin, Communism was to liberate humanity from want and oppression; as realized from 1924 to 1953 by his disciple Josef Stalin, Soviet totalitarianism was more ruthlessly oppressive, if possible, than that of Hitler. To paraphrase the eminent Soviet political columnist Melor Sturua, the Communists promised the Russian people heaven on earth but created hell instead.[1] Through forced collectivization in agriculture and a series of unrealistic "five-

1. Melor Sturua, "How a Tyrant Made Us Believe in Him," *Parade Magazine,* 28 July 1991, p.4.

year plans" in industry, Stalin sought to bring about the instant modernization of a backward Russian economy.

The full extent of the crimes committed against the peoples of the Soviet Union by the "evil genius of perfidy" (in Sturua's words) defies comprehension. Stalin's madness and inhumanity were revealed in part through Nikita Khrushchev's so-called Secret Speech at the XX Congress of the Communist Party of the Soviet Union in February 1956. These revelations, which were leaked to the West and received wide publicity, sent a psychological shockwave through Communists everywhere. Yet Khrushchev's catalog of Stalin's crimes was incongruously selective. Included were the massacre of most of the delegates to the Party Congress of 1934 and of 70 percent of the members of the Central Committee elected by that Congress. It also included the shooting of almost all Soviet army officers above the rank of colonel and the destruction of innumerable real or imagined political rivals, especially during the purges of the 1930s. Not included were such crimes as the forced incorporation of three Baltic countries into the Soviet Union, the partition of Poland with Hitler and the deportation of more than 1,000,000 Poles to Soviet concentration camps, the murder of almost 12,000 Polish officers in the Katyn forest, the intensification of Jewish persecution, and the eradication of the Volga-German republic.[2] It is generally believed that during Stalin's reign of terror as many as 20,000,000 Soviet citizens were incarcerated in "reeducation camps," as the forced-labor camps were euphemistically known from the time of the czars.

2. Large colonies of Germans had existed in Russia, especially on the Volga River in the district of Saratov, since the time of Catherine the Great (1762–96). Despite a large outmigration in the latter 1800s and early 1900s, Russian Germans numbered about 1.75 million in 1914 and owned an estimated 22 to 25 million acres of land. Efforts were made in the 1930s to disperse the German colonists, and during World War II all the remaining Volga Germans and most Russian-German men from South Russia were deported to Siberia or Kazakhstan.

The completion of the gigantic steelworks in Siberia in the 1930s, however, confirmed the blind faith held by Hilda and her husband in the benevolence of Communist leaders: the metallurgical plant had been built at great human sacrifice, but it had been built by the people for the good of the people; the steel it produced would be used to construct bridges, railroads, factories, and homes for the benefit of all. But their euphoria was cruelly dispelled. Like so many other Russian intellectuals, Georgi fell victim to Stalin's paranoia as one of the "enemies of the people" who might have constituted a threat to the dictator's power in time of national crisis. That Stalin's goal was the destruction of their entire families is clearly revealed by the metaphor of his command: "The enemies of the people must be torn out by the roots." Not long after Georgi's arrest Hilda was separated from her children and sent to a forced-labor camp. *Torn Out by the Roots* presents her vivid recollections of the stark terror and unrelieved suffering endured by the mostly innocent men and women in numerous death camps during Stalin's purges and World War II.

Although Hilda Vitzthum was sentenced to only five years of incarceration, she actually survived eight years of torment in labor camps, followed by two years of almost equally grueling and degrading toil in administrative exile before she was permitted to return to freedom in her native Austria with her son, Ruslan. (Her two daughters had died, one shortly before and the other immediately after her arrest.) She owes her almost miraculous survival to a remarkable combination of factors, including her ability to benefit from the healing beauty of nature under the most grim and hopeless conditions; exceptional physical stamina and moral integrity; her indoor work as a nurse, which sheltered her somewhat from the killing heat and cold of the taiga;[3] and

---

3. *Taiga* designates the evergreen and coniferous forests of the subarctic. Many Soviet prison camps were located in these forests, where the prisoners were literally worked to death cutting timber.

especially her loving concern for others—her fellow inmates and their orphaned children, her dying patients, the famished Russian peasants in desolate villages, and above all, her son.

For three decades Hilda Vitzthum found it almost impossible to discuss the terror of life in forced-labor camps in remote Siberia—partly because of the enormity of the experience itself and partly because of the inability of her Austrian compatriots to comprehend such inhumanity even after the horror of the Hitler years. In the course of time, however, Stalin's madness became known to people of the Soviet Union and to the Western world. Despite a promise exacted from her by Communist authorities never to reveal what she had undergone in the Gulag,[4] Hilda at the age of eighty felt morally obligated to record the deeply moving story of her *via dolorosa,* which ended, however, not in defeat but in the victory of integrity and compassion.

Although not a professional author, Hilda Vitzthum is a very effective writer. She developed her writing skill partly through the habitual composition of verse, which she began while still a pupil in elementary school. During her confinement in Russian camps, she worked on a long narrative poem about which, unfortunately, she tells us little in her memoirs. Furthermore, she profited greatly from the libraries in the wealthy homes in which she had worked as a domestic servant in Linz and Vienna. It was probably from her extensive reading that she acquired certain compositional skills and techniques that increase the persuasiveness of her moving account. She consistently relates events from the perspective of the camp prisoner thoroughly isolated from the outside world. Thus, for example, she records with surprise, bewilderment, and consternation the temporary compact between Hitler and Stalin, for, as mentioned above, she naively regarded Communism as the absolute negation of fascism and

---

4. *Gulag,* the acronym for the Chief Administration of Corrective Labor Camps, became a designation for the entire penal system under Stalin.

a firm bulwark against it. In the introductory chapter of her autobiography Hilda briefly describes her home life in a small subalpine village. Her mother is characterized as a woman of exceptional *Güte*, which has the sense of "compassionate goodness and kindness." As a petty imperial official, Hilda's father exemplified the virtues of loyalty and fidelity associated with the civil service of Austro-Hungary. His early morning hikes in the Alps with his children contributed not only to their physical strength and endurance but also to their appreciation of the beauties of nature.

This brief, idyllic chapter of Hilda Vitzthum's life was shattered by World War I, but its prefigurative function in her life story soon becomes evident to perceptive readers. The qualities of body, mind, and heart that she developed during childhood stood her in good stead in the vicissitudes of her incarceration. One example for many: we repeatedly have occasion to recall her characterization of her mother as Hilda endeavors to assuage the agony of her dying patients with no other medication at her disposal than her *Güte,* her compassionate kindness and goodness. It is also this quality that enabled her to create so many memorable thumbnail sketches of her fellow sufferers.

Since *Torn Out by the Roots*, as the subtitle indicates, is based largely on reminiscence—the written memoranda to which she refers cannot have been extensive—it is uneven in narrative richness and vividness; these episodic differences, of course, are reflected in the style. For the most part Hilda Vitzthum's colloquial language is highly readable. Not infrequently she waxes eloquent, especially when she describes the beauties of nature or gives vent to dismay or moral indignation at the senseless cruelty of Soviet oppression. And occasionally she achieves a degree of terseness that cannot be excelled, as in the initial sentence of her book.

Today Hilda Vitzthum's memoirs are especially timely in this era of precipitous change in Eastern Europe, where multiparty politicking, vociferous and violent, now goes on apace. The head of what President Ronald Reagan called the "evil empire" has been awarded the Nobel Peace Prize. *Doctor Zhivago* has finally been published in Russian, and the author's son has been permitted to accept the Nobel Prize for Literature that the late Boris Pasternak felt compelled to decline in 1958. And survivors of Soviet concentration camps, as we saw on our television screens, met publicly in Moscow to commemorate their less fortunate fellow victims of Stalin's holocaust. In view of such developments there is a real danger that people in the West will be tempted to doubt the veracity of factual reports of Stalin's savagery, especially as they come to recognize that the chimera of monolithic world Communist domination that haunted them for decades was largely a fabrication of the British and American press magnates Lord Beaverbrook and Henry R. Luce.[5] Certainly no discerning reader of Hilda Vitzthum's autobiography will succumb to such a temptation.

The general theme of the literary series in which Hilda Vitzthum's memoirs appeared in Germany was defined by its editors as "the encounter of the individual human being with the system of Communism." Hilda's husband, Georgi, came to the bitter realization that under Communism "the system is everything; the individual is nothing." Hilda herself finally "gave up seeking logical reasons" for the massive destruction of human life all around her. Nevertheless, like Alexander Solzhenitsyn's Ivan Denisovich, Hilda was intent on surviving. Almost miraculously she remained faithful to her duties as mother and nurse and maintained her personal dignity and her integrity as an individual human being. Despite the decade of cruel repression to which she was subjected by Stalinists, she never developed a blind hatred for the Russian people (who, she said, suffered more

5. See W. A. Swanberg, *Luce and His Empire* (New York: Scribner, 1972), esp. pp.75–78, 91–92, 99–101, 107–8, 212, 350–60.

than she did) or for the basic tenets of social democracy as she understood them. At last report, in 1992, Hilda Vitzthum was engrossed in the translation of her autobiography into Russian from the original German.

In conclusion, it is a pleasant duty to acknowledge my indebtedness to Elsie and Herbert T. Thomas for their help in the preparation of this volume. Herbert Thomas produced an essentially finished version of the map that enables us to visualize Hilda Vitzthum's almost endless peregrinations from one remote concentration camp to another—a total of over 40,000 miles, mostly in unheated cattle cars with barely enough bread and water to sustain life. Both Mr. and Mrs. Thomas helped me with the English rendition of Russian names and obscure words, including camp and underworld slang (whenever necessary, obscure names and unusual words are explained in footnotes). Elsie Thomas, associate professor of libraries at the University of Nebraska–Lincoln, not only called Hilda Vitzthum's memoirs to my attention while they were still in manuscript form; she also conducted all necessary correspondence with the author and with Professor Michael Voslensky, Director of the Institute for Contemporary Soviet Research, in Munich, which first published this book, under the title *Mit der Wurzel ausrotten*.

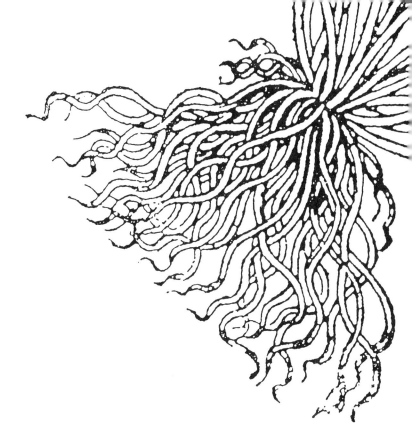

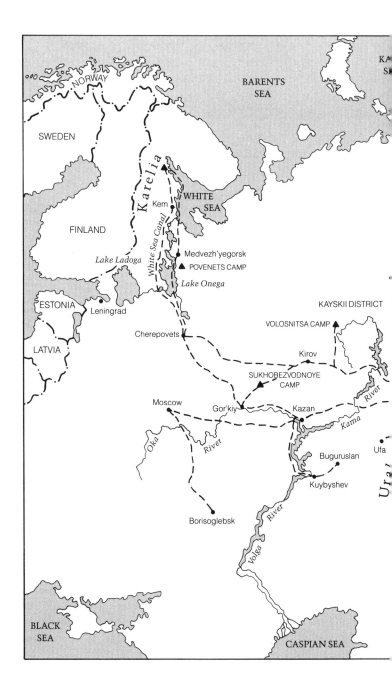

From Vienna to Siberia

I was born into a time that was fraught with the coming convulsions of the century. But the little market town of the Upper Austrian Hausruck district in which my parents lived still retained an afterglow of a time that was not good, perhaps, but peaceful and still untouched by the general fever. There was scarcely any industry in Frankenmarkt. Craftsmen and farmers supplied the people with their products.

My father was a royal and imperial official in the local court and enjoyed a certain public esteem, although not because of his economic position, since his salary was modest and we didn't even have a house of our own. For his milieu my father was a far-sighted person. He was very liberal in his views, and I have much to thank him for. He was full of ideas, jovial, and always made things lively. He taught us children to swim when we were still young and took us on hikes into the large forests, as far as the lakes in the Salzkammergut.[1] Often he roused me and my brother

---

1. The Salzkammergut is a region in north-central Austria renowned for the lake and mountain scenery that have made it a summer tourist attraction. It derives its name (literally, "salt domain") from the numerous salt deposits.

Hubert, who was a year younger than I, at three o'clock in the morning so that we could observe the sunrise from the nearby mountain. Father was very fond of music. He had a good voice and sang in a chorus he had founded himself. He took great pains that we children should develop our singing voices and learn to play musical instruments.

My mother was a simple peasant girl who had met my father when she was working as a housemaid at the home of the owner of the local glass factory. She came from a respected family. Her grandfather had been honorary burgomaster of his village. Even today it gives me pleasure to think of that friendly farmhouse of my grandparents, with whom I spent some of the most beautiful days of my childhood. My mother was the oldest of eight children. I remember her as a beautiful woman of great kindness, a quality that also characterized her sisters and my grandparents. I had two sisters and one brother. My mother did her best to give us a good upbringing according to the demands of the time. She was devout without being hypocritical, and we children enjoyed the homey atmosphere that she knew so well how to create.

Unfortunately, this happy childhood came to a sudden end. In September 1913 my mother died after suffering briefly from the so-called "galloping consumption." Before she died she exacted a promise from me, as the eldest, to look after my brother and my sisters.

For the sake of the children my father soon found it necessary to marry again. He chose a middle-aged, single woman from a distant village who had been recommended to him by acquaintances. His remarriage coincided with the outbreak of World War I, and for us children there now began a war from within and without. With our stepmother in the house we no longer felt at home. She made us feel all too clearly that we were merely tolerated. Since my father's work had greatly increased because of the war, he was seldom at home and did not know how bitter life had become for us. We didn't dare pour out our troubles to him, and he was much too gentle to prevail over his wife. But our stepmother did not hold back her complaints about us; again and again she tried to make our father think badly of us.

Even though down deep in his heart he didn't believe her, still it was simpler for him for the sake of peace to put up with his wife's complaints and occasionally to scold us. The situation compelled us children to stick very closely together; more and more I became the rebel in the house. I could no longer bear to see the injustices done my brother and sisters, and I defied my stepmother. Finally there arose a wall of hatred between us that could not be surmounted.

My mother had planned for me to become a teacher, but there was only an eight-year primary school in our village, and because of the war, study at a higher school had become difficult. My stepmother, moreover, was absolutely opposed to any kind of vocational training for me, and so I left home upon completion of primary school and thereafter earned my own living. Mostly I worked as a nursemaid or housemaid. At that age I was a very timid girl and had difficulty in defending myself against the whims and vexations of my female employers. Having left home so young, I was very unhappy during the first years. My time was at the disposal of strangers, whose demands on me exhausted me physically. In those days, nursemaids and housemaids were lucky to have a few hours to themselves on Sunday. And so I had at that time only one pleasure: reading! I secretly borrowed books if there were bookcases in the homes where I worked. In order not to be betrayed by the light, I made do with stubs of candles. Housemaids who read books were not liked.

In Linz, where I had my first employment in the home of a merchant, there was a granddaughter in the family by the name of Julia, who attended the secondary school for girls. We became friends, and it was she who introduced me to history, art, and the theater. Nevertheless, it was not easy for me to live in that house, for Julia's grandmother was an unrelenting mistress. Still,

I would probably have endured it there for more than a year if my stepmother had not suddenly become ill, so that I had to return home. I remained there for only a few months, however, for it was no longer home to me. I continued to correspond with my father, whom I deeply loved, and we got to see each other several times, but I never again returned to the house of my parents. Instead, I left for Vienna.

Julia Zehetner and I, however, remained close friends. During her student days in Vienna, we often got together. Even after she had become a teacher in the same secondary school she had attended as a pupil, our friendship continued, though we were parted for years before her premature death in the 1950s.

It was my brother Hubert who had persuaded me to join him in Vienna at that time. It was not difficult to find work as a housekeeper. Hubert had wanted to become an electrical engineer, but since no such apprenticeship was available at that time, and he didn't have enough money to wait very long, he had to be content with an apprenticeship as an amber turner.

The first time I set foot in the apprentices' quarters, located behind an old building in the Hirschengasse in Mariahilf, I was horrified. In a booth near the entrance sat the home assistant, a former army corporal. The apprentices had to report to him whenever they left the building and tell him where they were going. Permission to leave was limited, and in the evening they had to be back early. Whoever was late or in any other way violated the household regulations was punished with confinement to these quarters on his day off. A gloomy winding staircase of stone led to the second floor, directly into the bare common room. In the middle of the room stood a board table surrounded by plank benches. In little wall closets the apprentices kept their meager personal belongings and their eating bowls. Beyond this was the sleeping hall: a row of iron bedsteads, straw sacks covered with gray blankets. A crucifix on the whitewashed wall was the only decoration. The impression was that of a prison.

When I had seen these rooms and the pale, undernourished apprentices who loitered about here, and when my brother and I were again in the miserable stairwell, I began to weep bitterly. I was affected not only by the pain of seeing my brother in such a degrading situation but also by our common fate, of which I had never become so keenly conscious as at this moment. As a housemaid I was decidedly not well off, but in the lordly manors I usually had a small back room or at least a corner in the anteroom for myself, and it did not look like an army barracks there. And my food was certainly better than what the apprentices got in the public distributions of relief meals. I stinted on food in order to save as much as possible for my brother, who came to see me every Sunday. Whenever I had time off, we went walking together.

The vexations that the apprentices had to endure in these quarters soon led—it may have been late in 1919—to a revolt. In this time of revolutionary mood in "red Vienna" such lodgings seemed to the apprentices to be a vestige of hated former times. All the dammed-up rancor in these young men burst forth. Beds and other odds and ends of furniture were smashed and thrown out the window.

My brother was regarded as one of the ringleaders. To what extent he really was, I can no longer say. At any rate, he lost his apprenticeship and had no roof over his head. Our father came to Vienna, and at his intervention Hubert was reinstated by the master turner and moved into the headquarters of the turners' guild, which was run by Mrs. Zelinka, wife of a turner. Only a few apprentices lived there, and the manager and especially her husband, a Social Democrat, turned out to be fine human beings. With this family my brother came to feel almost at home.

Because of the revolt all the former apprentice quarters were closed, and the demand of the apprentices that the municipality of Vienna should provide apprentice lodging was met.

My brother's experiences touched me deeply and spurred me

on to improve my own depressing and degrading situation. I had succeeded in finding work in a textile factory and lodging with a caretaker and his wife near my brother, even though it was for the time being only a bedstead in their room-and-kitchen apartment.

Through my brother, who was a member of the Socialist Youth in the sixteenth district, I soon came in contact with the Socialist Youth movement and thus also with the political discussions that were going on with such intensity during the difficult years of complete political change following World War I. In those days, of course, we all believed in the realization of socialism. The only question in dispute was whether this would be achieved through revolution or by peaceful means. It can be regarded as an irony of fate that in the discussions I attended, the appearance and the argumentation of S. Schlamm impressed me so deeply that I decided on the more radical way and joined the Communist Youth of which he was the leader. Today, Schlamm is remembered as a rabid anti-Communist.[2]

About that time, the groups of National Socialists and their competitors, the Home Defense Force, supported by the government, were on the offensive. More and more frequently, workers' meetings and marches were unexpectedly attacked; workers were beaten and even shot. Bitterness increased among the workers at this unpunished rampaging of fascist gangs and led to the events of 15 July 1927.

When members of the Home Defense Force who, during a demonstration in Schattendorf, had killed a disabled war veteran and a child, were acquitted of the crime, this incited an enor-

---

2. "Willi" Siegmund Schlamm, Austrian propagandist and journalist, in 1938 fled to New York, where he joined the inner circle of converted Communists (including Whittaker Chambers) who inspired Henry R. Luce in his crusade against "godless" Russia and world Communism.

mous uprising. The workers spontaneously left the factories and went to the Ringstrasse to demonstrate.[3] On the morning of this day, as I was riding to work, the streetcar suddenly stopped halfway there. Columns of workers were already marching in the direction of the Parliament building and the Law Courts. Everywhere, mounted police were trying to scatter the demonstrators. A large garbage truck was driving along in the vicinity of city hall. The demonstrators forced the driver to park the truck crosswise on the street to block it against the police. Benches were brought from the city-hall park to form barricades.

A police station near the city hall had been stormed. I saw a policeman being beaten. But there were still some level-headed persons there who admonished the attackers, so that the policeman eventually escaped. The press of the crowd was so strong that it was impossible not to be carried along. From a distance I could see that several demonstrators had forced their way into the Law Courts. With cheers and shouts they threw piles of documents out of the windows and set fire to them. To be sure, the agencies housed in this building had not been directly involved in the acquittal of the killers, but the workers wanted to strike a blow against the administration of the law, which was anti-labor.

Here and there I bumped into friends and comrades. All of them had been surprised at the spontaneity of the protest. No one was certain of what it would lead to, how it would end, or what could be done. Carried along by the crowd, we were inspired by the courage of the Viennese workers to protest, and all the more so when we learned that strikes and demonstrations were taking place here and there throughout Austria.

In the afternoon, Seitz, the mayor of Vienna, tried to ap-

3. The Ringstrasse is a circular road that almost surrounds the central city of Vienna. It is lined with parks and important buildings, such as the imperial palace, the state opera, the Burgtheater, and the stock market.

proach with the firemen on one of the engines dispatched to put out the fire.[4] Just as the fire engines were clearing a way, the police suddenly began to shoot into the crowd without any warning. I was in the group near the Parliament, and a bullet whistled past the ear of the man beside me. We didn't have any idea where the shot had come from. Whether we wanted to or not, we had to fall back.

On the following day I was again on the streets. The strikes and demonstrations continued, to be sure, but the situation was already quite different. The workers had been pressed farther and farther from the Ringstrasse. My memory of this second day has faded, but my recollections of that evening are still vivid. I went to Hernals, where the last bitter confrontations with the police had taken place; but when I got there, everything was over, and the police were patrolling the streets.[5] My walk home was a sad one. Our small group of friends, who had come together, had to disperse, since one was allowed to walk the streets only singly. Each of us was searched, with hands raised, for weapons. But who in those days owned weapons but the police? The demonstrators had defended themselves only with stones or whatever other objects they could lay their hands on.

That evening I returned to my lodging with feelings quite different from those of the morning before. In contrast to the more than ninety victims who had almost all been shot to death by the police, and whom we had to mourn, the police suffered only a few casualties, and some of those had been struck by bullets from their own ranks.

It was deeply moving to see more than ninety coffins before the main entrance to the central cemetery, as well as the sad

4. Karl Seitz was mayor of Vienna from 1923 until 1934. Confined to the Mauthausen concentration camp by the Nazis in 1944, Seitz was made honorary head of the Social Democratic party upon his release in 1945.

5. Hernals is a working-class district northeast of the central city in Vienna.

survivors and the severity of the police cordon. Friedrich Adler spoke. I saw this son of Viktor Adler, the murderer of Stürgkh, and secretary of the Second International—who appeared to me to be surrounded by a halo—only this one time.[6] His speech seemed colorless. But who among those present, regardless of party affiliation, was really conscious of what was buried with these victims? Who could really imagine all that was yet to come!

Following these July events we returned to the routine of everyday life. Work was resumed. The fascist gangs, however, had become more brazen. Until then, they had seldom marched in Vienna and the industrial areas; now, it was precisely these cities that became their favorite arenas.

I had finally succeeded in acquiring a vocation. I had completed a nursing course at the University of Vienna hospital, where I studied under Professor Holzknecht, a pioneer in the field of radiology. I was now a certified radiology nurse and worked in a radiology laboratory.

Following their completion of school and vocational training, my two sisters had also come to Vienna, and so we were all together again. In the autumn of 1927, at the age of twenty-four, my brother died from a severe cardiac valvular defect, which had made itself noticeable during his apprenticeship years of hunger and fatiguing work. I had been closely attached to him; we had, after all, experienced together those first difficult yet fulfill-

6. Friedrich Adler (1879–1960) was an Austrian advocate of the workers' councils but opposed Bolshevik influence. Sentenced in 1916 to life imprisonment for the slaying of Count Karl von Stürgkh, he was pardoned in 1918. From 1923 he served as secretary of the International Socialist Workers' Parties, first in Zurich, then in London, and after 1935 in Brussels. His father, Viktor Adler (1852–1918), was a Social Democrat who advocated federalism, autonomy for all the peoples of the Austro-Hungarian empire, universal suffrage, and the unification (*Anschluss*) of Austria with Germany. A lifelong friend of Friedrich Engels, he edited the Socialist *Arbeiterzeitung* ("Workers' Paper") from 1899 until 1918.

ing years in Vienna. His death affected me all the more deeply because I was always sure he would not have died so young if we had had a real home, where he could have enjoyed care and consideration. Instead, he had had to do hard labor.

During all these years I remained active in the Communist party, which I had joined early. As a member of the antifascist committee, I was arrested one day in the autumn of 1929 as I was leaving the radiology lab. At that time the police were more concerned with the opponents of fascism than with the fascists themselves. I was accused of high treason. To be sure, I was freed again, but I lost my position as radiology nurse even before a verdict was reached, since the daily press had carried news of my arrest.

After this it was impossible for me to find work in my profession anywhere. Therefore, at the suggestion of the party, I took the opportunity of going to Moscow in October to take a one-year course at the Lenin School.

It was still the old Moscow that I got to know. Of course, many of the forty-times-forty churches—as they used to say— had been torn down, but the tall, mighty Church of the Redeemer on the Moscow River near the Kremlin was still standing, as were the old monastery on Pushkin Square (which at that time housed an antireligious museum) and the tower near the Sukharyev Market. With its old narrow streets, its low wooden houses among which here and there a church or an old palace towered, and its beautiful broad boulevards, Moscow presented a singular picture. Districts with houses built around the turn of the century were reminiscent of European cities, yet the total picture was still typically Russian. There was little that was new, and even that was still under construction.

Yet all this engaged me little at that time. I thought only of the future, and that could only be very promising, since I would be in the Lenin School with students from all over the world. I can recall meeting students even from Africa and Asia.

I had arrived somewhat late, and classes had already begun. My group was made up mostly of Germans (among them Max Hölz), plus German-speaking Swiss, Netherlanders, and several Scandinavians.[7] Instruction began at eight and continued with brief interruptions until two o'clock. In the afternoon we had time to assimilate what had been presented and to read supplementary material. The major subjects were political economy, historical materialism—the courses of greatest interest to me—and the history of the Russian Bolshevik party, which was regarded as the model for all Communist parties. There was a separate course in "Problems of Leninism," which we learned according to the book by Stalin. The program of instruction was thus clearly defined, but how much latitude there was for individual interpretation or ideas depended on the various teachers. I recall with pleasure our instructor in political economy; Segal was a brilliant pedagogue who really knew how to acquaint us with Marx's *Das Kapital*. In 1937 he and many other instructors and colleagues of the school were arrested. Many were probably put to death.

The class periods were often very lively. All the students in my group were active members of their own Central European Communist parties and raised specific questions to be discussed in connection with the various themes. Among other things they broached problems they had encountered in their personal experience. I too took part in discussions of all topics with enthusiasm and diligence.

To the extent that we could surmount the language barriers—sometimes with the help of translators who might be present—we tried to engage in conversations with comrades from other

7. Max Hölz (1889–1939) was a German Communist terrorist who was sentenced to life imprisonment in 1921. Upon being pardoned in 1928, he emigrated to the Soviet Union. He died, allegedly by drowning, in Gorky in 1939.

countries and continents and to learn something about their problems.

In addition to specific courses there were presentations of a more general nature in the main auditorium, in which all students participated. A simultaneous translation system made it possible to translate what was said immediately into the four world languages; for other large groups of students—for example, the Chinese—there were special translations. The speakers were leading comrades from the Comintern and Profintern or, when there were questions about the first five-year plan or other topics important for the Soviet Union, leading Soviet politicians.[8] During my stay, we students were allowed to attend a conference of the Comintern that took place in this auditorium. In this way I had the opportunity to hear the first great speech that Thälmann, as leader of the Communist party of Germany, presented before this forum.[9] I am afraid I remember nothing of this speech.

During this time there still prevailed an atmosphere in which it was possible to discuss questions and to advocate one's own point of view—though in 1937, as I said, many teachers were arrested and probably even killed. In the Lenin School, too, differences of opinion within the Comintern and the various Communist parties were expressed. These opinions concerned pressing fundamental political questions of the time, such as the problem of the united front, the assessment of Social Democracy,

8. *Comintern* is the acronym for Communist International, the world organization of Communist parties (1919–43). The Profintern was the International of trade unions.

9. Ernst Thälmann (1886–1944) joined the German Communist party in 1920 and became its chairman in 1924. He regarded Social Democracy as the chief enemy of his country and advocated the subordination of the German Communist party to the Communist party of the Soviet Union. Arrested by the Nazis in 1938, he spent the rest of his life in concentration camps and was murdered in Buchenwald in 1944.

and so forth. Yet even then, those who did not embrace the official—that is, the Soviet—point of view were ostracized. Hardest hit were segments of German and Dutch comrades, even some among the party leadership. One member of our group was the wife of a Dutch party leader who belonged to the opposition. Suddenly she was treated like a leper. There were quite a few black sheep like that in the school, most of whom, however— and it must be said to their credit—did not abandon their positions in spite of the disparaging treatment they received. At that time I was still among the naive who believed that the leadership, especially of the Soviet party, could not possibly err, though I had a more tolerant attitude toward those who held differing opinions and could not condone the severity of their condemnation. This condemnation had no influence on my friendship with the ostracized, and yet the blinkers that we wore helped us again and again to come to terms with things that we basically could not quite understand or approve of.

Even then it happened that some of these "deviants," members of the illegal parties of Poland or Romania, were not permitted to return to their homes (they were mostly illegal aliens) but were sent to work somewhere in the hinterland. If these comrades did not succeed in leaving the Soviet Union before 1937, they were among the first victims of the Stalinist terror.

Most of us regarded party discipline as so final that we did not comprehend to what extent this "democratic centralism" was becoming more and more of a fetter that held back all opinions except those that the well-installed party bureaucracy permitted.

It was certainly not a matter of chance that the suicide of Mayakovsky occurred at that time.[10] To be sure, I did not yet

---

10. Vladimir Vladimirovich Mayakovsky (1893–1930) was generally known as "the poet of the Russian Revolution." Stalin labeled him the "best and most talented poet of our Soviet epoch." Although a loyal Communist, Mayakovsky became increasingly disenchanted with the opportunism and

know or understand his poetry sufficiently, but most of us in the school knew that he was regarded as the poet of the Russian Revolution. News of his suicide was very depressing to us. Mayakovsky's body lay in state for several days in the House of Authors on Heart Street, which ran parallel to Vorovski Street, on which our school was located. We could see the long lines of persons who came as though on a pilgrimage to view his body. On the day of the burial the funeral procession passed through Vorovski Street, and we could observe it from the roof of the school. To our surprise the procession was not long. It was not until much later that I could completely comprehend the tragedy of this event.

When I arrived in Moscow in the autumn of 1929, there were still many small stores and workshops. In the bakeries one could still buy good *piroshki* and pastries, and in general there were quite a few things to be purchased in the shops.[11] This changed shortly afterward, however. Not long after my arrival I had to take my watch to the watchmaker, but when I went to fetch it, the shop was closed. A note on the door informed me where I could get it—in a miserable alley lodging, where I found the thoroughly intimidated watchmaker and received my watch. That was how I discovered that all small stores and workshops had just then been closed. Suddenly there was nothing left in Moscow to buy except rationed goods in the state stores. No trace remained of the craftsmen. When we discussed this in the school, it was explained to us that small-scale trade and crafts were a

---

stupidity of the Russian police state. His last play, *The Bathhouse* (1930), which was banned from the stage, was a persiflage of Soviet regimentation and bureaucratization. Unrequited love and general frustration brought about his suicide in Moscow in 1930.

11. *Piroshki*, or *pirogi*, are Russian turnovers with a filling of meat, cheese, or the like.

hindrance to the development of socialism. We accepted the explanation without serious misgivings, because this was the time of the first five-year plan, whose scale and significance had been convincingly presented to us in the school.

But also in another, personal respect my attendance at the Lenin School came to be significant for me. In this school I met the man with whom I truly desired to share the rest of my life.

Georgi Shcherbatov was a Russian and belonged to that group of Russian comrades who, upon graduation from Sverdlov University, had been assigned by the party to the Lenin School, where they were to devote themselves to international problems.[12] They were among the best university graduates. Since Georgi was a member of the school administration and during assemblies sat with the directors, it did not take long for me to become aware of him. His handsome, frank, and congenial face radiated confidence and trust. When our group was sent to the Urals for practical training in the summer of 1930, I was happy to learn that he was to be the leader.

There were only four women in the group, which numbered almost thirty. Among the men there were several half-baked fellows as well as older, mostly married comrades who had formerly been active as rather high functionaries in the parties of their countries and in general maintained their dignity. Yet after months of loneliness and the unaccustomed, strict school discipline, some of them were not indisposed to use the weeks together in the railroad sleeping car in which we lived for a bit of flirting. The compartment in which we four women sat was adja-

12. Founded in 1919 as part of the Communist party's educational network, which coexisted alongside what the Bolsheviks regarded as the "bourgeois" system of schools and universities established in czarist times, Sverdlov University offered high-level courses in Marxist thought for Soviet party members, but it could not rival the regular universities in traditional education.

cent to that of the leader, who shared his compartment with our translator and adviser. This man was a student at the Institute of the Red Professorship and had a command of several languages.[13]

Maria, a Romanian, and I—the youngest of the four women —were courted the most. Maria soon became friendly with a German comrade who in the school belonged to the branded opposition. Maria had endured much for the sake of her husband, who was among those sent to the hinterland. Perhaps the pressure that weighed on these two brought them together. Although I was not entirely disinclined to forming a close friendship with a comrade, there was no one who was really appealing to me. So I usually took refuge, when I was especially beset, with the two Russians, whom I found more interesting and to whom I felt attracted.

Our leader and our interpreter were essentially different from most of the other comrades, some of whom were often presumptuous. Both had risked their lives for the cause, and both were accustomed to leading and organizing. But quite aside from this, it was Georgi's personal qualities that strengthened my affection for him. Although I could speak very little with him, and that only with the help of the translation of the "Red Professor," our conversations were for me uncommonly stimulating and interesting. I admired Georgi's quiet, modest, and natural behavior, his endeavor to make himself understood by everyone and, above all, to understand them. His natural, strong appearance, a straightforwardness that inspired me with confidence, and the assurance with which he mastered all the organizational problems during the trip impressed me.

His task was not easy, for the program that we had to com-

13. The Institute of the Red Professorship was established under Communist party auspices as a graduate school for party members who, it was hoped, would gradually replace the "bourgeois" professors in the regular universities and higher specialized institutes.

plete was very comprehensive. We inspected old and new plants and some under construction, as well as the most important administrative districts, such as Sverdlovsk, and newly organized collective farms. We became acquainted with the problems of the smaller ethnic groups in Ufa, the capital of the Bashkir Autonomous Soviet Socialist Republic in the southern Urals. While inspecting the old Ural steel works such as Zlatoust and especially Nadyezhdinsk, we were reminded of the circumstances that had prevailed during the time of the czars. Working conditions had changed little during the thirteen years that had elapsed since the Revolution. The eight-hour day and new labor legislation had been introduced, to be sure, but no improvement had been made in the technical equipment of the plants: many difficult tasks still had to be performed by hand, and the workers had scarcely any protection from heat and smoke. For the most part, housing was still as miserable as before, although there were a few new clubs and kindergartens. Zlatoust, in the southern part of the Urals, was at least surrounded by beautiful forests, but Nadyezhdinsk, located in the eastern part, was one of the most disconsolate places I had ever seen. It lay in a barren, raw region, and the workers' living quarters seemed even more wretched than those in Zlatoust.

Still, the often dismal impression made on us by the Ural industry, which had been significant even in the days of the czars, was largely compensated for by grand plans for new industrial plants, some of which were already under construction.

Magnitogorsk impressed us most of all. We saw before us a gigantic construction site that extended for kilometers in length and breadth. There were only a few administration buildings and scarcely any dwelling houses—just barracks complexes for the constantly growing number of workers—but huge concrete foundations and enormous excavations gave us a notion of the future size of the planned work, and long ditches for the sewer system helped us imagine the extent of the evolving city. We also viewed nearby Magnet Mountain and could see how the high-grade iron ore was obtained through open-pit mining.

From the presentation of one of the engineers we learned that Magnitogorsk made up only one part of the larger Ural-Kuznetsk Collective Steel and Iron Combine. The plan called for two equally large metallurgical installations intended to complement each other, to be built in Kuznetsk and Magnitogorsk. In their foundries the high-yield ore from Magnet Mountain would be worked up. Freight trains would transport the ore to Kuznetsk and, on their return run, bring coal from the Kuznetsk Basin to Magnitogorsk. Since none of us knew much about technical matters, we were not disturbed by the fact that this exchange took place over an expanse of 2,300 kilometers. On the contrary, we were intoxicated by the large numbers, and the concept of blast furnaces that would pour out 1,200 tons of steel daily appeared to us a confirmation of our hopes that the Soviet Union would soon be a highly industrialized country. Programmed by a year of political cramming, we saw in these data the most important prerequisite for socialist development.

How the Soviet administration functioned in practice we then learned at a reception given by the party leadership of the local soviet.[14] Usually, one of the leading functionaries read a report with many numbers, which were often very impressive. In reality, of course, these statistics did not convey any real meaning to us, yet they fit into the pattern of notions we had developed through propaganda and study in the school. We also inspected one of the first rural communes, which made a miserable impression upon me when I compared it with our Austrian farms. We had to stay there overnight and were terribly bitten by bedbugs. But even an army of bedbugs cannot penetrate the armor of ideology.

14. A soviet, a governing council theoretically elected by the people to represent them, could be local, regional, or national in authority and function.

During these weeks we were almost overwhelmed by what we had experienced. We had become acquainted with a part of Russia and its problems and had gained some idea of the great expanse of this country. We had grown conscious of the fact that beyond the Urals there extended gigantic regions that were geographically and economically quite different.

Since we practically lived in the sleeping car and, because of the great distances, spent not only the nights but also often days in it, there arose lively discussions and conversations. We bombarded our two Russian friends with questions, and their explanations contributed much to our understanding. The manner in which Georgi endeavored to respond to our questions caused my attraction to him to become a real attachment, all the more when I noticed that he was not indifferent to me. What had begun quite gradually on this study trip continued in Moscow and finally developed into strong affection. When I had to return to Vienna in 1930 after the completion of the course, it was a difficult parting, but both of us quietly hoped that ways and means could be found for us to come together again forever.

The following years in Vienna were the only ones in which I was professionally a political activist. As an instructor I visited various provincial organizations and became more closely acquainted with that circle of people who had undertaken to work as Communists in an environment in which this certainly was not easy.

I was living in Austria illegally at that time. In addition to my first indictment, a further charge had been filed against me. The party had several times made use of my name during my stay in Moscow and had listed me as editor of the party organ. By then the *Rote Fahne* (Red Flag) had frequently been impounded or penalized by order of the court.

I seized the opportunity to travel to Moscow again, not merely to escape arrest—the jails were not yet the horrors they became during the Hitler period—but above all for personal reasons. I was to work in the women's secretariat of the Comintern. This never came to pass.

For the first time I felt a strong desire to have a child. Until then I had always dismissed such thoughts; after all, I regarded myself as a professional revolutionary who had no right to personal happiness. Now, however, neither Georgi nor I could see any contradiction between our feelings and our task. It seemed a matter of course, therefore, for me to accompany the man I loved when the party, at his request, assigned him to one of the most important construction sites of the first five-year plan: the Kuznetsk Metallurgical Collective Combine in Siberia. Since I had studied at the Lenin School, I was accepted, as a member of the Austrian Communist party, in the Communist party of the Soviet Union (at that time such a thing was still possible), and the Central Committee of that party commissioned me to take charge of the cultural work among the numerous aliens working in Kuznetsk.

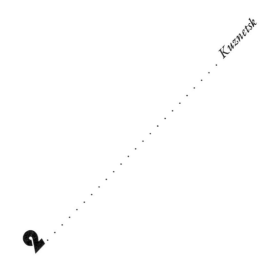

I was excited and full of expectations when we set off for Siberia. It was elevating to learn that this vast region, previously known to me only as a place of banishment under the czars, was to become an important living center of socialist construction. Since Magnitogorsk had made such an impression on us, Kuznetsk seemed to be a suitable place for us to begin life together.

On a radiant spring day we boarded the train in Moscow. The weather remained springlike as far as Kazan, the first station of our journey. We rode past small cities and extended villages that lay embedded between large cultivated fields and meadows, interrupted only by shallow lowlands and an occasional strip of forest. At Kazan we crossed the Volga, and the first thousand kilometers lay behind us.

The journey continued toward the Ural Mountains; the terrain became more barren, the air more biting; spring seemed to have remained behind. As the train carried us over the Urals, we could feel the puffing and the pounding of the locomotive up every steep ascent. Our eyes remained fixed on the trees of the dense evergreen forests that blanketed mountain and valley. The ground was still covered with snow; here and there we saw smoke from factories. When we arrived at Sverdlovsk, the second station of our journey, we had completed the second day and the second thousand kilometers.

A short distance beyond Sverdlovsk the Urals came to an end. Quite suddenly the train was gliding across the West Siberian lowland. Here and there a strip of earth or ice-covered bogs peeked through the snow. In the distance the land seemed to blend with the horizon. The Irtysh River, which we crossed at Omsk, was still covered with ice. The river ran along the lowland plain like a ribbon, and the old city of Omsk lay before us quite flat. A few brick buildings and the steeples of churches jutted forth above the low wooden houses.

Near the small railroad stations we saw the high grain elevators in which the wealth of grain from these steppes was stored every year and from which the wheat, which thrived here, was transported. At sunset the steppe glowed in shimmering color, from the most delicate pink to the deepest violet, and this continued for a long while until the last shimmer was swallowed by the darkness of night. I would never have believed that the steppe could be so charming.

Early in the morning we crossed the Ob River on a steel bridge that had been erected during the construction of the Trans-Siberian Railroad. This brought us to Novosibirsk. There we remained for a day, for Kuznetsk belongs to the Novosibirsk district, and we had to register with the district committee.

Between the low but solidly built log houses we walked to the newly constructed brick building of the party committee. There were in Novosibirsk only two buildings made of stone: the residence of the district soviet and the old jail, which, however, I did not see at that time.

Since the spring thaw had just set in, all the streets were waterlogged. Only along the buildings were there planked walkways, which substituted for paved sidewalks. There was, after all, plenty of wood, since the taiga was not far away.

If we had not received two tickets, reserved for party members, through the district committee, we—like our fellow passengers—would perhaps have had to wait for days at the station. The beleaguered railway stations best revealed the migration of peoples that collectivization and the first five-year plan had precipitated in the Soviet Union. Entire families with bag and baggage lay around the waiting rooms for days before they could by hook or by crook find space on the few passenger trains that were running. It was scarcely possible even to reach the path that led to the train platform.

Freight transportation had top priority at that time. Without interruption, the freight trains—some of them almost a kilometer in length—rolled past carrying building material, machinery (mostly from abroad), and other freight from the central regions of Russia toward the great construction centers, to which not only every nail but at first also every fireproof brick had to be transported.

Even with reservations it was not easy to get possession of our seats on the overcrowded train. From Novosibirsk to Kuznetsk we still had to travel through the rich Kuznetsk Coal Basin. Since the train was late, we were still traveling in the dead of night. The stations at which we stopped were only weakly illuminated with petroleum lamps. Suddenly a sea of lights appeared. We believed that we had reached a large city. It was Kuznetsk.

When we got off the train, we heard a deafening din in the distance. For the train, full to bursting, this was the end of the line. In this huge, milling throng we succeeded in getting a simple Siberian carriage, which took us to a newly completed hotel, one of the first four buildings to be constructed of bricks in this future city. We were barely able, with great effort, to get places to sleep. They were ordinary iron beds, but they had white sheets. Water had to be fetched from a water line located a considerable distance from the hotel. Farther away was a simple privy made of boards, fortunately with a dividing wall for women. For hot water we had to stand in line at a large boiler that was also located some distance away. Unboiled water was not to be drunk under any circumstances.

What a view greeted us when we came out of the hotel in the morning! There was not a trace of a city to be seen. The broad and enormously long valley that lay before us, surrounded by low, flat-topped hills, was simply and solely a construction site.

Of the four blast furnaces that were to be built, two half-finished structures towered above all the other building complexes; the large coke oven as well as the power plant had progressed furthest, but as yet one could scarcely imagine what their final appearance would be. About a thousand men were burrowing deep in the clayish earth with picks and shovels. One after the other, like a chain, small Siberian horses pulled up the wagons loaded with earth. Involuntarily, I thought of the Tower of Babel: human beings of the many nationalities of this gigantic country tried to communicate with each other in various and sundry languages—mostly through scarcely articulated cries. Peasants who had previously scarcely ever seen a machine, Kirghiz people who had never before used tools, nomads, men banished from their native soil—all were there.

They were excavating for the foundations of the kilometer-long rolling mill and for the huge steel mill with thirteen Siemens-Martin furnaces. They were already erecting the iron frameworks for the gigantic workshops. In addition they were excavating for and working on the far from small auxiliary buildings, such as the foundry, the fire-clay factory, and the mechanical colliery. At some distance from the plant itself, two large brickworks, which were to produce bricks for the construction of the entire city, were nearing completion. Deep ditches were dug the length of the valley to the Tom River; along it lay pipes that were meters in diameter. With this pipeline the necessary energy for the plant and the future city was to be obtained from the river, which flowed along on the other side of the valley. The provisional electric generator was run by means of oil-burning engines, whose noise was constant. The work went on day and night. Gigantic floodlights illuminated the work sites, and it was their light and the deafening din of the motors and the welding machines that had created the illusion of a great city upon our arrival. The collective combine at Kuznetsk had been planned by the American firm Fryen, whose engineers took part in the construction in a supervisory and advisory capacity. Several of them remained in Kuznetsk until some of the most important units went into operation. At this time only America had plants of such a capacity as were built in the Soviet Union within the framework of the first five-year plan. Kuznetsk was the first plant of such dimensions to be completed in Siberia.

Socialism no longer seemed to us to be only a utopia, for here we could see a manufacturing plant arise that formed the basis of industrialization without capitalists, one in which everything was to serve the people and to belong to the people. What un-limited possibilities the industrialization of this vast land with its natural resources seemed to guarantee for the progressive devel-opment of a better society. The construction of the plant itself was for us a convincing fact. We felt that we were important little wheels in this machine.

Many foreigners, skilled workers and technicians, were already involved in construction and especially in the temporary work-shops when I arrived. More and more followed. They came chiefly from Germany, but there was also a sizable contingent of Austrians—especially Viennese and Styrians—which may even-tually have numbered several hundred. One group, mostly Ger-man architects, planned the new city under the direction of the special group of architects in Moscow, in which also many for-eigners were cooperating (including Gropius).[1] It was their in-

1. Walter Gropius (1883–1969), equally famous as educator, author, and architect, was probably best known in Europe as the founder of the Bauhaus

tention to achieve a certain standardization of the new cities to be built during the first five-year plan.

Some of these foreigners came to the Soviet Union in order to escape the unemployment that prevailed in Europe at this time, but there were also Communists, socialists, and antifascists who wanted to take part in the realization of socialism. It was not easy for any of them to adapt to and cope with the unaccustomed, difficult living conditions, but the general enthusiasm of these years was so great that even the soberest person was seized by it.

The qualified Russian cadres of Kuznetsk came from industrial areas such as Leningrad, Moscow, and the Donets Basin; all these individuals made up a truly interesting collective. Most of the construction workers came from the villages. The forced collectivization that had brought agriculture almost to a standstill forced entire families to leave their homes. Such persons sought fertile regions, and Siberia had been spared from the drought. The great fertility of the vast, sparsely populated region enticed people from far away who hoped here to find the promised land. Those who worked here could count on receiving a ration of bread for themselves and their families, and that meant much in this time of hunger.

The large new buildings still required many laborers. When construction work was completed, however, only those workers were to remain who were necessary for plant operation and production, and only for these people were living quarters to be built.

For this reason housing upon our arrival consisted of the cottage quarter for technical and administrative personnel—well-built, one-story log cabins located on the upper part of the hill above the work site—and an extensive barracks settlement be-

---

in Weimar. As an officer in the German cavalry, he was awarded the Iron Cross in World War I. In 1934 Gropius secretly left Nazi Germany, and in 1937 he became a professor of architecture at Harvard University.

hind the plant buildings in the lower part of the valley. There were not nearly enough of these primitive, temporary barracks to shelter all the construction workers, however, and since each one consisted of a single room with rows of beds, they did not provide living conditions suitable for families with children. Therefore, the largest number of workers lived in self-made earth hovels, which were located around the barracks settlements. If the barracks made a cheerless impression, these earthen huts, which were scattered about in a completely arbitrary manner, appeared still more depressing. They were crowded together, usually had only one room—one part of which was dug somewhat lower into the ground than the other—with floors of stamped earth. The walls were made mostly of wickerwork or, with good luck, of boards smeared with clay. Several pasted-in glass panes served as windows. Leftovers from the wood used in construction or boards stolen from the poorly guarded supplies of building material served as roof and doors. To be sure, because wood was floated down the Tom from the nearby taiga, it should not have been in short supply, yet there was not enough available for everyone.

Water had to be brought laboriously from a great distance. The latrines, too, where there were any, were located far away. Since there were no sewers, waste water, like the ashes, was poured out in front of the huts; in the winter the frozen trash piles were as high as the low roofs. Some people had a cow or a horse tethered nearby, as they had formerly done when they lived in peasant cottages. The huts of the Kirghiz and other nomads rather resembled yurts, the round felt tents used by nomads in central Asia. The nomadic women, although they no longer were veiled, still wore long pants beneath their dresses. In the evening they sat before their hovels with little cans and pans and washed their bellies. If they had meat—usually mutton—they kept it outdoors on long poles.

On the other side of the river lay the old city of Kuznetsk, where there were well-built log houses, a distillery, a school for beekeepers, and the spacious wooden villa of the former owner of the gold sluice (gold was still being mined at some distance from Kuznetsk). Old Kuznetsk had once been a place of exile, and descendants of exiles still lived there. On a hill above the city stood the ruins of a fortress from the time of the czars, to which at that time prisoners had been transported. On the inner walls the rings to which the convicts had been chained could still be seen.

Because of the shortage of shelter near the construction site of Kuznetsk, some workers had preferred the housing in this old city (which was better suited to Siberian conditions), even though the city could be reached only by means of a ferry over the river, and the road from the ferry to the plant was several kilometers in length. The number of those who found housing there was not large.

The first thing we had to do was report to the party committee, whose offices were located in the vicinity of the plant administration. My future work had been determined by order of the Central Committee in Moscow, but the local party committee had to make decisions about Georgi's work.

I endeavored to look after the cultural affairs of foreign workers and technicians to the extent that this was possible under the circumstances. Since all the earlier cultural activities in Kuznetsk had been designed for Russians, only a few foreigners could participate in them. So they got together in the Club for Aliens, and in time a modest social life developed. My primary task consisted in explaining to the foreigners why living conditions were still so harsh and what difficulties still had to be overcome before a normal way of life could be achieved in Kuznetsk. The foreign workers had individual work contracts, lived in real housing units, and received better food.

Later, after I had acquired a mastery of Russian, I taught German at the technical school for metallurgy. Then I taught social studies at the school for master workmen, and finally I worked in the plant library.

It was during the initial years that life was most difficult, yet the general atmosphere was such that I still recall them with pleasure. A frank and friendly atmosphere prevailed; we had many friends; all sorts of things were discussed, and people were filled with hope.

Naturally, we could not continue to live in the hotel very long. We were truly happy to get a room in one of the log houses in the so-called upper colony, where we shared the apartment with another family. Even though there was no running water or indoor plumbing, we nevertheless had a kitchen and a large tile oven that kept our room comfortably warm in the winter.

Georgi had been received with open arms by the party committee, since he was one of the few party activists with a thorough education. From the very beginning he was called upon when there were difficulties that involved the entire plant. In order actually to solve the problems instead of merely giving orders, as so frequently happened, Georgi began to study at the metallurgical institute.

He had already learned English well at the Lenin School, and through constant contact with foreign students he had become acquainted with problems of capitalistic countries. This had created a certain basis for our mutual understanding. He understood my views and knew how to acquaint me with Russian problems.

He always sought and found contact with the human beings around him, and thus he had many friends. Since he was self-willed and independent in his thinking, he did not, as so many did, become a yes-man. The assurance with which Georgi approached the problems assigned to him and the manner in which he solved them not only strengthened my trust in him but also gave me a certain sense of security, which I had formerly lacked when I mostly depended on myself.

Although his work and his metallurgical studies left him little free time, Georgi read much. He loved Russian literature, but in addition it was primarily American authors whom he read with great attentiveness. America fascinated him. He had not learned English with no reason in mind. (It was therefore not mere chance that later, when he developed a severe meningitis and lay unconscious, he again and again imagined himself to be in America.) The pioneering spirit of the American settlers, and the democratic development that the consciously revolutionary segment of the Russian intelligentsia and of the Communists strove for, engaged especially those who vividly remembered the compulsion and constraint under the czars and had fought for a free development of their society. It was for this reason that they thought the foundations for the development of a new society could best be laid in the virgin vastness of Siberia.

All the more reason, then, that Georgi was troubled by the steady reorganization, the constantly changing directives from Moscow, as the result of which every local initiative was paralyzed and things that were really necessary on the spot were not given proper attention. He had already found it difficult to resign himself to the manner in which the collectivization of agriculture had been carried out. Since he knew from personal experience the scant productivity of the small farmer, he realized the necessity of a collective form of agriculture, but the manner in which it took place—whereby existing farm production was destroyed before the prerequisites for its transformation were created—was completely incomprehensible to him.

Georgi was concerned above all with human beings. He saw why the Russian peasant, who had not long before escaped from serfdom and for whom the Russian Revolution scarcely more than ten years earlier had brought land distribution, now clung to his plot of land, as small as it was. This peasant must have felt the recent measures as despotism. Georgi saw how agriculture was so severely damaged by forced collectivization that hunger and distress resulted from it. Often he said to me, "How can Stalin be so cruel!" For Georgi, the task of the party consisted in the education of the masses. Therefore the party should have more confidence in the people, should endeavor to convince rather than to dictate. "With such policies they can only make enemies," he often observed with deep compassion.

I myself faced these conditions with utter lack of comprehension. My position was more like that of an observer for whom everything was still new and unaccustomed and who therefore could not quite penetrate to the heart of the matter.

Georgi felt ashamed whenever he saw in what misery the workers lived here, in the earthen dugouts that they had excavated themselves and that were protected in the winter only by a thick cover of snow. Often we could see them distributing the snow so that the bitter cold would not penetrate their huts. In the spring, when the snow on the slopes melted, the ice on the river broke up, and an enormous volume of water poured through the valley, it was precisely the area where the earth hovels were located that was deluged. All who fled with their families and animals found meager shelter in the clubs and barracks. When they could return again, the water had destroyed their hovels and carried off their few boards. Now they had to excavate and build their huts anew.

Because of this annual flooding, the plant itself had been constructed on the broad, slowly rising elevation where it could not be reached by the masses of water. The new city, too, had been planned in such a way that it was protected from flooding. At such times contact with the old city was often interrupted for days on end, since the ferry had to suspend operation. Only after a bridge and a streetcar line had been constructed was the connection assured.

Georgi, who was especially distressed by the misery of the workers, endeavored shortly after our arrival in Kuznetsk to expedite as much as possible the building of the planned city. First as chairman of the soviet and party supervision committee—an institution dating back to the revolutionary period and liquidated in the course of centralization—and then as party secretary of the building committee of the new city, he saw to the procurement of building material; thanks to his efforts, construction proceeded rapidly from 1932 on. One street after the other developed. Sewers and water lines were laid. The construction of the central heating system was hastened; coal, after all, was to be found right beside the plant, directly beneath the surface. While concentrating on the construction of houses, streets, and sewage systems, we could not forget cultural establishments. Thus a moving-picture house, a theater, and a large clubhouse were built as well.

The chief goal, however, remained the plant. Daily, the two monstrous structures we had seen on our arrival came to look more and more like blast furnaces. The construction of the gigantic coke oven and the electrical plant was accelerated, for without coke and electricity not even the first furnace could be put in blast.

The steel mill and the rolling mill were still incomplete—their iron framework towered into the air—when, on 3 April 1932, the first furnace was set in blast. Its construction had required twenty-three months. For Kuznetsk it was a festive occasion, one for which the workers had toiled day and night, even when winter temperatures plunged to more than forty degrees below zero. For us this was an experience that I vividly remember after all these years. When the first of the thirteen Siemens-Martin furnaces poured forth steel, we were filled with a consciousness of victory. It was indeed the work of human beings who, housed in earthen dugouts and enduring hunger and cold, had yet in such a short time created something so prodigious.

It was precisely because of this feeling of victory, which filled all of us, that we paid little attention to the critical comments made by our foreign co-workers. At that time I, like so many others, lacked the technical knowledge to understand them, but later I often recalled these statements. The foreigners, who were used to a normal, rational way of working, could not understand why individual buildings had to be completed at such a forced pace. This, after all, led to an enormous increase in building costs and even to a senseless waste of human resources as well as material. Expensive equipment and materials—the machinery for the electric power station came mostly from Germany, the first fire-clay from Czechoslovakia—that could not be installed because the power plant was not yet constructed were haphazardly stored somewhere outdoors. Later, when they were needed, they could be found only with great difficulty and, because of the Siberian climate—rain, snow, and severe cold—had often been damaged.

Similarly, it was difficult to understand why work on the tunnel that was to be constructed underneath the plant, so that traffic between the upper and lower parts of the city would not pass through the plant area itself, was not undertaken until winter, when the temperatures were very low. Work in the solidly frozen earth was extremely difficult. Furthermore, because of the cold, the concreting of the tunnel floor, ceiling, and walls required expensive protective measures that would have been unnecessary at any other time. Obviously, given such hasty, forced work, accidents were unavoidable. In one such accident, one of the beloved work-brigade leaders met his death. For the prevailing mood at that time it is revealing that a poet, who was the editor of the plant newspaper, dedicated a farewell poem to him.

To be sure, in any such huge project with such poorly trained workmen, accidents would be inevitable, but there were also accidents for which there was no excuse. During the construction of the coke oven, for example, a meeting was held on the inner scaffolding one afternoon during the change of shifts. The wooden scaffold, which had already reached a considerable height, could not bear the weight of all those people and collapsed. Several men were killed and many were injured.

The second major accident occurred shortly after the second

of the two blast furnaces was put into operation. At this time two additional furnaces were under construction, and a temporary shelter where workers could come to get warm was still standing between the tracks of the two operating furnaces. As sometimes happens immediately after a furnace has been set in blast, there was a stoppage of slag in the drain following the tapping of the furnace, and instead of flowing into the slag cars standing on the track, it poured with tremendous force over the stockade directly onto the shelter, in which many workers just then were warming themselves. The force of the torrent was so strong that no one could be rescued. The dead were buried with honor in a mass grave near the upper part of the plant.

In 1934–35, when the last of the four furnaces had been put in blast, the thirteen Siemens-Martin furnaces had been completed, one rolling mill after the other had been set in operation, the cast-iron plant and the mechanical colliery had been completed, the fire-clay plant had long since been producing fireproof bricks and tiles, construction work was coming to an end, and housing and living conditions were increasingly improving—at this time the social climate began to worsen. The enthusiasm of the period of construction gave way to the daily problems of production.

Many of the construction and excavation workers, who no longer had any means of subsistence, had to leave again with their families. Their severance pay was a mere pittance; I doubt if it amounted to more than one week's wages. There was no unemployment compensation in the Soviet Union, so unless they had already been hired for other construction work, there was nothing left for them to do but to seek employment somewhere else at random. This meant riding the train and waiting and sleeping in stations for days and weeks. Still, with the exodus of these workers, the earth hovel settlements also partially disappeared.

On 1 December 1934 we wanted to go away on vacation. During the night Georgi awoke, and we saw that his face had become encrusted with a thick ulceration. Early in the morning we went to the doctor, who referred Georgi to the dermatological ward of the hospital with a diagnosis of erysipelas. Erysipelas occurs frequently in Siberia; the skin, which is assailed by the severe cold, is easily susceptible to such an infection.

Since there were as yet no antibiotics, erysipelas was treated in the time-honored manner: iodine was painted around the infected area. After just a few days Georgi's face cleared up. Strangely enough, however, just as he was to be discharged from the hospital, altogether different symptoms appeared. Georgi became terribly agitated, even confused, and had to be transferred to the neurological division. His condition rapidly worsened. When I visited him, he said things that were quite incoherent, and he rolled his eyes. I became very fearful, for Georgi's condition deteriorated from day to day. He lay there like a piece of wood, recognized me less and less often, and related the most fantastic things—that he had been riding on horseback the entire time because he was being pursued, and similar delusions. I realized that he would perish here, for the doctor interpreted his behavior as animosity toward himself and his staff.

I hurried to the party committee and to the board of health and convinced them that it was impossible to treat Georgi in Kuznetsk, where the hospital was merely a provisional arrangement housed in several barracks, was not yet completely organized and equipped, and lacked experienced doctors.

Georgi's friends understood at once that he was suffering from a serious ailment and that the doctor was probably unable to make a correct diagnosis. To transport Georgi to Moscow in his condition was impossible, for he could not endure the four-day journey. The decision was therefore made to send him as quickly as possible to Tomsk, as were all the complicated cases in Kuznetsk. Since the ambulance was not available, I took Georgi to the railroad station with the help of a nurse and an orderly. We made a bed for him in a compartment of a railroad carriage that was uncoupled at the Tayga station and switched to a train on the Tayga-Tomsk line. This meant several hours of anxious waiting.

When the Trans-Siberian Railway was constructed, the people

of Tomsk had for some reason been passed over. Formerly one of the richest and most modern trading centers of western Siberia, the city lost much of its economic significance when this vital line bypassed it. Only its university, founded in 1888, lent it distinction, though the city did later regain some of its luster through the establishment of a number of industries.

All the while, Georgi remained completely unconscious and stiff. Every three hours he had to be given an injection to strengthen his heart. The day-long journey almost became a race with death. Late in the evening we arrived at Tomsk. The railway station was quite far from the city. In the middle of a Siberian winter—it was January, the snow was deep, and it was very cold—I telephoned desperately for an ambulance, but in vain. There was nothing else to do but bed Georgi in an ordinary peasant sled, the only kind of conveyance available at the station. I knelt trembling beside him and continually checked his pulse to see if he was still alive.

The hospital to which Georgi was to be admitted was locked, and no one answered our knock. Finally, in one wing of the building, we found the emergency ward, which was open. When he saw how sick Georgi was, the paramedic consented to call the doctor on duty, who by chance was a professor in the neurological department. When the doctor examined Georgi, he immediately diagnosed his condition as a combined meningitis and encephalitis. He declared that the man was half dead and that there was no point in admitting him to the hospital. In response to my entreaties, however, he had him taken to the ward. With a heavy heart I went to find my hotel, there to undergo the usual disinfection and wait for the coming morning without a wink of sleep.

Early in the morning I made my way back to the hospital. I had to wait a while until the professor had me called, but what I saw in the meantime gave me a feeling of confidence. This was a real hospital, well built and well equipped. Yet the professor's words shook me badly. "My dear woman," he said, "you have brought us a man who is half dead. I don't know whether we can still do anything for him. He is living completely on the injections he gets. He reacts to nothing and doesn't eat or drink. I can't hold out any hope for you, but I assure you that we will do everything we can."

I was permitted to remain with Georgi during the day, since he was in need of very special nursing. After several days a small room was made available, and I could remain with him day and night. For several days Georgi continued to receive three cardiac injections daily, but gradually he needed them less and less frequently. Only with great effort was I able to get some cranberry juice and crackers softened in milk into him—the only nourishment he received. Since at this time there was as yet no specific cure for meningitis, treatment was limited to suitable diet and cardiac medication. When the blood tests were favorable and his heart continued to improve, the doctors began to believe that Georgi would survive. But even if he could withstand the infection, there remained the danger of paralysis or of damage to the nervous system. In Siberia such infections were very frequent, and they were usually fatal. Moreover, the survivors often remained handicapped for life.

The weeks that I spent beside Georgi's bed were weeks of desperation and yet of faint hope. I could at least feel certain that the doctors were doing everything they possibly could.

One day, after weeks of anxiety, I suddenly heard Georgi begin to cry like a little child, and I asked him what had happened. I was deeply moved when he said to me, "My beloved Hilda is dead. As we were riding through the swamp, she suddenly sank down, and I could not find her again." "Who am I? I have been beside you the entire time!" As though coming from a great distance he looked at me. Then he seemed suddenly to recognize my voice, and after he had stared at me for a long time, he seemed to recognize me too. From that time on he began gradually to recover. But although he was already asking for food by then, he did not always recognize who gave it to him. He had no idea of how he had come to the hospital. Sometimes he didn't quite know who he himself was. In response to questions asked by the professor, he gave different answers from day to day, just as he held the professor to be a different person every day.

When he fully regained consciousness, Georgi was found to have suffered no permanent damage, despite his enormous physical weakness. It was not until April that he had sufficiently recovered to return to Kuznetsk. Although his powerful physique had overcome this serious affliction, his convalescence after our return lasted for many more weeks before he could resume his work.

While Georgi was confined to his bed in this weakened condition, our lovely, lively daughter Natasha, then almost two and a half years old, one day poured hot water from the teakettle over herself. The burns were so severe that she could not be saved. Again I experienced days of anxiety—this time, however, in vain—at the bedside of my daughter. How we had loved her! Georgi again suffered a severe breakdown, and I had to muster all my strength in order to comfort and console him. We went to the Caucasus for a few weeks in order to recuperate.

August had come before Georgi again took up his work. After the murder of Kirov the situation in the country had greatly changed.[2] The difficulties to be overcome in order to establish normal production in the plant represented additional sources of tension. Many things that had remained concealed through the hectic work of construction now came to light.

2. Sergei Mironovich Kirov (1885–1934) was a dynamic Russian Communist leader who attained a position of power rivaling that of Stalin. His assassination in Leningrad marked the beginning of the Great Purge (1934–38). Nikita Khruschchev's widely publicized "secret speech" of 25 February 1956 implied that Kirov's assassination had been engineered by Stalin himself.

The personnel were poorly trained. Machines and installations had mostly been imported from abroad, and the foreign erectors and mechanics had left. Equipment had not always been properly protected from the Siberian cold, and the plant operated with great losses, yet Moscow demanded strict fulfillment of the quotas. Now and then, the workers' insufficient knowledge and experience caused debacles, which management tried to counter with pressure. Beginning as early as 1936, engineers and other plant personnel were arrested from time to time. People became uncertain and suspicious. Constant reorganizations and changes in personnel forced them again and again to adapt to new situations. These difficulties were said to arise from growth, but the explanation did not change the fact that morale constantly deteriorated, that people became more and more anxious and, in conversation, ever more reticent.

The first great shock occurred when the director of the plant, Engineer Frankfurt, did not return from an official visit to Moscow, and we learned that he had been arrested. Frankfurt, a man of great authority, had been in charge of construction from the very beginning and enjoyed the confidence of everyone. A member of the party from the time of the czars, educated, experienced, energetic, he had known how to fill people with enthusiasm for their work. All had seen in him an outstanding personality. In the entire country people prided themselves on the fact that the Kuznetsk metallurgical complex had been constructed in such a short time and was already producing iron and steel for the industrialization of Siberia. Now the man who had made the greatest contribution to the creation of this plant was branded a criminal!

That greatly disquieted Georgi, who was already apprehensive. Among other things, it was reported that Frankfurt had been reproached for wasting funds earmarked for the construction of the plant by organizing a celebration when the first blast furnace went into operation.

It had indeed been a great day for all who had performed the difficult task. The best workers had been awarded prizes, and in the clubs and eating houses there had been celebrations with banquets, wine, and vodka. It was precisely the feeling of recognition for their accomplishments that had filled the co-workers with new eagerness to work. There was still much construction work to be done, and daily life had been difficult enough. In any case, all of this lay well in the past, and it could not have been such a grave transgression; there must have been something else behind Frankfurt's arrest. It was the uncertainty that was so disquieting. Then the new director arrived, Engineer Butenko, bringing with him a group of young metallurgists who had been trained in the Soviet period and had earned their first medals in the Donets Basin. With Butenko began a struggle to fulfill the production quotas that left people little time for reflection. The party secretary of Kuznetsk, Khitarov, was recalled somewhat later; he was transferred to Magnitogorsk, where the local secretary had been arrested. Khitarov, the former secretary of the Communist Youth International, was a Georgian who in his early youth had been active in the Ruhr area; he was a man of caliber and at the height of his career.

As yet we saw no connection between the arrest of Frankfurt and the transfer of Khitarov, but with these two actions the two best minds of Kuznetsk had been eliminated.

Khitarov was later arrested in Magnitogorsk, as was Butenko in Kuznetsk. Even Shklyar, one of the bemedaled engineers who had come to Kuznetsk with Butenko, and who succeeded him there as director, did not escape this fate—along with several thousand colleagues at the plant.

Georgi and I decided, despite the terrible loss we had suffered, to have another child. In March 1936 I gave birth to our son, whom we named Ruslan. Like Natasha, he was a beautiful, healthy child. It may have been because of him that—although I had resumed my teaching duties—I could not pay sufficient attention to all the things happening around me.

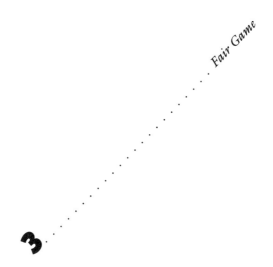

3

Following his return from a visit to the construction site in 1929, Vladimir Mayakovsky, the "poet of the Russian Revolution," composed a poem about the founding, the building, and the people of Kuznetsk. He concluded his poem with the proud and confident declaration of the workers, whose "lips were blue from the cold": "Four more years, and at this site will stand *Gorod Sad*, the 'Garden City'!"

In 1937–38, 5,000 workers and builders of Kuznetsk were arrested. In the "First House" of this garden city, which had become the headquarters of the NKVD, they were interrogated, tortured, and sent to forced-labor camps for ten to twenty-five years.[1] Many of them were shot to death.

The construction of the Kuznetsk Metallurgical Collective Combine, as it was now named, was rapidly nearing completion. All four blast furnaces were already on blast; most of the thirteen Siemens-Martin furnaces were producing steel; and the various mill trains of the rolling mill had been installed. Rails

---

1. NKVD, an acronym for People's Commissariat of Internal Affairs, designated the Soviet secret police, 1934–43. Hilda inadvertently continues to use the acronym up to 1948.

for Siberian railways and other products came from the automatic mill trains. The last American engineers had long since left Kuznetsk. Ivan Pavlovich Bardin, the chief engineer of the plant and one of the best metallurgists in the country, had been back from his study trip to the Fryen firm in America for quite some time. Many of the metallurgists of the plant no longer worked on the large construction sites but saw to the practical operation of the furnaces. In addition they continued to study, both to make up what they had formerly missed and to familiarize themselves with the technical aspects of their work.

The time had finally come for the people of Kuznetsk, who had built up their city in such a short time in heat and cold, to move from barracks and earthen hovels into comfortable dwellings. The essential thing now was to make the city a pleasant residential and cultural center. At last all the effort was to be rewarded! But things happened differently. Life became more and more uncertain and difficult. Georgi, who was now the cadre head of the plant and was informed about everything that took place in the plant and in the country, became increasingly more agitated and apprehensive. In his frank and open manner he did not conceal his thoughts and opinions from friends and colleagues.

The constantly increasing influence that the NKVD was gaining over people's lives filled him with uneasiness. Again and again men were arrested, but we never learned why. About some, nothing further was heard; from others we received news many months later and from far distant camps. We learned that most of them had been condemned to ten years of forced labor. They were branded as traitors and enemies, but we never knew what specific crimes they were said to have committed.

Georgi's uneasiness increased, for production, which had now come into full course, was constantly interrupted by these arrests. Experts, especially those who had become thoroughly acquainted with their duties, could not quickly be replaced. And

Moscow increasingly intensified its pressure and more and more demanded the fulfillment of quotas.

At that time I was not fully able to comprehend Georgi's anxiety. I was oppressed above all by the fate of my two sisters. Shortly before Hitler seized power they had gone to Berlin. Since both of them had followed in my footsteps and had become active Communists, they had been arrested there. Whereas my younger sister was soon discharged from custody, however, and was able to leave the country, the older one—she was married— was arraigned and sentenced to two years of penal servitude. Her child was born in the Moabit prison, but it was taken away from her several months later. When she was finally released and her child was returned to her, it was completely intimidated. Several months after the discharge of her husband from jail, they illegally went to Czechoslovakia, and I no longer received any information from them. Of course I was greatly worried on their account.

At the beginning of May 1937 I received an order from the party committee to check the library's foreign-language literature against a list they gave me and to remove all books contained on this list of prohibited items. None of the forbidden books was found in our rather modest holdings, most of which came from Soviet publishers of foreign-language literature. Nevertheless I was suddenly summoned to the NKVD. I was brought before an examining magistrate whom I did not know personally. I was quite taken aback by the manner in which he received me. He spoke to me as though I had committed a crime. His comments concerned my check of books in the libraries; he obviously believed that I had concealed certain books. This accusation and the tone of his questions dumbfounded me. I went home dismayed. Georgi was no less astonished and promised me to lodge a complaint, although he did not believe that anything would come of it. At this time the NKVD already carried more weight than the party.

At that time I was well advanced in pregnancy and the following day had to go to the hospital, where I gave birth to my Irina a few hours later. I had never had an easier birth. When I left the hospital after a week, Georgi's niece brought me home in an open, horse-drawn carriage of the kind commonly used in Kuznetsk. For no particular reason, just as we were driving over the bridge across the little river that separated the new city quarter from the barracks quarter, I turned around. Directly behind me in a carriage like the one we were in was the inquisitor who had recently questioned me. I had turned so quickly that I was able to catch him staring at me. His glaring eyes curdled my blood; he looked like a hunter who was about to make the kill. But I was able to escape him. The fact that I had just borne a child saved me. There was still a regulation against arresting a woman as long as she was nursing a child.

But now the baiting of Georgi began. It came directly from the NKVD. At the party conference that took place somewhat later, a member of the NKVD took the floor and accused Georgi of having glorified Hitler. A discussion of fascism had actually occurred some time earlier, but it was Georgi who had condemned fascism most strongly of all. Georgi did not let this senseless accusation disconcert him but simply asked for the testimony of those who had been present, so that the denouncer was brought into disrepute. At the conference the new party committee was elected, and Georgi received the highest number of votes.

But this was not the end of it. The secretary of the party committee, Ostrenko, a former construction worker and veteran Communist, had in strictest confidence informed Georgi about the background and the reasons for the arrests. Even though Ostrenko personally condemned everything that was happening here, as secretary of the party committee he was completely powerless to intervene. He did not even know from day to day what would happen to him. Later he was indeed arrested and died while awaiting trial.

In this summer of 1937 many alarming things happened. People still did not know what was behind them or what they would lead to. One day Georgi came home quite agitated. An order had come from Moscow to register all party members and all plant personnel with Polish names and to send the list to Moscow. "Now they are even making arrests on the basis of names," said Georgi with revulsion, for he knew why Moscow demanded such lists. I did not quite comprehend what he meant, for I could not imagine that what Georgi suspected could actually happen.

From then on we lived in the greatest uncertainty and tension until August, when I had another dreadful experience. Among the Austrians who worked at Kuznetsk there was a man from Graz. He was a widower, and his daughter, a pretty, well-mannered girl, had been reared in Graz by the Stolzes, a family of musicians. She had been engaged to a relative of this family. The young man, however, had not married her, and her disappointment had driven her out of the Stolz home. She had come to her father in Kuznetsk. In the meantime, however, he had married a Russian woman and had a child with her. So the daughter did not receive a friendly welcome there. Nevertheless she quickly learned Russian and was soon able to teach German at a grammar school. She was very happy about this and in general was content, for everyone treated this likable girl with the greatest friendliness. I too loved her very much.

Since her father had been temporarily transferred to a neighboring town, she now had the entire apartment to herself. One story lower in the same building there lived an Austrian family. One morning the wife in that family came to me in a panic and told me that the girl had been arrested during the night. As the girl was led away, she asked permission to give her valuables to acquaintances. The men who had come to fetch her had acceded to her wish, and thus the woman had learned what had happened. We puzzled about this for a long time but could not believe that the girl could be guilty of any crime. She was, after all, an Austrian citizen, and up to this time no alien had been arrested.

But things became still worse. Several weeks later there was a knock on the Austrian family's door at night, and when the wife opened the door, a man who spoke little handed her a note from the girl. It was a single cry of despair: "I am accused of espionage and am being kept in solitary confinement in a cold cell. They give me almost nothing to eat. Please believe me—I am innocent. Help me! Bring me at least some of my things and a little money so that I can buy some things. The man is one of my guards, the only one who took pity on me." The Austrian woman, who had come to me in terror, had been so frightened that she would not for anything in the world have risked taking the girl anything. She took the things the girl had left with her directly to the NKVD and requested that they be turned over to the girl.

For the first time I had heard something directly from prison, and I suddenly realized that this had nothing to do with real guilt. Rather, the purpose was to induce innocent people to confess to trumped-up charges. I now realized that we were at the mercy of the NKVD, and suddenly I comprehended all the comments that Georgi had made. Now I also understood why he had always said that I did not know what was going on in the NKVD. There had even been cases of suicide; indeed, at the beginning of the wave of arrests several members of the NKVD had taken their lives. To be sure, there had been only a few cases, for in reality it seldom happens that human beings take their own lives in order to escape committing atrocities. Georgi had many times assured me how happy he was that he had not had to serve in the NKVD. Since the functions of this organization had not previously been known to me, I had not understood why Georgi spoke of it with such abhorrence. It had, to be sure, not seemed to me to be especially respectable, yet I had looked on it to a certain degree as a necessary evil. While I was still in Austria, furthermore, I had regarded everything said about it as slander. Not without reason had Georgi frequently said to me, "How naive you are with your democratic way of thinking!" I had truly been naive.

By this time various foreign workers had been dismissed and deported. The foreigners were greatly agitated, for in those years a return from the Soviet Union was very dangerous for Germans and Austrians. Many had settled here for good, and some had even married. Frequently it was the most sought after specialists who suddenly lost their positions. They appealed to me, and I implored Georgi to do something. He really tried, but nothing could be done. The orders came directly from Moscow. In time all of them except the few who had become Soviet citizens were dismissed and deported.

Soon after Irina was born, I resumed my work in the library. My nursemaid was Mariechen, the daughter of a German settler. In the Siberian city and district of Slavgorod there were many German settlers. It was mostly precisely those peasants who had good farms, and thus many of them were simply denounced as kulaks, dispossessed, and dispersed.[2] Many had already been sent to work camps. In Kuznetsk too there was a group of Germans from Slavgorod. Those with families lived in the self-constructed earthen hovels. Mariechen's father had moved here with a large family. Mariechen was scarcely sixteen when she came to me. She had five brothers and sisters, and her mother had shortly before died of breast cancer. The father was happy that Mariechen could find such a good place to live; since she could scarcely speak Russian, she would otherwise have had to do hard physical labor.

2. *Kulak* (the Russian word literally means "fist") was the Communist designation for a farmer who employed one or more workers who were not family members. In 1927 Stalin confiscated all such family farms and collectivized them into kolkhozes. According to Stalin, the collectivization of Soviet agriculture required the liquidation of 10,000,000 kulak families. Many of these were German colonists, especially in the Ukraine and the Crimea.

Adults in families that did not know Russian could find only difficult, poorly paid jobs, but at least they received food ration cards. Since the children all had to attend school, they learned Russian and thus had the opportunity to study at special schools. In addition to a large school for trainees in metallurgy, there were in Kuznetsk several technical schools and special schools for adults that offered general courses in addition to professional training.

During the first years that we spent in Kuznetsk one-half of an average barracks had been large enough for the NKVD; its few members still wore simple military uniforms and greeted people in a friendly way, and the greetings were returned in a similar manner. But soon the NKVD acquired the first four-story building that had been constructed in the new city. Its members became more and more numerous and their uniforms increasingly more elegant. They received much higher food rations and were also better paid than anyone else. For this reason many persons wanted to work there, especially party members who had never acquired a profession, such as former army officers. The privileges that members of the NKVD enjoyed set them apart from other people. More and more it became a closed organization that everyone avoided as much as possible. And the "First House," as it was called, acquired an increasingly dreadful reputation.

At the same time as all this happened, life in Kuznetsk was becoming so unsafe that people scarcely dared venture outdoors alone even in the twilight. In one single night sixteen assaults occurred. The local police were scarcely visible and were powerless against the brigandage. I still remember several such attacks quite vividly.

At that time we were living in the upper cottage district, where individual log buildings were constructed in several rows running up the gently rising hill. They were one-story buildings, each of which had two stairways that led to six apartments. In the building located diagonally opposite and slightly above us there lived a colleague of the party committee with his wife and one child. One time when he was traveling on official business, his wife woke up and saw two men in the room gathering up everything that was not nailed fast. Almost paralyzed by fear, the woman tried to call for help. One of the men, however, pressed his knife against her breast, so that the woman had to look on quietly as they carried away all her possessions. She had to feel fortunate to have escaped alive. To lose one's possessions was especially bad at that time, since there was no way of replacing them.

On one occasion we had procured various provisions, which I placed between the window and the storm window. During the night I awoke and heard noises. I waked Georgi. He sprang up and hastened into the kitchen, from which the sounds were coming. There he saw a man standing in the window. He rushed at him, but the man without hesitation jumped out the window into a deep snowpile. He seemed not to have hurt himself and ran away. In the morning we found the plank leaning against the wall, which he had used to climb up to our window. The food, of course, was gone.

Another case, still more characteristic of the conditions at that time, occurred in another house on the same street. Our apartments each had a small anteroom, from which one could reach the kitchen and the other rooms. One evening when the apartment owner opened the door and entered the anteroom, he noticed that there was a man hiding behind the hall stand. Despite his fright, he had the presence of mind to act as though he had not seen anything. From the room in which his family was sitting he called the police. He was lucky; someone actually came and led the burglar away. On the following evening, as he and his family were eating supper, the doorbell rang. The man opened the door and to his amazement saw before him the burglar from the previous day, who brazenly demanded his cap, which he had forgotten. The police had released him because there was no room for him in their little primitive jail.

The court and the police were located in simple barracks, where there were scarcely any real jail cells. The NKVD, on the other hand, had sufficient cells for the prisoners awaiting trial in the basement of their large building. They even had a jail erected in the old city for their prisoners. There the innocent were locked up and tortured to make them confess to crimes they had never committed. For this there were sufficient personnel—but not to protect the population from the real criminals.

The criminality that was rife at that time was easy to explain. When construction was in full swing and there was no housing, it was difficult to register all the people who arrived daily from everywhere to escape famine. Top priority had been not employment but the food ration cards that every worker received for himself and his family. Now the rations were no longer sufficient, many persons could not find employment, and some preferred to keep body and soul together in other ways. And not all who came to Kuznetsk were in search of work; some were hardened criminals, who soon formed gangs and knew how to disappear in such a throng of people. Therefore, it took quite a long time before one of the most dangerous gangs, the "Kurilka Gang," could be cleaned up.

In the autumn of 1937 the non-Russians gradually began to be expelled. Among them were Austrian and German political emigrants, who could not return to their homes and therefore applied for Soviet citizenship. Thus it was with Franz Hobra-Prediger, a Viennese Czech who had charge of the technical direction of the automatic works. He was dismissed suddenly in the autumn of 1937. When he went to the Donets Basin in search of employment, he was arrested under unknown circumstances. He was never heard of again.

I vividly remember the fate of a German family from Jena. Franz Putscher had left his position with the railroad in Germany in order to participate in socialist construction and had come to Kuznetsk with his wife and two grown sons, one of whom had been a laboratory technician with Zeiss. As a mechanic Franz had been of especially great service during the construction period, when many improvisations had been necessary to keep tools and machines in repair. He was a simple, modest man who had always been a dedicated Communist. As long as Khitarov had been party secretary, things had gone well with the Putscher family, for Khitarov had a sympathetic understanding for the foreign workers. When the expulsions began, however, and an atmosphere of distrust against the aliens was created, the Putschers were not spared. But in their confidence in the Soviet Union they had acquired Soviet citizenship, since they were known in Jena as active Communists and therefore could under no circumstances return home.

As long as the arrests did not become massive, many persons believed that no arrests were made without good reason. The Putschers, too, were among those who had complete faith in the Soviet Union, and that is why they were especially agitated at the arrest of one of their friends, a man named Watz. An Austrian prisoner of war in World War I, Watz had remained in Siberia and married a Polish woman whose parents had fled to Siberia during the war. Since he spoke German well, he had been entrusted by the union with the work among aliens. He had an especially cordial relationship with the Putscher family.

The Putschers could not reconcile themselves to Watz's arrest. Ida Putscher even went to Moscow, to the Comintern, but her journey was ineffective. Watz had been arrested in connection with the woman from Graz, whom I have already mentioned. In the letter she had sent from prison there was this sentence: "I am accused of having committed espionage together with Watz." To the best of my knowledge, Watz never returned to his family. Since the Putschers, like so many others, believed that all these arrests had been inspired by local authorities, they decided to go to Magnitogorsk, where Khitarov was then party secretary. This was done at the insistence of Ida, the driving force in the family. Khitarov, whom they trusted implicitly, welcomed them, and Ida wrote to me several times in a very optimistic vein. Then we heard of Khitarov's arrest, and we received no more letters from the Putschers.

Later, in the work camp of Akmolinsk, I met a Hungarian emigrant from Magnitogorsk who told me that she had shared a cell in the prison at Sverdlovsk with Ida Putscher. The Putschers had all been arrested; Ida was completely deranged mentally and was said to have been placed in a psychiatric hospital. Of Franz Putscher the Hungarian woman could tell me only that she had heard he had died in prison. About the fate of the two sons she knew nothing.

In this connection I must mention one more person. Ernst Marulich, a Yugoslav from Agram, was a typical intellectual. Tall, haggard, somewhat ungainly, and of rather delicate constitution, he seemed like a figure from another world in his well-tailored suits and elegant topcoat, in which he shivered not a little in the Siberian winter. He had had to migrate to Russia because of his Communistic activity as a student. Why he had been sent to Siberia, of all places, I do not know—he was certainly out of place here. He first had to do cultural work among the aliens; later he had charge of the foreign office. In practical matters he had little experience, but he was so devoted to his ideal to the point of self-sacrifice that he remained virtually unaffected by the difficult conditions under which we had to live. We became friends. Georgi got along well with him, since Ernst was highly educated and was in every way a fine and decent person. He too did not, of course, escape arrest. As I learned later in prison, he was said to have suffered a complete collapse.

One day in the middle of October, when the number of arrests was constantly increasing and more and more acquaintances and colleagues were victimized, Georgi came home quite agitated. Although it had not come unexpectedly, he was nevertheless stunned when the director, Butenko, said to him, "Now it's your turn. You know I can do nothing to help you. I don't know how I can possibly get my work done. Almost all my electrical engineers are in prison."

Several days later—I had just returned from the library and was looking after the children—Georgi came home much earlier than usual. As soon as I saw him, I knew that the feared catastrophe had become reality. Tall, powerful Georgi, who had always been so light of foot, always so confident, now stood before me as though his limbs had become leaden. His face was gray and lifeless. We merely stood and looked at each other.

As usual Ruslan wanted to snuggle up to his father. He called, "Papa!" But there was no answer. Georgi remained standing before the child, looking at him seriously and sadly, so that the little fellow became quite uncertain. He kept looking up at him with inquiring and appealing glances. Finally Georgi lifted him up and hugged him. For a while he stood there, then sat down heavily with the child in his arms, and I saw that Georgi was crying. It was the first time I had seen him cry. Georgi had always regarded tears as something incomprehensible and undignified. Now he sat there with tears in his eyes and gazed at his son as though he were trying to imprint the boy's features on his mind. And then I comprehended the impotent despair that had overwhelmed him. He still clasped his child in his arms; the four walls of our apartment still enclosed us; but this very night all this could end forever, and we might never see each other again.

Until this moment I had been unwilling to admit to myself the possibility of such an atrocity, but now it was real.

We still had to wait for the party meeting, but we knew that it would be merely a formality. A few days later we both went to the meeting and were promptly expelled from the party. As usual, a member of the NKVD proposed the expulsion on the basis of alleged incriminating evidence against Georgi. I was merely asked if I had known a certain Austrian prisoner of war who had remained somewhere in the Kuznetsk Basin following World War I. Although I answered in the negative—I had never heard of him, nor had I been at that place—my answer was brushed aside with a malicious, suggestive gesture. No one, of course, dared say even a word in our defense, just as no one voted against our expulsion. In the face of the comedy I could not hold back my tears. It was so dreadful that the very same persons who until recently had treated Georgi with such respect, and many of whom addressed me merely as "Hildushka," now voted for our expulsion. But the expulsion was not the major issue. We could, after all, be happy not to belong to a party whose leaders helped or even caused such things to happen. We no longer had to take part in such meetings and to raise our hands for the expulsion of a close friend—the alternative being the certainty of being overtaken by the same fate the following day.

We returned home, knowing that the only thing we could do was to wait for Georgi's arrest. As difficult as it was for Georgi, he seemed to be more composed than I. I was completely beside myself. In the course of a few days I had grown terribly thin. Again and again Georgi impressed on me what I would have to do after his arrest: to think only of the children, to take them to his brother immediately. He did not conceal the fear, however, that I too might be arrested. "At least save Ruslan," he said. "In any event, get him away from here. Irina is too small; she can't live without you. She will die."

The days that we lived through were frightful. Immediately after his expulsion Georgi sent a protest telegram to the central commission of the Central Committee in Moscow and another one to Eikhe, who was still secretary of the Novosibirsk party committee and knew Georgi well. Of course, he received no reply. "If I were merely a lackey in America, nothing like this could happen to me," he said frequently in those days. "I could at least take my wife and children and go somewhere, if I were expelled without guilt. I could, of course, put a bullet through my head, as the municipal school supervisor recently did when he was accused of being a former Trotskyite. But if I did that, people could say that the accusations against me are true, and then matters would be even worse for you and the children." But matters could not have been worse than they were.

The NKVD was not long in coming. It was just after midnight. Georgi was still lying awake in bed. Just as I began to wash Irina's diapers, the doorbell rang. I quickly ran to Georgi. Once more he implored and encouraged me. I could not tear myself away from him, but the ringing of the doorbell became more insistent. I went to open the door. Two acquaintances stood there. They brusquely pushed me aside and told Georgi why they had come. They began to search the apartment. I could not help crying. Only now was I fully conscious of the fact that here I was far from home, without hope or protection, with two small children. I also realized that I had to go on living, had to live for the sake of the children, even though in this moment I had a premonition that I would never again see Georgi. Because of the noise, Ruslan awoke in his little bed and cried. Georgi could scarcely tear himself away from the child. It took quite a while until the search was completed. What they were actually looking for, I do not know, for there was absolutely nothing in our apartment that could have yielded any clues. We had long ago burned all Soviet magazines and books containing articles by persons who had been arrested or convicted. As late as 1935–36 there had been contributions by Radek, Bukharin, and other writers whose works now were banned.[3] At that time there was an enormous assault on books in most homes.

3. Karl Berngardovich Radek (1885–1937), like Trotsky, was an influential politician and a brilliant pamphleteer. A journalist of international stature, Radek served *Izvestia* as editor for foreign affairs from 1931 until 1937, when he fell victim to the Great Purge and was sentenced to ten years' imprison-

Finally the degrading rummaging around was over. I packed every conceivable useful thing for Georgi, and we took leave of each other. How hard it was to let him go, when I knew that I would never see him again. I cried incessantly. Bewildered, I stood there in my pain after the door had closed. Yet only a few minutes later the doorbell rang again. Georgi had persuaded the men to let him return to speak to me once more. He implored me not to forget what he had urged me to do and not to speak to anyone about it. He knew how indignant I became about injustice and how easily words got past my lips. Evidently, he had asked the men to tell him truthfully whether I was to be arrested, and they apparently had assured him that there were no charges pending against me. Thereupon he wanted to warn me again not to commit any indiscretion that could be even a superficial reason for my arrest.

It was late in October when this happened. Georgi had reached the age of forty this year. On his birthday in June he had stood before me, bursting with strength and brimming with energy, and had said that we should postpone his birthday observance until the October festival, for then it would coincide both with the completion of twenty years of party membership on his part and with the twentieth anniversary of the October revolution. This celebration never took place.

No one knew what happened to the arrested men. Like most other women—those who had not yet been apprehended themselves—I ran to the NKVD. Furthermore, I tried to get the money that was still owed to Georgi, since I had been dismissed at the library. I sold everything I could possibly spare. After all, I had

---

ment. Some sources state that he was shot to death following a mock trial. Nicolai Ivanovich Bukharin (1888–1938) was a prominent economic theorist. Expelled from the Communist party in 1929, he was shot to death after a mock trial during the Great Purge.

to go to Georgi's brother, and I did not want to arrive there with empty hands.

Things went with me as with the other women; we could learn nothing about our husbands. I was still living in our home with Georgi's niece when one day in the middle of December I received notification that I had to be out of the apartment within a few hours and that I was to leave the furniture there. It was the coldest time of the year. So with both children and my transportable goods—a bed and a crib—I was loaded onto a sled and taken to an unheated shack. It is not hard to imagine what kind of place it was, for it had remained unused despite the dire housing shortage that prevailed in Kuznetsk at that time. The walls were covered with a finger-thick crust of ice, and except for a primitive stove in the middle of the shack there was nothing else there.

How fortunate that Kuznetsk was well supplied with coal! The newly constructed buildings all had central heating. Now I had to do everything possible to save my children from freezing. I kept the fire going in that kitchen stove day and night, and I moved the children's beds close to the stove. The apartment that we had furnished with such toil and pain went to the NKVD man who had arrested Georgi. He regarded everything he had taken from us as well-earned booty, for when I returned the day following our evacuation for the provisions that I had forgotten in my haste and that I needed for the children, he refused to let me have them.

Weeks later I was summoned to the NKVD. A woman from one of the barracks stayed with the children. I was conducted to an inquisitor who handed me a letter from Georgi, in which he asked me for news about the children and myself and why I had not yet gone to his brother. The inquisitor demanded that I write Georgi on the spot that I was with the children, for—so he said—someone had told Georgi that I had been arrested. As ignorant and naive as I still was at that time, I naturally wrote him a reassuring letter, even though I knew I had been involved in the legal proceedings, since I was not permitted to leave Kuznetsk. I was permitted to go to the NKVD again to receive Georgi's acknowledgment of my letter; I was also permitted to send him food and money—his unpaid salary, which was suddenly given to me. I received one more letter from him which I have saved to this very day:

I am well. Don't worry about me, and take care of your health for the sake of our children. I have received everything you sent me and need nothing further. You have actually sent me too many provisions and other things. (You must be very sparing with the money.)

My health and state of mind depend on what happens to you and the children. If you succeed in getting to my relatives with the children and if you are healthy, I too shall be healthy and calm.

Therefore I beg you again to do everything you can to inform me by telegram and letter about your trip and your arrival, and whether you and the children are well. If I know that, everything will be as I wish. As soon as possible I shall give you information about myself. You know that all my thoughts, all my feelings, my entire being are with you and the children. I am firmly convinced that you will do everything to keep the children alive and healthy. That is all I wish to say.

Remain calm and healthy.

I kiss you, the children, and Nyura.

Your Georgi

6 January 38

P.S. Don't send me anything else, neither money, nor food, nor other things. Do everything you can to get away as quickly as possible.

With kisses,

Your Georgi

These lines were the last sign of life that I or his relatives had of Georgi.

Now nothing could hold me back. I left with the children at the end of January 1938. At this time railroad stations were closely guarded, but at every train departure there were crowds of people. I put on a kerchief and an old coat so that I resembled a *babushka*.[4] I also disguised the children in such a way that we looked more like the other passengers who in those times thronged the stations. Georgi's niece, who had moved in with a friend when I was evicted from my apartment, bought the tickets for me, checked the belongings that I could not carry, and went to the station with me. Thus I left Kuznetsk, worried and fearful that I might be detected and brought back. And indeed, on this four-day journey I did have to pass two controls. I was able to prove my identity both times with my personal ID card, which was the only document I had, but naturally I was terrified each time. In Moscow we had to wait until the next day for our connection, so we spent the night in the station. We did not arrive at the little station of our destination until the evening of the next day. Georgi's brother Grigori was waiting for us.

---

4. *Babushka* is here used in its literal sense of "grandmother."

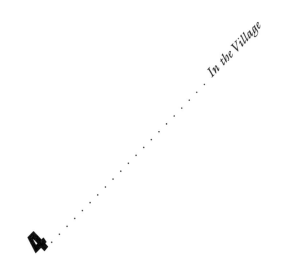

Grigori drove us to his place in a simple kolkhoz sled.[1] The village Kostin-Otdelets was located sixteen kilometers from Ternovka station. It was in the district of Voronezh, not far from the city of Borisoglebsk. The modest hut of the simple kolkhoz farmer would be my only refuge and a home for my children for several months. Grigori and his wife, Natasha, gave me a friendly reception. What touched me especially was the fact that Natasha, as soon as we had exchanged greetings, said, "Stalin did this, didn't he?" Her words expressed what many were thinking at that time.

I had met Georgi's family on a visit in the winter of 1933. His oldest brother, Grigori, owned his own hut. At that time the youngest brother, Nikolai, lived with his wife and their three children in one room of the parents' two-room cottage. He worked as a brigade leader on a distant kolkhoz. During World War I, Grigori and Georgi, who was more than ten years younger, had been in the same regiment. Grigori had served as a private, whereas Georgi had risen to the rank of corporal. In the Red Army, Grigori served for a time in the unit that was commanded

1. Kolkhozes were collective farms.

by Georgi. On the kolkhoz Grigori was a simple and diligent worker. His own place was small: it consisted of the few acres of land the kolkhoz farmers were permitted to keep, one cow, and a few chickens.

I was very sorry that Georgi's parents were no longer alive. His mother had died of pneumonia a few months before, and Georgi had regretted very much that because of the tense situation in Kuznetsk, he had been unable to go to Kostin-Otdelets. His father had died just a few weeks before my arrival. It seems likely that he had heard something about Georgi's fate. In order to make a coffin for him they had had to take a few boards from the floor of the parents' room, since there was nothing else available in the village.

Before the Revolution the Shcherbatovs, who had owned very little land, had worked for an estate owner named Malakhov. Georgi's father, a man of initiative, had planted a large orchard, which brought the family additional income. The sons, as soon as they could, had to work on Malakhov's estate, but the father had seen to it that they all attended the village school. This was something that not all parents did in those days.

A patriarchal order prevailed in the family. In 1902 Grigori, at the age of eighteen, had married a girl his age, Natasha, who had been selected by the parents. Then both of them had worked on the Malakhov estate. This marriage remained childless. During the war, when Grigori had been in the army and Natasha had worked in the home of the estate owner, she had borne her only child, Nyura. Grigori reared this child as though it had been his own and never betrayed the fact that he was not the father. I do not believe that Nyura ever knew it.

During the Revolution most of the peasants in this village had joined Makhno.[2] The estate-owner Malakhov had been shot

2. N. I. Makhno led a peasant anarchist army in the Ukraine during the Russian Civil War. Although quite independent of the Reds, his forces opposed the landowners and fought against the White armies.

to death by them. The Shcherbatovs, who had not taken part in plundering and whose two sons had served in the Red Army, were an exception in this village.

The father had been a man of very venerable appearance. He was not so tall as his sons, but with his long, white beard and Russian shirt he had reminded me of portraits of Tolstoy. He had spoken little but thoughtfully, always listening attentively to the person with whom he was conversing; I had often been astonished at the logic of his objections when he interrupted Georgi's lavish speeches about the plant construction at Kuznetsk and his great visions of the future. As little as I had understood in the few days we were there, so much the more did I have to think of his father's words later. Our visit had been just after the drastic collectivization, and suddenly there had been nothing to buy. The old man had reminded Georgi that although they had formerly had to work very hard, they had nevertheless been able to celebrate their festivals and to lay back reserves for poor harvest years, whereas now they lived from hand to mouth and badly at that. Life had not merely been completely transformed; it had almost died out.

The Shcherbatovs also had a daughter who, to the sorrow of the family, had had an affair with a worthless fellow during the war. The man had had to enter the armed forces, and while he was in the army, she had had a child. She had named it Misha. When she became pregnant again, however, she had gone to a quack for an abortion, and this had led to her death. Her friend had later married, and the old Shcherbatovs had kept the little boy. Georgi had always sent money for him. As long as the parents had been alive, the boy was well taken care of, but when they both died, one so soon after the other, he had been passed back and forth between Nikolai and his own father, who had several other children by his wife. If Georgi and I had not been so harassed at that time, we would probably have taken him in. When I came to the village, Misha was about thirteen years old, and as long as I lived there, I looked after this unusually intelligent, well-behaved, and studious boy. He lived with us, and Ruslan was very fond of him. His later fate was similar to that of many other young fellows; as a soldier he was sent to the front, where he was soon killed.

Georgi had told me how he had once been playing in front of their cottage, where he had been instructed to take care of his three-year-old brother, Nikolai. All of a sudden Nikolai, who had been playing near the well, disappeared. In great fright Georgi screamed at the top of his lungs. The mother rushed from the cottage and without a moment's hesitation had sprung into the well into which the little fellow had fallen. Neighbors hastened to pull both of them out of the well, which was several meters deep. Nikolai had broken out his front teeth, and his mother had broken a foot. But after this event she had been more highly respected, not only by her family but by the entire village.

Kostin-Otdelets, which extended for several kilometers and had, as I was told, over ten thousand inhabitants, was a typical village of the central black-earth region. On both sides of the broad village street stood small, mostly one-room cottages. There were only a few brick houses, most of them built in the center of town, in the vicinity of the church. The straw-roofed cottages were made of clay or of wickerwork smeared with clay. The windows consisted of a single pane of glass. On the coarse plank floor stood a bed. In the corner was a table with benches and sometimes with chairs. The Russian oven occupied almost one-fourth of the space. Especially in the winter it served as a sleeping place for the entire family.

The fireplace was located far inside the oven, and all pots had to be pushed in with the help of a handle fastened to a long pole. Since the pots were mostly made of cast iron, this was heavy, difficult work. In addition to food for the family, fodder and mash for the animals had to be cooked or warmed. Through the strain of this work many women became ill (prolapse of the uterus was especially frequent). The oven kept the food warm all day—often until late at night. As fuel, people used dried cow manure, straw, and what little brush they were allowed to gather in the woods. The forests were state property, and no one was permitted to fell trees.

Here for the first time in my life I encountered real poverty. Even the poorest cottagers of my home country could not be compared with the people of this village. The Austrian cottagers all had more than one room to live in, and most of them had more than one cow in the stable. Our cottagers also had outdoor toilets, so that it was not necessary to go to the manure pile or behind the house to relieve oneself in full view of the neighbors.

Here there was scarcely any kerosene for the tiny lamps. Whether one wished to or not, one had to go to bed early. The water from the draw wells was so hard that it could not be used for washing. Soap was in short supply, and there were no detergents. Since I had to bathe the children and wash diapers or clothing every day, I had to melt snow in the oven in the winter and collect rainwater in the summer.

It was lucky for me that I had been able to send by train the few belongings I had rescued. Grigori had driven to the station in the sled to fetch them for me, and so I had at least a bed for myself, a crib, a child's bathtub, and some household necessities. In Kuznetsk I had once stood in line for a long time in order to get hold of a manual sewing machine, and this came in very handy. In Vienna I had learned something about sewing and tailoring, I could knit well, and so I could earn a little something here. It was not so much a matter of money as of provisions, which were in scant supply.

Because I was worried about my children, I soon learned to adjust to conditions here. Furthermore, I felt more secure with Grigori and Natasha than in the shack in Kuznetsk, despite the electric lamp—my only luxury there—and an abundance of coal for fuel.

Nevertheless, life was very difficult. I was among strange people under strange circumstances, and sometimes I felt I had been abandoned by the whole world. Since I found it difficult to accept help from others, I did everything I could to provide for the three of us myself.

Georgi had two old friends with whom he had served in the Red Army. I had met both of them during our first visit here. One was a farmer who lived not far from us. He was one of the few persons in the village who had not joined the kolkhoz. With his wife, who did sewing while he did odd jobs, he managed his little farm well and was able to support his family. Since he was a veteran of the Red Army, he had remained unmolested so far, even though things were made difficult for the few persons who were not in the kolkhoz; most of them had simply been dispossessed and deported. He and his wife always treated me very well. Georgi's fate had depressed and disquieted them very much.

The second friend was the chairman of a kolkhoz that was located some distance away. When he learned that the children and I had arrived, he sent his wife with a carriage so that we could spend a few days with them. He lived in a somewhat better house, which probably had once belonged to a rich villager and now was the property of the kolkhoz.

As I knew from Georgi's accounts, the three had been close friends, their friendship having begun in the imperial army. They had been recruited at the same time and had then served together in the Red Army. They had gone through thick and thin together and had borne and shared difficulties. Each of them had been wounded several times. With one of them Georgi had been captured by the White Army, where they had been saved from death only by chance: one of the guards was from the same region as they, and at the very last moment before they were to be shot he let them escape. On another occasion the three had succeeded at the peril of their lives in fighting their way out of an encirclement by the White Army.

Since I already knew so much about them, there was always much to talk about when I stayed with these friends. Yet the conversations with Fedya, the farmer, had quite a different character from those of the chairman of the kolkhoz. Fedya felt that all the ideals for which he had fought had been betrayed. He rejected collectivization and had the courage to oppose it. He did not join the party and was greatly worried about the future.

The other friend, who put forth every effort to promote and advance the kolkhoz, was no less worried when he saw that the Communists who performed their duties honestly were suddenly engulfed in mistrust. Even in the villages arrests were made. Party members and other influential persons were the first to disappear. If, here and there, one of these was still left, this was regarded as a matter of chance. People lived in constant fear.

In the few days that we spent at the home of the kolkhoz manager, he and his wife did everything they could to make life less difficult for me. They gave me some provisions and a *pood* of rye before they brought us back to Grigori.[3]

Until the weather got warm, I lived at Grigori's house, but when it was no longer necessary to heat the Russian oven, I moved into his parents' empty cottage. I placed my bed over the part of the floor from which the planks for the father's coffin had been taken. Since I had brought a Primus stove along, I used it for cooking. I had to be very sparing with kerosene, which was scarce, but the tractor driver from the kolkhoz sometimes sold me some of the little he was able to divert.

Although Georgi had implored me to go to his relatives immediately after his arrest, he had also warned me urgently: "You cannot be too careful there. The villagers will steal everything from you. You have no idea what thieves there are there." I was soon to experience how right he was.

While I was living in the parents' cottage, a distant relative of

---

3. A *pood* is a Russian unit of weight equal to 36.11 pounds avoirdupois.

Georgi's came to visit me under some pretext or other. It was around noon, and I had just fed the children and put them in bed for a nap. Since I had been sewing, the sewing machine was standing on the table. About sixty rubles lay in a small drawer—a great deal of money at the time. Just as the relative was about to leave, I noticed that the money was missing. Although she tried to slip away quickly, I had the presence of mind to scream so loudly that the people next door could hear me, and with the help of the neighbors I succeeded in getting the money back. This experience made me cry terribly.

From that time on I lived in constant fear, especially at night, for the door of the cottage opened directly toward the street and could be secured inside only by means of a hook. Besides, it would have been child's play to climb in through the low windows.

Whereas the paupers of Kostin-Otdelets exploited every opportunity to commit their crimes, there were many, like Georgi and his friends, who from a deep sense of conviction fought for a better life and for the freedom the Russian people had never known. The difficult life in this village taught me to understand many things.

Grigori and Natasha came to help me whenever they could. Ruslan was especially fond of Grigori, and although only two and a half years old, he invented all possible pretexts to run over to his cottage. Once, when he had gotten away from me, I went after him on the village street. In summer it was thickly covered with grass, since there was scarcely any traffic. People tied their young animals to long ropes there and let them graze. I saw Ruslan approach too close to a young bull. The bull sprang at Ruslan. I ran to him in terror. Ruslan was frightened to death and screamed at the top of his voice. The bull had knocked him down, but except for his fright he had suffered no harm.

Nikolai's wife (he himself was seldom at home) and their children, who lived next door, were always good to me as they were also to Misha, who frequently stayed with them. I was astonished at the miserable conditions under which children grew up here. They seldom had a change of clothing or underwear; there were not always enough shoes for everyone. Early in the morning the women cooked the cabbage soup for the whole day. Every ten or twelve days they baked rye bread. From time to time there was also some porridge, and the people were happy when they had it.

Since kerosene was always scarce, I once tried to heat the Russian oven on a hot summer morning. But when the smoke rose from the chimney, the neighbors came running; they were afraid that sparks might set the straw roofs of the surrounding cottages on fire. I never dared do anything like that again.

I was in every respect a foreign body in the village. The children gaped at me and treated Ruslan and Irina like beautiful dolls that did not belong to them. Everything was incredible for them, but also for me. Even though I could express myself in Russian and understood everything they said, my pronunciation as well as my appearance and my conduct were quite different. Only with difficulty could I accustom myself to what for them was routine.

I was not a member of the kolkhoz, nor could I be admitted to it. I had applied for the position of German teacher in the village school, but when I appeared before the local soviet, I realized immediately that they would not dare appoint me. They told me I could find work in road construction about ten kilometers distant. My children were growing. Both were beautiful and bright. How Georgi and I had longed for these children, and how happy we had been to have a boy and a girl. And with what sorrowful, anxious eyes did I have to regard them, now that the bleakness of my situation became clear to me. It was a life completely without prospect; the Kuznetsk NKVD had already inquired about me. I could be taken away from my children at any moment. I became increasingly more aware of the fact that there was no place where

I actually belonged. More and more keenly I felt that I was even more deprived of rights than all the others.

At the beginning of summer there were scarcely any potatoes left, and there were still no vegetables. The grain and the groats were soon exhausted everywhere. So one day I made my way to Ternovka, the station town, where there was a store in which allegedly there was something to buy. But even there I found nothing but groats. Previously I had gone to market with some neighbors in a rather distant village, where many farmers had come together from the surrounding villages. Yet there too almost nothing was offered for sale except millet. I had bought a *pood* of millet at that time. By chance there were lemons in the store in Ternovka. They were expensive, but I bought several.

Scarcely had I returned from Ternovka—I had covered more than thirty kilometers to and from that place on foot—when both my children came down with dysentery, regarded in the village as one of the most dangerous diseases. Every year it carried off many children, for there were neither sulfa drugs nor antibiotics. In the clinic, where a field surgeon was on duty, they actually had only herbal teas, which were ineffective. But they did have "beautiful" placards on the wall: "The enemies of the people must be torn out by the roots!" At that time walls everywhere were "decorated" with these and similar posters, but here with my deathly sick children I truly sensed the significance of this threat. Naturally, the medicines I received at the clinic were of no help. The children had a high fever, threw up everything they swallowed, and excreted blood and water.

Even when Ruslan had been quite small and there had been little fruit in Siberia, he had been used to drinking lemon juice. At that time the lemons had come from the Caucasus, and during the Spanish Civil War also from Spain. How fortunate now that I had walked the long road to Ternovka! I gave the children the juice of the lemons, and it worked like a miracle—the children recovered. At this time I was still nursing Irina, since there was no safe milk in the village, and I knew about the danger of an infection—especially in the summertime. Although the child could by then eat everything, the milk was the iron reserve. And with what relish the child nursed in the morning and in the evening.

At first I had been horrified to see Russian women nursing their children often to the age of two years. But in Kuznetsk there was no dairy, and the milk that could be bought was often sour. So I came to understand how sensible Russian mothers were in nursing their children so long.

How difficult life in the village was at this time is shown by something I saw in the summer of 1938. As I was on my way with little Irina to the Board of Control in Moscow (a kolkhoz wagon had taken us along to the station at Ternovka), we came past a potato field. In this huge, level field there was an entire brigade of kolkhoz workers busily digging out potatoes. But the potatoes were only the size of plums and far from mature. I was astonished and could not help asking why they were already harvesting the potatoes. The answer was that they had been ordered to deliver the potatoes to Moscow immediately. I could hardly believe it. Having grown up in farming country, I knew something about harvesting various crops. If we needed some early potatoes, we carefully dug a few of the larger ones here and there by hand and took care not to disturb the others. But to harvest potatoes that were not even half grown was a terrible waste. Even in the village, potatoes were a luxury at that time. The old ones were almost gone, and the farmers did not yet dare to harvest the new ones from their own tiny patches.

A second experience on this journey revealed to me the sheer brutality of my situation. To make the trip, I had had to purchase a reserved ticket on an express train. When I occupied the seat with Irina (each seat was also a sleeping accommodation and thus occupied the entire bench), I saw in the upper berth an NKVD officer with the characteristic blue cap. It was already toward evening when we got to Ryazan, where the train stopped to take on coal and water. As soon as we pulled into the station, I noticed that something unusual was happening. Beside the tracks, huddled closely together, was a crowd of people—women with babies on their arms, children, and old people. Some distance away a long column of prisoners was being led to cattle cars standing beyond the station. I saw pale, emaciated figures whose appearance reflected months of imprisonment and torture. A chain of guards in close formation with leveled rifles and barking dogs on leashes escorted them. Women called out the names of their husbands, who were among the prisoners. They cried and screamed. Some of them had thrown themselves down on the ground; some kneeled and begged the guards to let them give their husbands some food and articles of clothing. But the guards, their guns at the ready, did not even look at them. They merely repeated their customary warning: "Not a step to the right, not a step to the left; otherwise you will be shot immediately!" Now and again a prisoner who recognized a face among the weeping women would raise a hand to wave. They all tried to look at the women and to turn their benumbed faces toward them. But the guards merely drove them on all the more.

I shuddered to think that Georgi had been treated like that, but even more terrible for me was the sight of these lamenting women who ran along beside the train, crying and screaming. As our train was pulling out, I could see how the first prisoners to arrive had to kneel down by the cattle cars, while the women were forced away from the area.

Since I had Irina on my arm, she had also seen everything. When I stepped away from the window, I was so agitated that I could not hold back my tears and loudly voiced my indignation at this cruelty. Then the NKVD man leaned down to me and said emphatically, "They are guilty and are getting what they deserve. There is no reason to pity them."

At the Board of Control in Moscow, to which I had already submitted a detailed appeal, I again mentioned the telegram that Georgi had sent them following his exclusion from the party. But again I was unable to get any definite information. They consoled me by saying I should receive an answer as soon as they had discussed the matter.

I spent the night with friends of Grigori's in Moscow. I also looked up my Austrian friends to ask for their advice. I sensed at once, however, that I was speaking to deaf ears. And so I returned a day later, convinced that there was no escape from my situation and that I now had to be prepared for all eventualities.

Not until September 1938 did I receive a letter informing me that I had to appear before the Board of Control in Novosibirsk for the discussion of my case. Even the date was fixed. I was required to present a precise description of my work in Kuznetsk, and it would therefore be necessary for me to go there first. This notification was sent to me from the Board of Control by registered mail. It deeply disturbed me, even though I could not yet know that the Board of Control had acted on the direct orders of the NKVD. It seemed to me impossible not to comply with this summons, especially because I knew that questions about me had already been directed to the local village soviet.

With a heavy heart I set out. Again I took Irina, since I could not very well burden Natasha and Grigori with the care of two children. In the village there was at this time barely enough food to live on, and after the serious illness of the children I had not been able to bring myself to wean Irina. The milk, after all, had contributed so much to her recovery. Now that I had to travel, she would be all the more dependent on my milk; it was very dangerous to give children the food, especially the milk, that was sold in the stations. But the most important reason for taking Irina along was the fact that I had to travel to Kuznetsk by way of Moscow, and I strongly hoped that my Austrian friends, whom I really wanted to see, could do something for me. I wanted to leave Irina with them, not only to spare her the journey but also to secure protection for her in case I was arrested. Furthermore, it would be easier for Grigori to fetch her from Moscow than from Kuznetsk. And so in Moscow I went with anxious heart to find my friends. But they refused to keep Irina. Even when I had been at the Board of Control in Moscow the first time, they had treated me as though Georgi had been guilty and had not been arrested without good cause. Like many others, they were afraid—and not without reason, for so many had already been arrested.

It is difficult to describe my feelings when I set out with Irina for Siberia. Scarcely nine months had passed since I had left Siberia with the children, in constant fear of being arrested during the journey. I thought of my hopes and expectations when I had first traveled this route with Georgi. Now I still had no information about him and had to fear the worst for him and also for myself.

Irina and I were still together, and I took delight in the many words she could already speak and in the friendly smile with which she greeted all fellow passengers. With what joy she drank the milk from my breasts; it was indeed the only warm food I could give her on this journey.

The closer the train, with relentless speed, brought me to Kuznetsk—I had neither eye nor ear for the many well-known places we passed—the stronger my feeling of despair became, and the more clearly I realized that there was nothing and no one who could offer me help and protection.

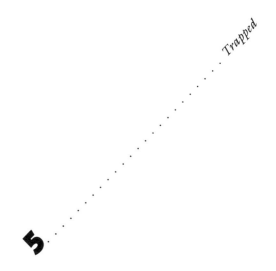

5

It was evening when I arrived in Kuznetsk. I had no other choice but to look up an acquaintance. She was terrified to see me, but she could not bring herself to send me away. As much as we had to tell each other, there was nothing that could have given me even a wisp of hope. She too was without information about her arrested husband. Expelled from her house, she now lived in a room in one of the barracks. After the children had fallen asleep, she told me in a low and uncertain voice, excited and fearful, about everything that had happened meanwhile in Kuznetsk.

After my departure the arrests had not ceased. Not only managers but also workers and even unskilled laborers had been apprehended. As hopeless as my own situation seemed, just so depressing was it for me to learn what had happened to all the persons with whom we had worked together and with whom we had carried on so many friendly conversations.

From the many sad individual fates there arose a frightful picture. Almost all those who had built the steel plant, under the most trying conditions, had disappeared behind the walls of the "First House" (the NKVD building still bore this name, in Russian *Pervyi Dom*). And many of those who had replaced them at the plant had likewise been arrested. Most of them were never heard of again. People knew about executions by shooting but never learned the names of the victims. After long months of waiting, news of some prisoners came from distant forced-labor camps, and it was regarded as great good fortune if the sentence was only ten years of hard labor, for in most cases it ranged from fifteen to twenty-five years.

In recent weeks, to be sure, there had been fewer arrests, and in the most recent ones the wives had usually been spared. Apparently the planned quota of arrests had just about been filled. But the lives of the women who remained "free" were far from secure. Very few were permitted to find shelter with relatives. Most of them were evacuated from their homes, resettled, and often permitted to engage only in the worst-paid kinds of work.

The steel plant, which we all had built with much love and great expectations, also suffered as a result. In the atmosphere of anxiety and insecurity, in which anyone could be accused of "wrecking," all initiative was extinguished, and the few trained personnel who remained were unable to fulfill the production quotas, much less to utilize the plant to full capacity.[1] The atmosphere of fear had also prevented my acquaintance from answering my letters and warning me. It was fully clear to both of us, however, that such a warning could not have changed matters.

The next morning I carried out my orders by immediately going to procure my service record. I was told to report at three o'clock to the cadre division, where allegedly a discussion was to take place. I had no real hope, yet things could not continue as they were.

On other occasions when I had had to leave Irina, she had not taken it so hard, but this time she ran after me all the way to

---

1. "Wrecking" was a popular Communist term for various kinds of real or alleged sabotage. The work is usually rendered as "sabotage" in this translation.

the door, calling "Mama, Mama," and she cried terribly when I closed the door behind me. In the last few days so many strange experiences had assailed her that she had not yet been able to adjust to the new environment and the strange people. Her mother was the only fixed point to which she could cling. With confused feelings I left Irina in the care of my acquaintance's son, but I did not then think that I would never see her again.

The meeting took place in the department of which Georgi had once been head. Georgi's deputy as well as his secretary had already been arrested, and the deputy's wife had given birth to her third child at this time. In the room adjacent to Georgi's former office several men sat at a long table. I knew two of them well. The chairman was Pinin, who had once worked with Georgi. Georgi had done much for him. Pinin had been expelled from the party, and Georgi had personally assumed responsibility for him. He had him reinstalled in his position and arranged to have his expulsion annulled. The second man I knew also owed his professional advancement to Georgi.

The men sat there as though they were to sit in judgment of me. In their faces I saw no trace of warm, human sympathy—only triumph. Yet I had never done them any wrong but had always treated them as Georgi's friends. How resigned I had already become. What remained to me in a foreign country without protection of any kind? My only goal was to save my children and, as long as I remained free, to do all I could for Georgi's vindication. At the very least I wanted to know what they had done with him and where he was.

But my modest hopes vanished as soon as one of the men declared that there could be no discussion of Georgi's rehabilitation, for his crimes had been proved and he had been sentenced to twenty-five years at hard labor. I, however, should have recognized him as an enemy of the people and exposed him; consequently, I was also guilty.

My God! What was more flagrant—the twenty-five-year sen-

tence or the realization that such an honest man, completely devoted to his country, could be charged with crimes that would
justify such an outrageous punishment? What had Georgi already
had to endure, and what still awaited him? I looked these men in
the face. That they were not ashamed even to say such things—
these men who knew how hard Georgi had worked and who he
was! No! Suddenly I no longer felt meek and resigned. I had
been wounded enough, but I would never have performed such
servile services.

Indignantly I shouted that Georgi had never committed a
crime and that I consequently could not have exposed him. I
asked where he was, and if I could at least write to him. But the
men declared that they did not know, and they told me to wait
outside the room until they decided what kind of service record
they wished to issue to me. Stunned, I left the room. What I had
heard was shocking enough—but more was already awaiting me:
an agent of the NKVD declared unceremoniously that I was under
arrest. For whom had this farce been performed? They had pretended to grant a hearing in response to a petition. In reality
they had merely demonstrated the close connivance between the
Board of Control of the Central Committee and the NKVD and
the fact that there was in the entire Soviet Union no court of
justice to which one could appeal.

At this moment I had only one duty: to provide protection
for Irina. I implored the NKVD agent to take me to her so that
I could make arrangements for Georgi's relatives to fetch her.
But my entreaties were in vain. The agent made me get into an
automobile, and he drove me to the railroad station to get my
suitcase, which was still in the baggage office. Then he drove me
to the jail. Georgi had been right when he said that I would not
be able to save Irina. She was not even one and a half years old. I
never saw her again, and all my recollections of her are combined
with the painful scene of our final farewell.

As soon as the jail door had closed behind me, the NKVD agent took a document from his pocket. He pretended to be in a great hurry. I begged him once more to take me to my child, or at least to permit me to advise the woman in whose home she was, but he categorically refused. He read from the document: as a member of the family of an enemy of the people and a traitor to the fatherland, I had been condemned to five years in a forced labor camp by the special commission of the NKVD in Moscow. "Five years! My children! What will happen to them?" Of course I was not allowed to read the document. I had to surrender my possessions, and I was put into a cell completely filled with double-tiered plank beds. The women lay there, crowded close together, and upon my entrance they all sat up in astonishment. Before I could comprehend what had happened to me, all at once some of them addressed me by name. They were horrified to see me appear there so suddenly. At first I did not recognize anyone. These women, confined here for months, had changed so much that it was difficult for me to identify them.

The women on the upper plank bed made room for me, moving closer together to open a narrow space. I was completely dissolved in tears. My eyes were swollen shut from weeping, and I merely stammered incessantly, "My children, my children!" Although the others were in an equally depressing situation, they were very sympathetic and took great pains to comfort me.

But how could I be comforted when I had had to experience within a few hours what the others had been prepared for for months? These women did not yet know their sentences. They even hoped, perhaps, to be freed, since they had remained here for such a long time.

It is understandable that it took a while for me to become concerned about my cellmates' situation. To be separated from my child and then to hear immediately that it was to be for five years was, in spite of all I had already experienced, just too much. Because of my isolation in the village following my departure from Kuznetsk, I scarcely knew what had happened here in the meantime or what fate the people were facing. All I knew was what my acquaintance had told me during our few hours together. As deeply as that had shocked me, it was still not so overwhelming as the grief that I now underwent in this cell.

Here I saw the wife of the chairman of the state soviet. Her husband had been arrested at the same time as Georgi; she, somewhat later. She had spent over ten months in this jail and had experienced and witnessed a great deal. For interrogation, prisoners were taken to New Kuznetsk; the jail was located in Old Kuznetsk. In the basement corridors and on the stairways to the rooms of the inquisitors, people came in contact with one another, and there all of them had soon learned to say much with a few words and gestures.

During my absence, decisive events had occurred. Most of the builders of Kuznetsk had passed through this jail. A majority of them had already been transferred elsewhere. Those who had been sentenced by the *troika*[2] had been sent to labor camps, but some had been taken away without having been sentenced, and it was this that had nurtured the wildest rumors. Some believed, to be sure, that they were to be tried in Novosibirsk, but some assumed that they had been shot without a trial, and this assumption was not unfounded; indeed, it was in part correct.

What Lebedeva told me helped me to understand Georgi's situation. She too had been interrogated and ordered to write her husband that she had not been arrested. Lebedeva had not wanted to make life even more difficult for him. Had he learned that she had been arrested, he would have known that the children had been put into an orphanage, since they had no close relatives in Siberia. And that is actually what happened. Naturally, Lebedev had learned that his wife was also in prison and

2. Under Stalin, *troikas* were specially constituted courts composed of three judges. They generally handed down severe sentences to anyone accused of a political crime.

succeeded in getting this message to her: if he did not make the false confession demanded of him, they threatened to arrest his wife; nevertheless, he refused to confess because he knew for certain that his wife had already been arrested.

Now I understood the maneuver that they had carried out with me—why I was suddenly summoned and given letters from Georgi, and why they had permitted me to send him money and other things. It also became clear to me why Georgi had insisted that I send him a telegram as soon as I reached his brother's place. I had, of course, done so.

And now I could also understand something else.

All the women in the cell had been astonished when I suddenly landed in jail directly from a state of freedom. Months before, they had read on the walls of the common toilet and of the hallways of the remand prison: "Hilda, where are you?" with Georgi's signature. I was the only Hilda in all of Kuznetsk. Since all the wives of the arrested men had been picked up immediately or soon thereafter, the people in prison were convinced that I had suffered the same fate.

Now one piece of the puzzle after the other fell into place, and I understood ever more clearly what had happened and how. Georgi, of course, had believed nothing of what I had written him, for he must have found out how they had tried to deceive Lebedev. From all this I could now guess what methods were used to force men, who were not so easily frightened, to make false confessions.

Most of the women had already been sentenced and sent to the work camps. All whom I met here were still waiting for judgment to be pronounced, something that was done after their husbands had been convicted. Since the inquisitors did not have an easy time with men of this caliber—prisoners who were not prepared to sign the confessions in spite of the torture to which they were subjected—it often took a long time to conclude a case.

When the NKVD agent read my sentence, I noticed that it had been pronounced on 7 July 1938, almost three months before my arrest. The fact that the local NKVD had been assigned the task of arresting me had given me three more months with my children, for to come and get me at the village where I had been living would have been too bothersome. It was, after all, much easier if the bird simply walked into the cage.

What we all felt and thought at that time can perhaps best be illustrated by the history of a little piece of paper. Since I had already been convicted, I was spared a long stay in the Kuznetsk prison. It was long enough, however, to permit me to learn what had happened in this one year, during which about 5,000 human beings had passed through this little prison. The prison was actually only a rather large, oblong barracks, which had been erected early in 1937. At that time people jokingly said that it was to be a vacation resort for administrators. We had all laughed at this joke, but the joke was not the result of pure chance. Considering how overcrowded this cell was, one could understand how many persons could pass through in such a short time. It was not even possible to turn around without causing one's neighbor to do likewise. After months of living like that, all the women I knew had become disfigured beyond recognition. Although still relatively young, most of them, like Lebedeva, had grown gray or even white.

I also learned something about the fate of the girl from Graz. When she was in solitary confinement, which was regarded as one of the most terrible forms of torture, a guard had taken pity on her and had occasionally given her something to eat. He was the one who had brought the note that horrified us. When the girl had again returned to the common cell, she had naively told one of the women lying beside her about this note. This woman, a Communist and the wife of the likewise arrested administrator for plant supplies, promptly reported the story to the inquisitor; in her opinion, she said, the girl was a spy. By doing this, she hoped to prove that she herself had been accused without reason.

The guard had been arrested immediately and now had to share the fate of the other prisoners. The girl had had to endure many months of the most terrible interrogations and tortures. She had been loved and pitied by all. One day she had been called out of the cell, and it was assumed that she had been expelled from the country as an alien. Upon my return to Austria, I could unfortunately learn nothing about her, because I had completely forgotten her name.

Of the many things I was told, one incident especially perturbed me. While several women were standing in the hallway of the court awaiting interrogation, one of the men who happened to be there had very cautiously slipped them a tiny rolled-up piece of paper and had requested that they throw it from the train when they were transported back to prison (women could conceal it more easily on their persons than men, who were constantly subjected to frisking). But during the trip back, the women had not succeeded in doing so. They had tried several times while being transported back and forth, but always without success. Still, they had kept the note hidden in the cell in the hope of sometime being able to throw it out of the train. When once again the customary room inspection was carried out, however, one of the women became frightened and swallowed the note. In these searches literally everything was turned upside down and inside out; every crack in the wood, every opening between the planks of the beds, was examined.

But all the women knew the content of the note from memory. It was an appeal to the people of Kuznetsk, which read approximately as follows:

We, former Communists, leading functionaries of the party, of the soviets, of the unions, and of the plant, are being accused of committing acts hostile to the people and of engaging in sabotage. We assert that these accusations are lies, and that the NKVD inquisitors employ the most cruel measures to force us to make false confessions. We are subjected to torture for hours on end, must stand barefooted on the cold floor, and are deprived of sleep and food. If anyone is committing acts hostile to the state, it is the organs of the NKVD, which wants to brand us honest men and Communists, dedicated to our country, as criminals. We appeal to you, the working people of Kuznetsk, not to believe the slanderers. Know that we have always been faithful to our ideals and will always remain faithful, no matter what may become of us. You, who know us and our work, believe us. We have fulfilled our duty according to the best of our knowledge and ability, and have honestly served our country and our people.

Among some twenty signatures was that of Georgi. It was the last sign that I received from him directly.

For me, these days were a concentrated dose of experiences that the others had acquired over a period of months but which was administered to me all at once. What could I still hope for after all this? The work camp, about which I knew absolutely nothing, would separate me from my children by several thousand more kilometers. In me the last faint hope of ever again seeing Georgi, my relatives, and my native country expired.

I suffered physically as well. Since I had still been nursing Irina, my breasts had become painfully swollen and had to be firmly tied off until the secretion of the mammary glands could be brought to a stop. It was a twofold torment because the physical pain was added to the grief of being separated from my children.

The separation from my children, the most severe trauma of my whole life, burdens me to this very day. At the time, I suffered this trauma, as well as the separation from my husband, even more strongly because my personal sorrow was intensified through fusion with that of all the other women. For us a world had collapsed, and the question "Why?" tormented our minds incessantly.

Quite early one morning, after I had been in the Kuznetsk prison for one week, I was taken away as the only woman with a group of men. Worry about Irina had so robbed me of my senses that I did not look around carefully, but it seemed to me that I did not recognize any of the men. Now I had to leave my child behind as I left this place. I had received no answers to all my questions and requests and had no idea what was to become of her.

We marched the entire distance from the prison to the station, crossing the bridge across the Tom River. I had to march at the front of a column that had the same kind of formation and the same kinds of guards as the one I had seen when the Kurilka Gang, which had committed so many crimes, was taken away. We marched past the buildings where I had lived, through the streets of Kuznetsk, the town whose origin and growth Georgi and I together had experienced with such great enthusiasm. This route was one of the most painful and shameful that I have ever traveled. At that time I did not yet know how many such roads awaited me. I think that in this brief hour I really understood for the first time to what baseness we were being subjected. On both sides of us marched the guards with guns ready to fire; behind us trotted the dogs, ready to pounce on anyone who made the slightest misstep. The commanding officer warned us that we would be shot immediately if we stepped even one foot out of line.

The horror was intensified when we were ordered at the station to kneel before the train car. On our knees we waited until we had been transferred to the train guards and were permitted to enter the car. In the car there was a young woman with an infant on her arm. Small children in a car for prisoners. Can there be anything sadder than that?

As the train pulled out, I could see through a grated peephole the smoking chimneys of the steelworks. The plant was alive, but we were to perish miserably, and our children would grow up without parents. Somehow our nocturnal arrival in Kuznetsk came to mind—the bright lights after the long journey through the darkness of night, the light that had greeted us with such great promise. What an abyss lay between then and now!

I never saw Kuznetsk again. But what I experienced there can be neither obliterated nor forgotten. The horror of this farewell and the fear of the future—yet nothing was so strong and so terrible as the painful concern for my child.

Akmolinsk

My memories of my first journey in a Stolypin car are far from good. I scarcely spoke to my companion, for both of us were in a state of shock. Furthermore, she came from the national region of Gornaya-Shoriya and spoke almost no Russian.[1] I can't recall when she was removed from the train, but she did not continue as far as Petropavlovsk. I constantly considered and reconsidered how I could get word to Grigori so that he could fetch Irina. In my purse, from which all my documents had been taken, I found a small scrap of paper and the stub of a pencil. I deliberated feverishly how I might throw a note from the train so that someone might find it and forward it. But all windows and doors were tightly locked, and I did not succeed.

From Kuznetsk to Omsk we traveled part of the same stretch

1. "Stolypin car" (alluding to P. A. Stolypin, prime minister of Russia, 1906–11) was prisoner's lingo for a railway passenger coach specially redesigned to transport convicts. Each car was divided into several locked compartments with gratings that enabled the guards to observe the prisoners at all times. The windows were blacked out.

Gornaya Shoriya is an area south of Kuznetsk inhabited primarily by members of a tiny ethnic group who speak a Turkic language.

that was familiar to me from my trips between Moscow and Kuznetsk. From Omsk we proceeded on a branch line to Petropavlovsk, where, three days later, we were put on another train. I was still virtually paralyzed from shock, and now made my first acquaintance with a provisional prison: that is, with filth, bedbugs, and such crowding that one was happy to find a place to sleep on the floor. I don't know why I was subjected to frisking there of all places. I had to help harvest crops for several days until a group had been formed that was to go to the Karaganda camp area. With several other women I was taken to Akmolinsk.

In Petropavlovsk I had lain beside Paulina Golubyatnikova. We had also worked together in the harvest field. Paulina was the only person who had noticed my emotional condition, and she had tried to be kind to me. Thus began my friendship with her.

In our group there were also women from Moscow prisons, among them several Germans from the Comintern. They had many interesting things to relate, some of them about persons I knew. These women had been sentenced not as family members but mostly according to Point 10 of the infamous Paragraph 58—because of hostile political agitation—almost all to ten years in labor camps.

Those of us who had been arrested as family members went only as far as Akmolinsk; the others were taken on to Karaganda.

The camp at Akmolinsk was designed exclusively as a camp for family members of "enemies of the people and traitors to their country." An overwhelming majority of the prisoners had been sentenced to eight years of hard labor. I was among the few who had received only five years; fewer still had gotten off with only three years.

When I arrived at Akmolinsk in October 1938, the camp was completely built. The first women, who had been brought there in 1937, had had to live in hovels dug into the ground, but now there was a large camp settlement of log barracks with the necessary outbuildings. The women themselves had done all the construction work except for the rafters. When I got there, the camp was badly overcrowded. There must have been more than 10,000 women living in the barracks. We, and all who followed us, had to sleep on the floor for a long time because the double-tiered plank beds that ran the length of the buildings could not accommodate all of us.

Akmolinsk, located in northern Kazakhstan, was at that time still a rather insignificant place. Not until later did it become an important junction, following the construction of a new railroad line through the Urals and of several industrial plants; the steppe was cultivated, and the name of the place was changed to Zelinograd. At that time, however, it was a real steppe with moorland and many swamps covered with high reeds, which spread out on all sides of the camp. The reeds were used as fuel, since there were no forests in the vicinity. The soil was very fertile.

Akmolinsk was not the only camp for family members. There was another one in Syzran on the Volga, one in the taiga near Omsk, and still others. Nor were all the women sentenced as family members put into the general camps; some were confined in high-security facilities.

The initial period of camp confinement is always the most difficult. When in retrospect I compare Akmolinsk with all the other camps where I was confined, it was certainly not the worst. But for me it provided the first impressions and horrors of a con-centration camp. By chance the first woman I met there was Mia Spitz, a good acquaintance from Vienna. She had been a kinder-garten teacher and had worked quite close to me in Grinzing. She had married a Polish student who had gone to the Soviet Union as an engineer. Both of them had been overtaken by the same fate as Georgi and I. Her only child, a boy, had been placed in an orphanage. I embraced her and desperately lamented my separa-tion from my children. As long as we were at the same place, we were close to each other. Mia had a fortunate disposition. She could see the bright side of every situation, was well acquainted with everyone, and was always well supplied with the latest news. She always knew how we should best conduct ourselves. Under the conditions in which we had to live, such a person was a real blessing. Mia's optimism was priceless.

I shall never forget Christmas Eve of 1938. Mia had somewhere gotten hold of a pot with a hot coffee-like beverage and a few spice cakes. We sat together in a corner of the barracks with two German women. Mia related several anecdotes and did not permit us to give ourselves up to our pain and sorrow. I was with her in Akmolinsk and also in Spasski; then we were separated. Mia spent the whole time in the region of Karaganda. How happy I was upon my return home to Vienna in 1948 to learn from her relatives that Mia was still alive. She was not permitted to return to Vienna, however, until after Stalin's death. She still had to endure many difficult experiences and was in very poor health when she finally came home. We have remained the best of friends until this very day. I still admire her unbroken optimism and her readiness to help.

But I also had a very unpleasant encounter in this camp. I met the woman who had denounced the girl from Graz and her prison guard to the inquisitor in Kuznetsk. I could not resist calling her to account for this. She asserted that it had been her duty to report this plot with the guard, since this connection could have been used for quite different purposes. I was horrified. How could a person who was convinced that she owed her own confinement in a camp to the caprice of bad luck so shamelessly cast suspicion on others? From then on I did not hesitate to show her how much I despised her.

When I arrived at Akmolinsk, especially strict discipline was still enforced. The worst thing about it was the fact that one might neither write nor receive letters. We knew nothing about our children, parents, or other relatives. Also the fate of our arrested husbands remained unknown to us. Especially the concern for our children weighed heavily on our hearts and minds. The uncertainty as to whether they had been put in orphanages or whether relatives had been able to care for them tormented all of us so incessantly that some women became very depressed.

Another part of this strict system was the daily muster. Every evening we had to line up in rank and file before the officer on duty and, one after the other, recite our name and sentence. With more than 300 women housed in each barracks, it took a long time to complete this procedure. Almost every evening one or more women fainted, but the camp command saw no reason to break off or to discontinue the muster. That we women had to perform very difficult tasks all day long could still be endured, for all this work was necessary to sustain life. But the daily muster was an act of sheer mockery.

It was not until late in 1939 that the special rules and the mail restriction were abolished. In a solemn manner we were officially informed that, as women sentenced as family members, we were not prisoners undergoing sentence but merely "restrained persons." Such delicate nuances were meaningless, however, since we were sent to the same general camps under the same conditions as other prisoners, as well as convicted criminals. And besides, no political prisoners or family members were released during the war, even when their term of confinement had expired. Nor were any of us discharged immediately after the war. Not until 1946 and 1947 did dismissals begin, and they were independent of the sentences. Moreover, those who were freed were not permitted to return to the central part of the Soviet Union nor to large cities.

In the general camps the convicted criminals often set the tone. By contrast, the "restrained persons" in Akmolinsk were mostly wives of former party and economic leaders, scientists, and artists. Many were highly intelligent women. Some of them were Communists. There were also aliens, wives of Comintern workers and of emigrated Communists, and also several wives of foreign—mostly German—technical personnel who had been obligated to become Soviet citizens.

Some of the women were not clear about what had actually happened and regarded the entire matter as a mistake and a temporary condition. Here and there, there were still zealous Communists who regarded themselves as innocent and all others as guilty, and who endeavored to prove their innocence at the cost of the others. In short, most of the women had not come to grips with their situation and still hoped for a great miracle. The most impossible rumors popped up, the most fantastic conjectures were formed, and these somehow whitewashed the cruel reality.

The women had been locked up because they would have been embarrassingly conspicuous through their sheer numbers. Furthermore, they had everywhere asserted their husbands' innocence, had run from pillar to post, had stood before prisons, and had engulfed the NKVD with their entreaties. Besides, housing was needed for the successors of the imprisoned personnel, for the staff of the NKVD, and for those who had lent themselves to making denunciations or providing desired eyewitness accounts. For these reasons, entire families had to disappear.

Many women who until recently had been socially prominent and had even held managerial positions were suddenly degraded to nothing. There were also women who were used to having their husbands make decisions for them and to relieve them of difficult tasks. Such persons could neither perceive that a return to their former way of life was unthinkable, nor could they imagine the possibility that they might not survive life in labor camps. To be sure, time was pitiless; it gradually taught the women to comprehend their fate, but in those days in Akmolinsk few of them grasped it.

By that time I no longer had any illusions and belonged to that group of women who viewed facts realistically. And yet how gladly we let ourselves be deluded when we heard the optimistic rumors that were disseminated there, even though we could not believe them for longer than a day. Life was too disconsolate, and so it was understandable that even the tiniest bit of information was often twisted into its opposite, into what was hoped for with such fervor and longing. The atmosphere of Akmolinsk found its most distinct expression during the preparations for the November celebration in 1938.[2] This celebration was taken very seriously. Dancers and actresses practiced diligently, and "poetesses" wrote texts. The entire camp command was to be present. The camp commander was especially esteemed by many of the women.

The club was overcrowded. I stood at the very back and saw little of the stage. But one presentation vividly comes to mind. One of the "poetesses" had revised the song "My Moscow," which was very popular at that time, for the camp, and I still remember one stanza: "And should it be necessary, we are prepared to plow with our breasts this land so large and wide." Then followed the refrain, "my Moscow." In this song lay all the faith and hope that still inspired the large majority of the women. But like everything else, the song faded out unheard and unnoticed in the empty loneliness of the Kazakh steppe.

Since several of the women in the camp had actually lived in the Kremlin, the story had already spread that Stalin had murdered his wife. Therefore I was somewhat surprised when I heard several years ago in Vienna that Alliluyeva had committed suicide.[3] We also had definite information at that time that the

2. The November celebration honored the anniversary of the 1917 revolution that brought the Bolsheviks to power.

3. Nadezhda Alliluyeva, married to Stalin in 1918, shot herself (or was shot) in her bedroom in the Kremlin in November 1932, following a quarrel with her husband at the home of Kliment Voroshilov. Alliluyeva had expressed dismay at the famine and terror rampant in Russia as the result of Stalin's forced industrialization and agricultural collectivization.

order to repress family members had been decided upon in the Central Committee of the party. How this decision was publicly propagated was shown by the placards that were displayed everywhere: "The enemies of the people must be torn out by the roots!" These words imprinted themselves indelibly on my mind, for after Georgi's arrest I came upon such posters everywhere. At that time everyone knew that "roots" meant the family members of the arrested men, and for this reason they were avoided like the plague.

A friend of Georgi's who had studied with Alliluyeva at the industrial college had told us about a friend of his, an engineer, at this school. One day the engineer had been picked up by the NKVD, and Alliluyeva had disappeared, never to be seen again. At that time I could not comprehend the significance of this story.

Akmolinsk was a world in itself and for many reasons a very impressive example of what a community of women can accomplish. Later, in the general camps, I experienced the terrible bleakness that prevailed in them and the squalidness of the men. By contrast, the camp at Akmolinsk created an impression of cleanliness and order. The women performed the most difficult tasks as a matter of course. Scarcely anyone shirked her duty. Many regarded it as an honor to do their best. Northern Kazakhstan, which borders on Siberia, has a raw climate. By November the temperatures can drop quite low. Water had to be drawn exclusively from deep wells. In emptying the buckets into large vats, which were transported on horse-drawn carts or sleds, the women could not avoid splashing themselves. In the terribly cold weather some were so covered with an ice crust that they looked like figures made from ice. With red hands stiff from the cold they held the reins of their horses and directed them to wherever water was needed.

I had been assigned to rush-cutting. Under the supervision of guards we cut the tall reeds, which served as fuel, until deep into the winter. As long as the temperatures were not very low, it occasionally happened that one of us broke through the thin covering of ice into the swamp water or into one of the bog lakes, some of which were very deep. Such individuals, of course, could return at once to the camp compound.

Women are resourceful. They can sew things together, do laundry with the scantiest soap ration, repair things; even in camp clothing, each one of us still radiated an aura of femininity.

Akmolinsk differed from the other camps that I was still to become acquainted with in that here a certain degree of community still prevailed. Most of the women had trusted acquaintances. They united to share things and to help each other whenever possible. One could knit, the other could sew.

The fact that only women lived in this camp had no immediate consequences because we were all so strongly shaken by the initial terror. Gradually, however, the younger women especially began to suffer from this unnatural situation. Conversation revolved more and more around the theme of "men," and this contributed greatly to the fact that the fantasies of many women were occupied with unfulfilled desires. All kinds of anecdotes were in circulation, some of a strongly sexual nature. Yet how different all this was from what went on in the general camps, and I cannot help feeling bitter when I think of the fact that the women from Akmolinsk were not spared such camps. Above all, we were protected in Akmolinsk from the greatest terror of the camps, the convicted criminals.

Since the inner administration of Camp Akmolinsk lay in the hands of women, there still existed a trace of humaneness, even though this community did not remain completely free from envy and resentment of those in preferential positions (such as the administration of the barracks, for example), or from spying and informing. But the intrigues were not yet systematized. The women were still absolute novices, completely lacking camp experience and routine.

I shall never forget the only case of a liberation from Akmolinsk. It was early in 1939. I returned in the evening from cutting reeds to find great excitement in the camp. One of the women had been singled out; she was to be set free the next day. Spirits ran high. It was said that this liberation would be followed by others. The excitement was intense. No one dared speak the sobering words—one sparrow does not make a summer.

On the following morning, immediately after roll call, all the women who had remained in the compound got together and accompanied the lucky lady to the camp gate. There they remained standing while the woman went to the administration office to get her papers. Through the spaces between the planks the women observed everything that happened outside. The discharged woman was still completely caught up in the news of her liberation and especially the joy of the others. With her few possesions in her hands, she was hardly able to grasp her papers. The camp commander, who handed them to her, said that he still had to read to her the order for her release. He held a document in his hand from which he read to her that her husband had died before the investigation of his case was concluded, and that she therefore could no longer be retained as a family member and had to be released immediately.

At first she did not quite comprehend what it meant; she stared disconcerted at the commander. Then he repeated to her in his own words that her husband was dead and she was free. Thereupon she was conducted out to the wagon. The women behind the gate were on the point of cheering until they noticed how downcast she was. When she reached the wagon, she glanced back at the gate, where she knew the women were watching. Then she could no longer hold back her tears. She made a sad, highly significant gesture and turned around. The wagon drove away; she did not look back again.

Through one of their fellow inmates who worked in the administration office, the women soon learned what had happened. The news did not fail to have an effect, for most of the women would have preferred to endure the camp, as difficult as that was,

than to know that their husbands were dead. Slowly they resigned themselves to the reality of the camp and gradually came
to understand that they would have to make the best of camp life
for a considerable period of time.

For a large number of the women who had come together at
Akmolinsk (belated contingents still kept arriving) there was not
enough work, especially in the winter when nothing could be
done in the fields. Whether this was the reason for phasing out
the special camps, I do not know.

In the winter of 1939 there was a registration of women who
had medical and technical training. As an x-ray nurse by training, I was among those registered. As early as February 1939 they
began to transport some of the women from the camp. Paulina
Golubyatnikova and I were among them.

Paulina and I had been together since Petropavlovsk and had
become good friends. A surgeon by profession, she came from
Moscow and had married a Ukrainian, who had been a minister
of the Ukrainian Soviet government. From the very beginning
we had made our beds together; in Akmolinsk they had been on
the floor for quite a long time. Paulina was truly a good comrade to me. She was a somewhat older, intelligent woman with a
quiet, mature personality. Whereas I had difficulty in recovering
from the terrors, she had better defenses with which to resist the
blows of fate. Like all her countrymen, she had not had an easy
life. She had great patience with me, and I could express myself
absolutely freely to her. She did not know what had become of
her husband. Her daughter, who had not been imprisoned, was
studying at a university. Afterward, when I was in other camps,
I several times received lovely letters from Paulina.

Our transfer from Akmolinsk produced something like an
atmosphere of liberation among the women of the camp. Most
of them, who could not yet comprehend what was being done
to them, still believed that everything would flit past—like a
ghost—and that life would be normal again. Since it was not

customary to tell camp inmates in advance what was to be done with them—and never why they were being transported or to what place—this uncertainty among the women of Akmolinsk, who had had little experience with camps, raised the most incredible hopes.

To be sure, there were always rumors, and all the more now because at the beginning of the year the camp commander had made the highly suggestive comment to the women that many changes would occur before the year was over. And naturally the women, still for the most part very naive, had interpreted this remark in an optimistic sense; they read into it the most impossible interpretations, just as they did the transfer of the first contingent, to which Paulina and I belonged. In the darkness and bitter cold we were crowded onto benches made of planks in open trucks. Everyone was greatly excited as we drove away. We were so tightly crammed together that I could not free my foot, which somehow had gotten jammed. The pain was terrible, and I asked the women to move somewhat so that I could free my foot. Either they really couldn't move or else they were so excited with escaping from here that they could think of nothing else. Fortunately, the journey was not very long, but I had screamed the entire time, and finally I had to vomit violently.

We were taken to the Akmolinsk railroad station, which was some ten kilometers from the camp. This first stop was not very promising. We were herded into one of the wooden stopover barracks such as are common throughout the Gulag. They were made of boards, the cracks filled with clay. There were tiers of unplaned plank bunks, and the entire place was swarming with bedbugs. But we did not remain there very long; the next evening we set out again.

We were stuffed into cattle cars equipped with plank benches and transported across Karaganda toward Karabas, the exchange point of the extensive Karaganda camp area. This took quite a while. Karaganda was situated more than 200 kilometers from

Akmolinsk, and from there to Karabas was about 100 kilometers farther. Cattle must be transported quickly or the animals may die, but human beings in cattle cars can often be left for long periods of time on railroad sidings, especially in the thinly populated camp areas. Who pays any attention to cattle cars!

All kinds of fantasies were exchanged during this long journey. Hopes were mingled with reality. When they ran out of topics for conversation, the women decided that each of them was to relate one of her most adventurous experiences. Since they began with the upper row of plank beds, and I lay on the lower one, my turn fortunately never came.

The most interesting aspect of this game was the fact that several women told about how they had deceived their husbands. The temptation to boast a little may have been involved, and perhaps also the desire to inject a bit of romanticism into the boredom of their domestic lives. Yet most of them recounted things they had actually experienced; I sensed that immediately. One of these stories especially comes readily to mind.

The woman who related it was a rather young, blonde, slender Russian. She had grown up without parents in the Moscow home of an elderly aunt who supported herself by sewing. When she was quite young, this aunt had made a match for her with a considerably older officer of the Kronstadt garrison. Young and inexperienced as she was, she had submitted to her fate, since her life until then had been miserable enough. Her husband was a decent sort of person; he treated her well, and they had one child. One time, however, when she took her child out for a walk, she met a young officer who immediately appealed to her. From this moment on an extremely strong attraction developed between them, and they met secretly for some time. When the young officer was assigned to a post far in the east, however, they decided to confess their relationship to her husband and to request a divorce so that they could go to his new post together. With a heavy heart but with a clear understanding of their situation, the husband consented. They were even able to take the child along.

She had now become a truly happy woman, but her good fortune did not last long. Her new husband was arrested. In fear of being arrested herself, she tried to appeal to her former husband for the sake of their child, only to learn that he too had been arrested. The child had probably been placed in an orphanage but, like most of us, she knew nothing about its fate.

When we finally arrived in Karabas after this time-consuming journey, we were put into barracks like the one at the Akmolinsk station, but here there was an entire settlement. Our group still remained together, separated from the other barracks, especially from the men's quarters. In Akmolinsk, where everything had been administered by the women, food had been prepared as well as possible and apportioned fairly. Here things were different. Here we had to make do with the usual camp fare and thin, watery gruel.

When the women discovered that there were men in the part of the camp that was separated from us, they assumed, as everywhere, that their husbands were there. A feverish calling of names and places began back and forth over the wooden enclosure. It was clear, however, that we would not have been sent to the Karabas camp if our husbands had been there. The prevention of such meetings was a well-calculated method of the Gulag, especially since our husbands were among those who were to be condemned to death. Some of them had already been shot; others had been sentenced to twenty-five years in the forced-labor camps of the far north or the distant east.

In any event, our stay at Karabas had a sobering effect on us women. Here for the first time we were together with other camp prisoners. Even though we were segregated, we were nevertheless on the same level and could therefore expect only what was in store for them: namely, to be sent to some part of the forced-labor camps in the Karaganda district, which was an area probably about the size of Switzerland.

To be sure, the disillusionment was far from complete, but the intoxication of hope that had dominated the women had already subsided to the level of very moderate expectation. We remained for several days in the barracks settlement, awaiting the arrival of another contingent of women from Akmolinsk. Quite early on 16 February 1939 a rather large group of our women, including Paulina and me, was assembled and prepared for evacuation.

Although it was winter and the cold had been severe, a sudden thaw set in. Our baggage was stowed on horse-drawn sleds, but we had to go on foot. In our generally poor footgear we plodded through the wet snow to Camp Spasski, about thirty kilometers distant. At noon we received some warm food and had a brief rest at a stopover on the way.

It was a terrible march. Several women who were close to collapse were put on the sleds with the baggage. From time to time, however, they had to go on foot because the horses could scarcely get through the thawing snow even without their extra weight on the sleds.

But at least we were not forced to march in the tight formations that were customary everywhere in the camps—we poor little sheep, where could we have escaped to? Our contingent sometimes stretched out. Some of the women fell behind, and so, divided into groups, we did not arrive in Spasski until after nightfall. The camp had been completely put in order for our arrival. As we could see in the weak illumination, there were no camp barracks here but real houses, made of brick. Deathly tired, we stretched out in the places assigned to us.

Spasski, a former English colony and copper works, had simple brick houses, like those in English working-class districts, and a well-built red brick hospital. The one-story building to which we were assigned may well have been an administration building.

Spasski was for us an interim camp during the phasing-out

period of all camps for family members, who until the autumn of 1939 had been kept in strict isolation. The women had been divided up so that their consignment to general camps could proceed more quickly. Since we had arrived during the winter, there was not yet much work to be done; still, the camp inmates had to be kept busy. So some of us—including me, for I was in work category 1—were assigned to a very difficult task, as a result of which I suffered an umbilical hernia.

The English copper works had had a well-constructed building of reinforced concrete which, at the time when we arrived, had been reduced to the foundation and several parts of the frame; the *lagerniki* who had formerly occupied the camp had demolished it.[4] Our task was to break up the concrete floor with iron chisels and to remove the iron parts embedded in it. Quite apart from the fact that the work was difficult, we suffered terribly from the concrete dust and from the icy wind that constantly stung our eyes. It was sheer slavery. Once the brickworks began operation in the spring, I was put to work there. It was not easy, to be sure, but at least it was better than this senseless destruction.

Some of the women were assigned to procure fuel for the camp. It can be asserted that the English had really left behind a long-term blessing: from the extensive mountain of ashes produced by the copper plant the women sifted out small pieces of charcoal. Some were even as large as plum pits, but most of them were only the size of small pebbles. Nevertheless, they were very good for heating; otherwise, there was scarcely any fuel in the bare steppe. Years ago, when I was back in Vienna, I met a man who had been a prisoner of war in Spasski until after the war. From him I learned that heating was still done there with charcoal sifted from the ashes.

4. Inmates of Stalinist camps or penal colonies referred to themselves ironically as *lagerniki*, which means "campers."

This then had become our lot. Often enough I thought back with a faint touch of irony to the impatience and the hope with which the women had scrambled to prepare for the departure from Akmolinsk. Nevertheless, Spasski too was—though less than Akmolinsk—something like an anteroom to purgatory. We were still together; there was still something like comradeship, solidarity, and the endeavor to make the best of prevailing conditions. Hell—the general camps—still awaited us.

At harvest time I was in the group of women assigned to making hay. We had to march rather far into the steppe, turn the mown grass, and then load it. The heat was altogether unbearable, and there was nothing in the wide steppe that afforded protection from the sun. Once, during the march of several kilometers back to the camp, a terrible hailstorm struck us. In our light, sleeveless dresses and with sunburned arms and backs, we were at the mercy of pounding hailstones the size of cherries. We could only throw ourselves down on our knees and try to pull the thin rags we wore over our heads. Nevertheless we arrived back at camp with cuts and bruises.

On the meadows there were large numbers of poisonous snakes, and we had to be careful at every step not to tread on them. They liked to lie under the bundles of hay. In our group there was a young Russian woman—a music student from Kharbin—who with great skill caught the vipers behind the head and thus got rid of them. The rest of us, of course, screamed in horror whenever she showed us a captured snake.

Scarcely had the hay been brought in when the steppe dried out. Moisture came mostly from the winter snow, and as soon as it grew warm, the grass began to grow luxuriantly in low-lying, marshy regions. The greatest part of the steppe, however, was covered with low bushes of saltwood. During the long, hot, dry summer months steppe fires often broke out. Once there was such a steppe fire near our camp, and we had to go out at night to put it out. We were loaded onto trucks and driven to the burning steppe. With firmly tied bundles of twigs we beat on the burning bushes until the fire was extinguished. This work did not seem as terrible to us as the fear of being surrounded by the fire on the steppe and smothering in the smoke, something that could easily happen in such fires. We were not the only ones sent out for this task. Trucks came from other camps, and some of the firefighters were men. Although we saw them for the most part only in passing—we were not permitted to have contact with anyone outside our group—the sight of the men caused not a little excitement for our women.

It was in Spasski, too, that I experienced an impressive example of resistance. Shortly after I had reached Akmolinsk, a rather large contingent of women from Georgia had arrived. These women were in a frightful condition, for they had been imprisoned for a long time. Before their departure they had been subjected to a humiliating procedure: all their hair, including the pubic hair, had been shaved off—by men. Shaven like felons, they had arrived in a state of utter collapse. Some of the women from that contingent also came to Spasski, among them Lorko-Panidze, a woman from a well-known Georgian family of noble lineage. I can no longer recall who her husband was or what her profession was. She was the only one, however, who had the courage to go on a hunger strike. Like most of us, she had submitted petitions to the authorities but had received no reply. When her hunger strike had gone on for several days, she was put in the clinic, and no one was permitted to see her. We crowded around the clinic in order to get information. After several more days her condition became critical, and she was transferred to the hospital. Naturally, she achieved nothing, but her example exerted an enormous moral influence upon us.

In Spasski, Paulina and I slept on the upper plank bunk in a room of the one-story house. My place was at the window, and from there I had a good view of the surroundings. Opposite us at some distance was the hospital. The English had built it simply, to be sure, but also in good taste, so that its appearance spontaneously aroused the most remarkable associations. For me it was a connection to the world I had known and loved. As simple as the building was, it was nevertheless well balanced and harmonious in its structure and thus formed a contrast to everything else that surrounded us.

In September 1939 I was sent to Dolinka with a large number of women. The special camps were in the process of being terminated, and thus Paulina and I were separated forever. Dolinka was a central compound of the Karaganda camp area. Most of the women came to Dolinka from other parts of Karaganda to be transferred from there to various other camps in the Soviet Union. These women had been registered according to profession. But things don't happen so quickly in camps. Almost two months passed before I left Dolinka. Naturally we had to work. First of all, thirty of us built a large ox stable. Then we helped to construct the new hospital. One of my tasks was to help insulate the ducts in the central heating system.

Finally, we were permitted to write and to receive letters. One day, when we returned from work to our barracks, a great surprise awaited me. There was a letter there for me! I was thus one of the first to receive information from the outside. It was an answer to the letter I had written while working in the brickworks at Spasski. I had given it to one of the truck drivers who hauled the bricks away. The truck drivers had been given permission to move about freely in camp territory, and several of us had asked them to mail letters for us. We had not had great hopes, of course, but the men had apparently understood our concerns and had found ways to dispatch the letters.

I was terribly excited when I picked up the letter. The other women surrounded me eagerly. The letter was from Georgi's niece, with whose parents Ruslan was staying. It began as follows: "Now we have finally received a sign of life from you. We had begun to believe that the same thing had happened to you as to Georgi, from whom we have heard nothing to date. Your boy is fine, but Irina died." When I read that, I burst into tears and began to scream about the bandits and murderers who must bear the guilt for the death of my child. Even the word "fascism" slipped out. The women were terribly frightened. They tried to quiet me down because of their fear, but nothing mattered to me.

Following my arrest, Irina had been placed in the Kuznetsk orphanage, whose directress I knew. At that time there was an epidemic of scarlet fever there, and Irina came down with it within a few days. She was taken to a hospital, where she died a few days later. Irina had been not quite one and a half years old. After the severe intestinal infection she had suffered, I had nursed her twice a day, for there was no pasteurized milk, and raw milk was the major source of infection. Too many things had happened to the little child at the same time—separation from her mother, changed surroundings, a different diet—and so she was unable to survive the sickness. During the course of the year I had directed several inquiries to the NKVD in Kuznetsk, hoping to find out what had happened to Irina, but had received no reply. A woman physician in Kuznetsk—a friend of the family—had taken loving care of Irina. It was she who answered the desperate questions of the relatives.

I was not the only one to get such sad news by mail; as other women gradually received letters in which their inquiries to the pertinent local NKVD offices were answered, there were quite a few shocking reports. Often, however, there was also welcome information. Many children were healthy, and some were even well looked after. About their husbands, however, most of the women could learn nothing.

Finally, at the end of October, a group of us—doctors, nurses, technicians—were prepared to leave Karaganda. In Spasski I had left behind all the women whom I knew well; then I had become well acquainted with other women through our common work; now I would also be separated from them. As was usual in the camps, we were not told where we would be taken. Usually one is informed of a departure only a few hours in advance and ordered to be ready.

When I was arrested, I had no suitable winter clothing with me, and so I had gotten a padded jacket in Akmolinsk. For my feet I made myself wadded outer stockings, over which I wore galoshes, since my shoes had quickly become useless while cutting reeds. Within a few weeks after my arrest I had grown terribly thin.

Now, like most of the others, I was outfitted in camp garb and had to await patiently whatever would happen next.

1

Each stage signified a new ordeal for me. In the prisoners' cars or cattle cars we sat crammed together; then we marched in formation, guards to the right and left of us with leveled guns, and behind us the panting dogs. Thus we marched through the streets, past people who turned away in terror or sometimes glanced at us with sympathetic eyes.

The Novosibirsk prison was a transfer point where transports coming from central Russia were routed to the far north, the distant east, or the remoter regions of western Siberia. It had already served this purpose during the time of the czars, but at that time there had never been such a large number of prisoners.

When we arrived in Novosibirsk, the railroad station—although rebuilt and larger than before—awakened sad memories: it had been the first stopover for Georgi and me when we went to Kuznetsk. Now I was being brought here as though I were a dangerous criminal.

After enduring the transfer procedure and the bath, we were taken to a small, overcrowded room. As in all camps there was nothing here but two-tiered plank bunks running the length of the room. Evening twilight was approaching, but there was only one weak light burning, and the only window was nailed shut with boards on the outside. Since the bunks were completely filled, we had to lie down on the floor, in the narrow space between the bunks. Here there was an inconceivable din, which at first almost deafened us. Finally, we realized that we were in a room full of adolescents. Beside me lay an engineer from Alma-Ata, with whom I had become acquainted during the journey.

The girls received us with the most obscene language; they were furious that we had disturbed them in their horseplay. We were horrified even more by their conduct than by their words. Some were half naked, and others were dressed like boys; at first we believed that there really were some boys with them. Some were so pale and underdeveloped that they still looked almost like children, but this did not prevent them from using the most fearfully abusive language.

For us, the worry about our children was probably the heaviest burden we had to bear. In addition, I still suffered from the depressing news of Irina's death. And yet it was thoughts of our children that fortified us most against all suffering. For their sakes we had to live, because they would still need us. Here in the prison we now became acquainted with one of the worst phenomena of that time—the *maloletki*. The word really means "minors," but the Russian term is also a concept.

During the Revolution, the civil war, and the difficult hunger years there had been many children who lived as vagabonds and who were called *bezprizorniki*. Gradually, this problem was addressed and an effort was made to help these orphaned and uprooted creatures find the "way into life" again. Now, however, there were the *maloletki*. In many fairly large cities in the newly developing industrial regions, gangs of adolescents had developed—wretched, frequently orphaned young people who had ganged up in the barracks and earth hovel areas and sometimes even in the schools around the large construction sites. Through compulsory collectivization and the consequent ruination of agricultural production, countless families had been forced to seek shelter and work throughout the country. These uprooted and pauperized people had often been unable to provide their children with security or even with a good upbringing. On the contrary, often enough they had encouraged their children to beg or even to steal.

During the years before my arrest I had experienced the operation of such a gang in Kuznetsk. It had rendered the city so unsafe that no one could walk the streets alone at night. Not only had people been plundered and robbed of their clothes; at the slightest trace of resistance they had been stabbed to death. When after many attempts the local police had finally succeeded in cleaning out the gang, it was discovered that they were all adolescents; they even had trainees. At that time, however, there was no longer any interest in studying this problem. The young people had simply been prosecuted and locked up; some had even been condemned to death.

But how could one incriminate young people who every day saw how innocent people were driven from their farms, plundered, arrested, shot to death, or sent to forced-labor camps, which for many was tantamount to the death penalty? How many children had been deprived of father, mother, or both parents? Then the young people had seen that the men who committed these crimes were decorated with medals, given preferential treatment, and materially advanced. Life had taught the children something different from what they had learned in school.

As a rule the young people who, like us, were arrested as family members, were not *maloletki*. In Akmolinsk there had been many girls to whom the *troika* had given the same sentences as the wives, because of the arrest of the father or a brother. In the other camps too I had again and again met such young people, but they had nothing to do with the *maloletki*. Young family members were usually sent not to the penal colonies but rather to the forced-labor camps.

The *maloletki* were a special category; so were the *urki*—members of the underworld—who made up a considerable percentage of the Russian population and therefore a significant number in the camps. The *urki,* also called *blatnye,* had adjusted well to camp conditions and lived there according to their own laws.[1]

For the most part, the *maloletki* were not the direct progeny of the *urki,* but through their confinement in prisons and colonies they developed new criminal blood. If juveniles were caught committing crimes, no matter how petty, they were put in jail, where they shared cells with hardened criminals and were finally sent to penal colonies. The colonies did not differ essentially from the work camps except that in the colonies the sexes were always separated. I already had a notion of what a penal colony was like, for there had formerly been one at Spasski and the camp personnel there had told us about it. Since there are no secrets in prisons, despite the strictest isolation, juveniles soon learned the methods and tactics of experienced criminals.

Because of the separation of sexually mature young people, homosexuality was rife among the *maloletki.* The girls paired off, with one member of the pair assuming the male role, which she stressed by manner of dress and behavior. Infidelity and jealousy frequently led to brawling. Even murders were not infrequent.

Deeply shocked at the first sight of the *maloletki,* we instinctively moved as close together as possible. Since the light bulb gave off only a dim light, it took us a while to get our belongings together and to recover somewhat from the terrible din. Whether we wanted to or not, we looked at the girls time and again and tried to understand what they were saying. Suddenly I heard the engineer beside me cry out in horror, "Tamara!" The call was directed at a slender, pretty girl, scarcely sixteen years of age, who was sitting on the upper plank bench directly over us. Since the

---

1. *Blatnye* (plural of *blatnoi* and synonym for *urki*) are thieves or members of the underworld.

ceiling was fairly high, she had almost enough room to stand up. Among all the girls she had already attracted my attention because of her shocking behavior and her especially loud talking and swearing, wherein she was most vigorously supported by a girl dressed like a boy.

She had heard her name and looked at the caller in astonishment. The engineer had been arrested together with a friend whose home she had frequently visited in Alma-Ata. They had been in the same prison and later had been transferred to Akmolinsk. Her friend was especially worried about her children, because she had had to leave a thirteen-year-old boy and a fourteen-year-old girl with her infirm old mother. She had done everything possible to get information about her children but, like the rest of us, without success.

Although Tamara recognized the engineer, she did not seem especially touched, but she did come down from the upper plank bed. "How come you are here, Tamara? Your mother is very worried. Where is your brother?" the engineer asked. "My brother is also here in the prison, but he is with the fellows," the girl answered unconcernedly.

The answer appalled us even more. The engineer was so benumbed that she could scarcely speak.

"How is that possible? Your mother thinks about you day and night. What about your grandmother?"

"My mother!"—the recollection seemed to tear Tamara out of the unruffled attitude with which she had reacted until then, and she began to relate: "How terrible it was that she was arrested right after my father. What we all then had to endure! No one was concerned about us. You know yourself how helpless grandmother was. Why did father and mother never write? When they were taken away, grandmother was very sick, and we had nothing to eat. There was no money left, either. And so my brother and I went to the market to beg. Sometimes, when no one had given us anything, we stole food. One time we were caught, and the police immediately locked us up. I got one year and my brother a half-year. When I returned, my brother was already at home and grandmother was dead. We continued to beg, and then we stole again. When we were caught again, I got two years and my brother one year. That's why he is here, too."

The engineer was shaken by these words. She hastened to explain the fate of Tamara's mother to her. "Your mother is in Akmolinsk. I was with her there until a few weeks ago. That is a work camp where she can neither write nor receive letters. She is worried sick about both of you. She tried everything possible to get news about herself to you and to find out something about you, but everything was in vain."

"A camp"—that was nothing very special for Tamara. She said, "We'll be sent to a camp again near Tomsk. That's where the big camps for *maloletki* are." For a moment, however, it seemed as though something in Tamara had been roused by this conversation, yet she realized that her mother, who was also in a camp, was unable to help her. She said a few more words to the engineer, then climbed back up on the bunk and was soon carrying on as before.

Tamara's father had been a minister in the Kazakh government. The girl had enjoyed a sheltered childhood and loving parents, though this scarcely seemed credible in view of her present behavior. Yet even now, not all traces of her good upbringing had disappeared from her pretty and regular features. Somehow or other these young creatures who had been utterly deprived of love and security, and were being tossed about in prisons and work camps, had to let off steam, and this often led to the most terrible excesses.

I cannot recall how this night passed, for the shock we had suffered blacked out everything else. We were awakened early the next morning to line up in the spacious prison yard, which gradually filled with hundreds of inmates. It seemed impossible that this prison could hold so many persons. We women, who until now had had hardly any contact with men in camps, were suddenly placed beside a group of men whose wanness and physical condition were the traces of a long stay in prison.

Several hours passed before all formalities were taken care of. The groups had to be drawn up, and documents and rations had to be distributed. Standing in the middle of this prison yard, I could not help wondering if something similar could have taken place here during the time of the czars. At that time there had surely been more criminals than real revolutionaries, but in no case had there been a category of innocent women such as we were.

I sought among the many tense faces to find an acquaintance, but I met only equally searching gazes. The men beside us had come from the Lefortov prison, the worst one in Moscow. They had endured a long period of confinement and horrible tortures. Condemned for the most part to twenty-five years, they were to be sent to the high-security camps in the distant east or the far north. It was a singular experience for these men to speak to women who were suffering the same fate as their own wives. Now they could relate everything they had experienced and suffered in prison.

For the first time it became clear to me that the purpose of all this was the extermination of an entire generation. All those who had belonged to the party before the Revolution, who had fought on the side of the party during the Revolution, and who had been the cultural and intellectual elite—all these had to die. Without wanting to glorify them—for some had already been partly corrupted by power—one must nonetheless admit that they had been the upholders of an ideal, had been animated by the desire to create a better and freer way of life. And along with them, numberless ordinary human beings, who through their labor had created what the leaders now prided themselves on, were also carried to their destruction.

A remark Georgi often made came to mind: "The system is

everything; the individual is nothing." It seemed to me that this sentence went to the heart of the matter, and nowhere did it ring truer than in this jailyard, which was full of human beings whom the system had struck down and who now helplessly awaited their coming fate.

I could not help thinking of the blind trust with which we had slid into this situation, for in spite of our doubts and our disapproval of certain incidents, we had always endeavored to find an explanation, and we had believed in the necessity of party discipline. I had been much more credulous than Georgi, who through his work and his utter dedication had comprehended the situation much better than I. At the time I had not grasped the full significance of some of his bitter comments. Now I stood face to face with men who could make Georgi's fate forcibly clear to me; they, at the same time, could gain from my accounts a clear picture of the lot of their wives and children.

Since Kuznetsk was known to everyone, and some of the men had known Director Frankfurt or others personally, they were especially interested in what I had to relate about that place. Those who had performed managerial functions in Moscow, in the party or in the ministries, could provide me with much information. Their prison experiences were among the worst I had heard of until then.

For me, this was an encounter at a crossroads; it made me more mature and fortified me against all future horrors. I was now fully convinced that only the consciousness of one's own dignity can help one endure boundless degradation, and that only the knowledge of the truth that exists, independent of everything, gives one the strength to survive.

We prisoners had not known each other previously, but we felt bound together through our common fate; and after these few hours we took leave of each other with heavy hearts.

It was not without reason that many of us believed it was better to be in a camp than to howl with the wolves outside.

Some people cannot comprehend why we did not rebel, but such individuals do not know how deeply demoralizing the effect of the camps was. The number who perished far exceeded the number of those who remained alive and sane.

After we had stood for many hours in the prison yard in almost wintry cold, waiting for the groups to be organized, the departure from Novosibirsk slowly began.

Then something happened that depressed all of us even more. While the adolescents were being assigned to their various groups, it happened that Tamara was separated from her friend. Thereupon, both of them began to scream loudly and demanded that they be kept together. Anyone acquainted with camp bureaucracy knows that such a thing is impossible; the papers had been processed long before, and once they were in the hands of escort guards, nothing could be changed.

When the girls saw that their pleas brought no results, they stripped off all their clothing without a moment's hesitation, despite the cold and the many onlookers. When the *urki* wanted to have their own way in the camps, they too resorted to such measures and even worse ones.

Both of them behaved so madly that it was impossible to dress them forcibly. Finally they were led off so as not to delay the departure of the others. This time, it's true, they did not leave with their assigned groups, but I doubt that they remained together.

This scene exerted a strong effect on us camp greenhorns, especially because Tamara was the daughter of one of us, of an arrested family member. The encounter with Tamara remained one of the most terrible recollections from my camp years.

Our group of women from Akmolinsk also divided. The engineer from Alma-Ata was sent farther east; three of us were assigned to the contingent for Tomsk. In Tomsk we marched—once more escorted by guards with guns at the ready and with barking dogs at our heels—into the filthy, bug-infested transfer prison. We had shared the cattle car with men, but in the prison we were separated again. We three women from Akmolinsk remained close together, still in too great a state of shock from our experience in Novosibirsk to work up interest in our new surroundings. When we left the camp at Karaganda, we were full of curiosity about our future fate, but this curiosity had now been more than subdued.

For me, the march from the station to the prison at Tomsk was above all a sad recollection of the time I had spent here with Georgi during his illness.

As usual we had to remain in the filthy hole for several days before we were taken on a branch line to the camp that was located about 200 kilometers from Asinovka.

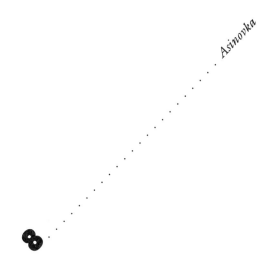

Asinovka

When we arrived at Asinovka, the region was already in the grip of a real Siberian winter. I had become accustomed to the raw climate in Kuznetsk, but my clothing was utterly inadequate. By the time I reached the bunk assigned to me after the long ordeal of admission, I was half frozen. In spite of my curiosity I was scarcely able to answer the questions assailing me from all sides, let alone to ask any myself.

It was not until the following day that I became acquainted with the camp. The individual buildings did not differ essentially from those in the camp at Akmolinsk. There were the same kinds of barracks, bathhouse, kitchen, mess hall, and other buildings necessary in a camp; only their arrangement was perhaps somewhat different, and there were more administrative barracks, since Asinovka was regarded as the central point of the entire camp complex. The real difference, however, was that here the men were in the same compound; even though the women's barracks were located next to one another, they were not separated from those of the men by any barriers. I estimate a high number of barracks for the prisoners, though still not so many as in Akmolinsk. They were, however, just as overcrowded; here too thousands were housed, because Asinovka functioned as a depot for the entire camp complex.

The very next morning we had to go to work in the nearby sawmill and woodworking factory. The timber was cut in the taiga camps along the Chulym and then floated down the river. It was processed at the Asinovka camp and then distributed from there. I was assigned to a relatively easy task: I had to calculate and record the number of cubic meters of wood loaded for transportation. The work area was enclosed on all sides by a high barbed wire fence. From the high watchtowers that stood at all corners, as in all camps, armed NKVD guards could watch every step we made. But within the work area we could move about freely, and this was a great advantage.

At Asinovka a good number of skilled workers were employed in the power plant, in the repair shop, and in the lumber mill, where they serviced the machines. These men were permitted to go to work with their own passes, and this was one of the few and special privileges of the camp.

Since my arrest I had come into contact with male prisoners only occasionally. In the prison yard of Novosibirsk the sight of the men had been depressing, but I attributed their appearance to long imprisonment and the conditions of transportation. Here, however, the impression was more disheartening than I could have imagined: in long columns the men went trudging off to work—emaciated, poorly dressed, unshaved and unshorn, huddled from the stinging cold in their dirty, often torn overcoats, and on every possible occasion uttering a flood of the most abusive language. I thought about Georgi and wondered whether he, if he were still alive, had to drag himself through cold and snow somewhere to the north or east. No news could reach him; he could write no letters.

Hopes and illusions that may still have been present somewhere in recesses of my consciousness were finally stifled by the brutality of everyday camp life. Contact with my home, my nearest of kin, was completely severed. Even the few connections I had still had in Akmolinsk had vanished. All that was left was the feeling that I was totally dependent on myself, completely given up to the mercy of the forced-labor camp.

One long, cold day I discovered the carpentry shop in the work area. From then on I hurried there during the noon hour to warm myself and to exchange a few friendly words with one of the carpenters, a former journalist from Birobidzhan. In Akmolinsk I had met several women from that region; from them I had heard with what enthusiasm Jews from everywhere had gone there to begin a new life. Now I learned that there too everything had been destroyed and the families torn apart.

When I returned to the barracks one evening I noticed a blonde woman on one of the benches reading the German-language edition of the journal *Soviet Literature*. I spoke to her, and we soon became friends. Her name was Ilse; she was from Berlin, and her husband was in prison in Hitler's Germany. She had been employed as a secretary in the tradeunion division of the Comintern. We soon discovered that we had a number of acquaintances in common. Ilse was in delicate health and worked in the tailor shop, which was located inside the compound.

One day during the daily march to work I came upon the former party secretary of the factory organization of Kuznetsk, whose arrest I had already heard of. As a former worker he had administered the strongest party organization in Kuznetsk, numbering close to 5,000 members. In addition, he had been a member of the city party committee. His name was Kulikov. Since he had been imprisoned at almost the same time as Georgi, he was able to tell me a great deal, though he had not been sentenced in the same group as Georgi. He had received a sentence of fifteen years. I was surprised that he had not been sent to a high-security camp and even more that he knew exactly how Georgi's downfall had been engineered and who had contributed to it. Since everything he said agreed perfectly with what I already knew all too well, however, I had to believe him. According to his account, Pinin had functioned as a stool pigeon during the entire time he and Georgi worked together. When I had been invited to appear before the so-called "commission" in Kuznetsk just before my arrest, Pinin's jeering manner had struck me as especially obnoxious, because I knew that Georgi had always regarded him as his friend.

When Georgi was elected chairman of the Control Commission upon our arrival in Kuznetsk, Pinin became his colleague. As far as I can recall, Pinin had come directly from the military. When the Control Commission was dissolved on orders from above—I think it was in 1934—Pinin was sent to Minusinsk, an important agricultural region, as party secretary. In fertile, western Siberia the harvest must be brought in quickly because the heavy rains often begin early, and then the grain can rot in the fields. For this reason the party committee of Novosibirsk sent its best and most experienced people there at harvest time. Georgi visited one of these regions several times during harvest season. I think it was during the autumn of 1935 that he was sent to Minusinsk because the harvesting was going badly there. When Georgi arrived, the party secretary—Pinin—and the chairman of the local soviet had just been dismissed from their posts and expelled from the party for nonfulfillment of the quota and for alleged drunkenness. Georgi remained there for several weeks until the harvest work was completed according to schedule.

Things looked bad for Pinin. For his sake Georgi appeared before the district committee in Novosibirsk, assumed responsibility for him, and gave him a position in his department. That is how Pinin was again accepted into the party.

Clearly, Georgi placed complete confidence in Pinin and spoke openly to him about his opinions. Therefore when close friends on the party committee confidentially revealed to Georgi that the NKVD had material at its disposal that included all his critical remarks, he could not imagine who might have passed on his comments to the NKVD. He had several friends with whom he spoke frankly, and so it was also difficult for him to form a suspicion. Pinin was the last person he would have suspected, nor did he think that anyone would try to set a snare for him with his completely objective statements. He had not advocated any counterrevolutionary views but had merely been critical of certain measures, most of which had come as commands from above. Kulikov now repeated Georgi's statements almost verbatim, and they were all too familiar to me. He informed me that Pinin had been summoned to Novosibirsk in the summer of 1937 for the express purpose of preparing the evidence against Georgi.

At that time Pinin had actually called me up to say that the military command (he was a reserve officer) had suddenly ordered him to report for six weeks of field maneuvers and that he had to leave immediately for Yuryevsk—that was the name of the place. He said it would serve no purpose if Georgi sought to intervene because the matter had already been arranged with all pertinent authorities. When I gave Georgi the information that evening, he was quite indignant, but Pinin had already left.

Obviously, Georgi's remarks did not provide the basis for the accusations against him—those had been fabricated—but they did serve the purpose of shedding light on his manner of thinking.

As much as Kulikov's knowledge about Georgi surprised me, I attributed it to the fact that Kulikov had been a member of the Kuznetsk party committee; this would account for his knowledge of many things. In addition, he had spent months in prison, where many more things came to light. He told me about other well-known persons who had also served as stool pigeons. It was not until later that I learned by chance how Kulikov had come to be so well informed.

Since I was still not well acquainted with the conditions of forced-labor camps, I sensed the uneasiness that prevailed in Asi-

124

novka but paid little attention to it because I did not know what it meant to be transferred from there to a compound situated in a more remote region of the taiga.

Although we were prepared for our transfer and were expecting it, it nevertheless took us by surprise. It was on December 25 that we were awakened even earlier than usual. The door was locked, a guard was posted, and the list of those to be transported was read. My name was on the list. All whose names had been called out had to pack their belongings immediately. Under close guard we were taken to a building emptied expressly for this purpose and were locked in. The feared transportation into the taiga had begun. In my ignorance I looked upon those preparations with a certain indifference. Could anything more terrible happen to me than what I had already gone through?

Only after I had spent several hours in the locked building did I realize that at least a third of the prisoners were convicted criminals, most of them fairly young. Up to this time I had never come into such direct contact with criminals. In the women's barracks in which I had lived there had been mostly political prisoners and *bytoviki*.[1] Although the *bytoviki* had been convicted of financial offenses or other misdemeanors, they had had nothing to do with real criminality.

Most of these women, except for those employed within the compound—for example, in the kitchen, the dispensary, or the administrative offices—did hard physical labor outdoors and returned in the evening weary and half frozen. And so the barracks remained rather quiet. The *urki,* too, behaved more quietly in the camp during this time. They knew that a detachment was soon to depart for a remote taiga camp, and since they very much wanted to remain in Asinovka, they tried not to make themselves too visible.

But when the die was cast, and those of us who made up the

1. *Bytoviki* were nonpolitical prisoners but not thieves. The word is sometimes rendered as "nonpolitical offenders."

detachment were all in one barracks, it turned out that more than a third were criminals, mostly younger ones. I had had an inkling of the crude behavior of the criminals in Novosibirsk, but what now took place in this barracks surpassed the bounds of the imagination. Screaming and cursing—I doubt if there is any language that has as much profanity as Russian. Much invective developed in the camps, which had become a permanent establishment in the Soviet system; for certain categories of people they represented, with short interruptions, their permanent places of residence.

While the rest of us quietly awaited what was to come, the criminals in their own way expressed their protest and attempted to avoid transfer by any means at their disposal. Most of us were ignorant novices, but the *urki* knew all too well what awaited them and what they were about to lose here. In Asinovka there had been many connections with the outside world. In recent transports from the prison there had even been inmates who arrived with their possessions in suitcases. They were welcome victims for the *urki;* they could be robbed and their belongings sold off. The greater the number of criminals who remained there, the better were their chances of organizing life in the camp and of terrorizing others.

As much as the camp administration favored the criminals and *bytoviki,* and as far as possible granted them the best positions, thieves could nevertheless not be trusted to work in storehouses. It was also difficult to put untrained workers in charge of complex machinery. Yet the lumber was urgently needed, and the plan quotas had to be met. To the extent that it could be done, then, the criminals were appointed brigade leaders, who did no work themselves except to force others to work and then in addition cheated them in the distribution of rations and pay. Whenever the influence of the criminals became too strong, however, the administration had to suspend these practices in order to provide a better balance among the inmates.

The *urki,* especially the young girls among them, had obtained colored pencils, whose fillers they dissolved in water. They drank the dyed water to make themselves vomit, or else they rubbed it into their eyes until they became inflamed. Then they began to scream terribly. Some of them inflicted wounds on themselves with sharp objects so that they bled. Although in general not much attention was paid to sick people in the camps, nevertheless the doctor had to be called, and some of these people were taken to the hospital ward. They had achieved their goal: they could remain in Asinovka.

We few women who were regarded as political prisoners and were still short on camp experience had gathered together on the opposite side of the barracks. All we could do was to sit on our belongings and endure everything as patiently as we could. It would have been too bad if any of us had even attempted to intervene.

Criminals were more or less subject to ordinary courts and laws. For them there were maximum penalties. Murder was of little significance, because for this crime they got no more than ten years. Furthermore, the *urki* stuck together, and when a murder took place in such a locked barracks, woe to anyone who might betray the perpetrator. He was killed—that was their law. And so camp murders were no rarity.

Like the criminals, who defended themselves in their own way, the other women were also greatly concerned about what was to happen to them. By now most of them had succeeded in establishing contact with relatives. Some had even received parcels. In response to the letter I had been permitted to write to Grigori upon my arrival, in which I had asked for some warm clothing, I had received a parcel several days previously containing a fur cap, warm trousers, and woolen underwear—all things that I could now make use of. Except for a few bulbs of garlic, however, there was no food in the package. From this I could see how badly things were going in the village.

With the departure of our detachment all these contacts would again be broken off. Some of the women had old friends in Asinovka from their prison days or even from before their arrest; from these they were now separated. Others had made friends there to whom they could not even say goodbye, for all our requests to leave the building were rejected. I was deeply agitated by what was happening in the locked barracks; unable to control myself, I was convulsed by a paroxysm of weeping.

In the evening the camp director arrived, accompanied by a train of officers. As he strode past me, I addressed him and complained about being subjected to such a humiliating procedure: "If I must leave, just tell me, and I'll go without being penned up here!"

In reply he merely smiled mockingly and said loudly enough for all to hear: "Just look at this fine lady. She doesn't like it here. But that doesn't matter. She'll soon get used to our sanitaria. They were really made just for such carefully selected people." Then I realized how completely abandoned I was, because his answer was tantamount to an exhortation to the criminals. With them the director spoke in a friendly manner. He even made some "witty" comments and listened to their wishes.

Then the five-day march began, about 100 kilometers through the wintry taiga, where there were no paths. Every day we had to plod about twenty kilometers through the snow. Behind us, horses drew the sleds with our belongings. We stayed overnight in abandoned peasant houses, where we were lucky if the windows were intact and the Russian stove could still be heated. We spent the nights, men and women, huddled closely on the floor.

In the depths of the taiga, villages were few and far between. As always when on the march, we received only bread and salted herring, but nothing to drink. When we did finally reach a village in which there was a draw well, we were not permitted to drink the unboiled water. It was too dangerous—what could they have done with sick people on such a march?

We marched in columns of two under very close guard. The

worst thing of all was when we had to relieve ourselves. We all wore felt boots and wadded men's trousers. For the men it was easy, but we women had to take our pants down. We could not step out of the column, neither could we stand still, or we would not have covered the daily assigned distance. Since we were marching with the men, the only thing that remained for us to do was to run ahead as far as possible, unbutton our pants while running, and try to be finished before the column caught up with us.

When we had set out from Asinovka early in the morning, we made up a long column of many hundreds of prisoners. As usual in the camps, there were fewer women by far than men. From time to time during the five days certain groups were called out and led off into various camp units in the vicinity. Finally there remained only several hundred persons, among them twenty women.

At the very beginning of our march I had noticed that Kulikov was among the men. Several times we succeeded in walking side by side so that we could converse, and I expressed my opinions to him quite frankly. It was the time of the war with Finland, and from the little information we could get, we knew that the general situation was difficult. I recalled that a letter from a Belorussian woman, which her relatives had given me to read, included this passage: "It was the most cruel winter we have ever had. It was so cold that our fruit trees froze, just as we did, for those of us who remained behind are suffering a similar fate. Everything has frozen from this cold, which has penetrated our lives. It is difficult to live in this cold world."

At that time Kulikov was still in good condition. He had received parcels from home, and his tasks in Asinovka had not been very difficult. In response to my comment that people who were not in camps also had to lead a difficult life, he replied that that was merely my opinion. I was astonished at this answer, because Kulikov surely knew as well as I did what we had heard daily from the new arrivals in Asinovka. Slowly, his strange behavior unsettled me, and I began to have second thoughts about various things. The mere fact that Kulikov had such precise knowledge about Georgi's arrest yet could tell me nothing of what had finally happened to him, even though they had been in jail together—this fact above all had made me suspicious. Did he not want to tell me the truth? After that conversation I avoided him. He marched with our group until we reached our goal. Then he was sent with a small detachment of men to a still more remote camp unit, about which everyone spoke with horror.

During our five-day march through the desolate, pathless taiga we did not know what landmarks our guards were using to find their way, and so we were constantly in fear of getting lost and of freezing to death during the night. Yet at times I could not resist the magic of the wintry landscape. When we reached a clearing and I saw the tall, snow-covered trees glittering in the noon sunshine, I was overwhelmed. Yet these were only brief moments, because the prisoners, the guards, and the dogs soon made me fully conscious again of where I was.

After marching for hours, we would occasionally catch sight of a village. At such times I was overcome by homesickness. I was reminded of my parental home, and never before had the recollection of my homeland awakened in me such a feeling of desolation and despair.

While laboriously dragging myself along in the middle of the column, I sometimes recalled what I had heard about prisoners who had been banished or sent into forced labor during the time of the czars. Before the Trans-Siberian Railroad was constructed, the prisoners had traveled by routes that led them through populated areas. But the political prisoners had been separated from the convicted criminals. Like many others, Lenin had hired a coach on his way into exile. Custody had not been so strict, and many had been able to flee from their places of banishment. The wives of the convicted political prisoners had in no way been mistreated then, and when they followed their husbands into exile, as Krupskaya did, they did so of their own free will.[2]

I had never before heard of prisoners being driven through the pathless taiga by guards with guns at the ready and by snarling dogs, and I had certainly not heard of wives of condemned political prisoners being treated as though they were dangerous criminals. What had formerly seemed cruel paled into insignificance in the face of what was being inflicted upon me.

Life in the central regions of Russia was familiar to me not only from Georgi's description but also from personal experience at close range. I had seen for myself how one peasant shack was built tight against another, and how the peasants had to use cattle manure for fuel instead of fertilizing their fields with it. I was aware of the constant hunger there, which the frequent periods of drought merely intensified. Since I knew all this, I could appreciate what the vast expanses of Siberia with their fertility, their mineral resources, their soil, their coal, their lakes and streams meant for the whole country.

Here a good and dignified existence could have been created for millions of human beings. It could have been done with the energies and resources used to maintain armies of guards, overseers, and stool pigeons. While the prisoners were constructing well-furnished and well-equipped quarters for their wardens, they themselves had to subsist under inhuman conditions and finally perish from hunger, torment, and slavish labor. In this way the land was not really made habitable; it was merely plundered.

It is hardly surprising that during this march scarcely a happy word was heard; there was almost nothing but scolding and especially powerful cursing. Yet there were some who mutually en-

2. Nadeshda Krupskaya (1869–1939) spent several years in exile in Siberia with her husband, Vladimir Ilyich Lenin, and shared many years of exile with him in France, Switzerland, and Poland.

couraged each other and some to whom the frequently used Russian proverb applied: "The world is not without good people."[3]

Among the women there was a nurse, who had come with me from Akmolinsk. We women did everything possible to stick together, especially at night. Since we slept in the same room as the men, we lay down close together and took turns doing guard duty. The nurse was well acquainted with one of the men, a former army officer, who often marched with us. He was always ready to help and watched over us at night. As we sat huddled together in a corner of a shack, stiff from the cold, it often took a long time until we had thawed out sufficiently to be able to sleep. At such times he would recite Pushkin's poetry to us. He could repeat from memory entire chapters of *Eugene Onegin*, *Poltava*, and *The Bronze Horseman*. Never again did I hear Pushkin performed with such fervor as in those nights in the taiga. Soon after our arrival I lost contact with the former officer and never heard of him again, but I did not forget his poetry recital.

It was late in the evening of New Year's Day when we reached our destination after our five-day, 100-kilometer march. In the winter there was no other access to these remote camp sites except through the taiga. The camp enclosures were all located near the river, and probably it was the frozen Chulym that had provided the landmarks for the guards. During the summer, felled logs were floated down to Asinovka, and boats provided transportation for people and goods. Yet because sailing upstream was always difficult, pains were taken to escort people on foot during the winter.

3. The proverbs frequently quoted by Russians are of several kinds: genuine old sayings handed down by word of mouth for generations, "instant proverbs" created on the spur of the moment, and literary quotations without source reference. The "proverb" about "good people" is credited to the popular and influential poet N. A. Nekrasov (1821–78).

The farther the timber cutting progressed into the depths of the taiga, the more difficult work conditions became there. Most of the people who did not die became sick and useless for such difficult labor. It was therefore necessary to make careful arrangements for a steady supply of replacements.

New Year's Day was one of the few holidays that were observed even in the camps, and so the inmates were free of work when we arrived. They surrounded us and bombarded us with questions. It took quite a while before we could respond to the questions of the people surrounding us. We were dead tired, but we had to undergo disinfection and take a bath before we received some warm food and a place on the barracks bunks.

On the very next day I had to go into the forest with the brigades. I was still so exhausted from five days of marching that I fell asleep immediately whenever I sat down. In addition, the clothing we had worn during the march had not been warm enough; by the end of each day we were so chilled that our feet merely moved forward mechanically. The nights had not been long enough for us to get really thawed out again. As a result we had constantly felt in need of sleep. Furthermore, our sleeping places had been so bad that we never felt rested; often we had had to sleep in a cramped position because there was not enough room to stretch out. On this march I had contracted scabies and discovered with horror that I had lice, which I was unable to get rid of for a long time.

After this march and my arrival at this camp unit in the depths of the taiga, I could understand why the *urki* had so violently resisted being sent here. There was nothing except the camp compound and the gloomy taiga; in the winter there was no communication even with Asinovka for weeks at a time. Admittedly, the camp provided wooden barracks, but by contrast with Asinovka, where there was a constant coming and going, everything here was much more depressing. The work in the sawmill, where we had been able to move about freely, had been an inestimable advantage. Here the few workers who lived inside the enclosure all had to fell trees or work on the construction of a narrow-gauge railroad. Again we had to remain in groups with the guards constantly ready to shoot, and we had to be outdoors from early in the morning until late at night. In the winter we were tormented by the cold. In the summer, when we sank down in the marshy earth at every step, we were plagued by innumerable mosquitoes.

As I soon noticed to my regret, the *urki* had the upper hand in this camp. They were the work brigade leaders and held the best positions within the compound. Even the cadre division lay in their hands. The bleakness of life in this camp could scarcely be intensified. The men whom I encountered in the taiga looked at us few women in amazement. Some of them also had sympathy for us, especially when they learned that we had had to leave our children, since most of them were fathers.

In the barracks in which I found lodging there were so many bedbugs that I could not sleep despite my utter weariness. But after several days I was relieved of my work in the forest. I received a pass permit to leave the compound in order to reach my new work place in the veterinary laboratory. This was located outside the barbed-wire enclosure on the edge of the taiga, adjacent to the large horse stables. I was also assigned a bunk in a separate room in the barracks in which only women were housed.

From this camp unit and the surrounding smaller ones, timber cutting was carried out on a large scale. Transportation required many horses, which dragged the felled trunks to the completed portions of the narrow-gauge railroad to the Chulym River. A large number of these horses had been infected with a form of anemia known as brucellosis, an incurable blood infection that is widespread in Asiatic regions. Since the sick horses did not perish immediately but only after a series of attacks of fever, which subsided again, they were again put back into harness following such attacks. They were subjected to constant blood checks in order to determine the degree of their illness and their potential for work.

The laboratory was housed in a small building. Except for a small vestibule it had only one room, in which our instruments and the microscope were kept. The doctor, Ivan Ivanich, also lived in this room, but I had to return to the compound every evening.

Ivan Ivanich was an exceptionally amiable, quiet, and somewhat shy person with whom I worked on the best of terms. Except for the taking of blood samples, our work was mostly carried out in the laboratory. I had to enter the results of various tests on a chart and keep the equipment in order. He and I worked together a lot and became good colleagues, but nothing more. I highly respected Ivan Ivanich for his restraint. Although he suffered greatly from involuntary continence, he understood that my emotional upset was still far too strong to permit any other feelings to arise in me. After his unexpected release from the camp I continued to work in the laboratory, where in addition to an older veterinary doctor, there were two young veterinarians. Unfortunately I was not shown the same consideration by them.

Soon after my arrival I learned that there was an engineer here, by the name of Ushatin, who had been well known in Kuznetsk. It was his task to build the narrow-gauge railway into the depths of the taiga. Apparently Ushatin had also heard of my arrival, so that a meeting between us soon came about. I had not only known him well; I had also been on friendly terms with his wife, a German woman from Riga.

Ushatin was an engineer of the old school. He had worked on the construction of railroad lines even before World War I and was among the builders of Turksib, the Turkestan-Siberian railroad connecting Siberia with Central Asia, which began operation in 1930. For this he had been awarded the Order of Lenin. In

Kuznetsk he had supervised the building of all streets, bridges, and the no less complicated transportation network within the plant itself. This tall, gaunt, reddish-blond man was to be seen everywhere; he was as much a part of Kuznetsk as the administration building, which stood before the entrance to the plant and could not be overlooked. His last great achievement had been the construction of the bridge across the Tom River, the bridge that connects the old city of Kuznetsk with the new city and the plant. Until then the ferry had been the only connection. There had been much talk about the construction of this bridge, since Ushatin had developed a whole series of completely new methods of construction in order to preclude difficulties arising from the annual inundations. Construction work on the bridge had taken about two years, and although it had been opened to traffic several months earlier, it was not completely finished until February 1938. Immediately thereafter, Ushatin was arrested. He had been prepared, for when the NKVD agents came to get him, his rucksack was packed with all his necessities, including boots, a sheepskin coat, and a quilt. In jail he was already expected, for during the hearings of those arrested earlier he had been spoken of as an accomplice.

Now he lived in a little room of the barracks with several other technicians who worked with him on the narrow-gauge railroad. Since he could move about freely on the work site, I looked him up several times, and he told me what had happened between the time of his arrest and his arrival at that camp. When he was arrested, his colleagues already had weeks of interrogation behind them, and so he learned from them what had taken place in the meantime and what the charges against him were. He was horrified at the condition in which he found his colleagues. All of them, without whom the plant could not exist and function, were accused of espionage, sabotage, participation in secret organizations, and more of the same. Ushatin told me the names of all those who had been convicted in one group—about thirty persons. I knew most of them. They were construction engineers, production engineers, heads of various divisions of the plant administration, and several technical directors. Kulikov had been a member of this group as well; Ushatin said little about him, but I paid no attention because we were not concerned at that moment with individuals.

Ushatin had never been in the same cell as Georgi, but through others he was well informed about him. He had also known the group to which Georgi had been assigned. The kinds of accusations had been about the same for all of them, just as they were subjected to the same methods of interrogation. Ushatin had naturally been subjected to the most terrible tortures. He had been interrogated uninterruptedly day and night. He had been forced to stand upright for hours, had not been permitted to sleep, and had received nothing to eat. Sometimes he had been made to stand, almost naked, on the balcony of a building in the Siberian cold. Some of the men could not endure the tortures of the interrogations, and knowing that there was no other escape, they signed the desired confessions. Most of them, however, did not do so. When finally the interrogations were brought to a conclusion, the captives were taken to Novosibirsk, where a mock trial was staged.

The court consisted of two or three rather high-ranking NKVD officers from Moscow. By chance the indictment against Ushatin was the first one to be read out. One point of the accusation reproached him for having sabotaged his newly constructed bridge in such a way that one of the pillars collapsed. Since the accused men had just been brought from the prison in old Kuznetsk to Novosibirsk, they had had to cross this very bridge, and as the builder, Ushatin had recognized every section while crossing it. Knowing that there was no hope of acquittal, however, he had become indifferent and interrupted the reading by shouting, "But we crossed that bridge by train just two days ago!" The court paid no attention to this interruption except that one of the inquisitors (all the examining magistrates sat at the court table) threatened to strike him with his fist.

At the very time when people all over the country were writing with pride about the great building achievements of the five-year plan, the persons whose contributions had been essential for the successful completion of the plant at Kuznetsk were "on trial." (Even today the well-built streets of Kuznetsk and the transportation network within the plant are a memorial to Ushatin.) The prisoners were not allowed to speak for themselves; instead, the accusations were based entirely upon the testimony of "witnesses." Most of the members of this group were sentenced to be shot; several received sentences of twenty-five years at hard labor in high-security camps; Kulikov was sentenced to fifteen years.

Ushatin was one of those given the death sentence. Immediately after the mock trial the prisoners were isolated from one another so completely that none was ever able to learn anything more about any of the others. Ushatin spent eighty days in the death cell, expecting every minute to be taken out and shot. But when he finally was taken out, he was sent to the taiga to build the narrow-gauge railroad. He was not told, however, whether the sentence had been commuted. Thus he lived like a dead man on leave.

One thing struck me as strange. Most of this group of specialists, including Ushatin, had not been members of the Communist party. Yet Kulikov, who was regarded as one of the group, had been not only a Communist but even a party secretary. I puzzled about this somewhat, but since so many unlikely things had happened at that time, I gave up looking for logical reasons.

I got to see Ushatin rather frequently, and we always had a great deal to talk about. His wife had left Kuznetsk with their daughter; she was one of the few wives of political prisoners who had not been arrested, at least at that time. Their daughter, if I remember correctly, was studying chemistry. His wife, who was staying with some of his relatives, worked as a cashier in a lunch-room. When Ushatin wrote her about seeing me in the camp, she asked him in her reply why she could not come here as well. Because of the strict postal censorship he could not tell her the truth about our circumstances; all he could do was indicate that such a thing was unfortunately not possible.

Even though the working conditions were not so difficult for me in the taiga camp, I had to endure considerable discomfort and injustice in the compound. At night the bedbugs did not let me sleep, and the criminals who lived in the barracks turned my life into a veritable hell. I had to leave early during the winter because I took the food along for my colleagues who slept at the veterinary clinic. In the darkness I laboriously waded through newly fallen snow, but at least my felt boots provided protection from wetness and cold. One morning, however, the *urki* attacked me. I did not let them intimidate me, but they threw me down on the floor and tore my felt boots from my feet. No one was there to help me, but probably no one would have dared to inter-vene anyway. I never received another pair of felt boots. Indeed, when I complained about their theft, I was told that I ought to replace them. Luckily I still had the wadded stockings and the galoshes. Nevertheless I suffered terribly from the cold without my felt boots.

One day the leader of the cadre division took it upon him-self to examine the belongings of all of us women who slept in the separate room in the barracks. Several days later my best things—the few that I still had—were stolen: my woolen dress from Vienna and the warm underwear that Georgi's relatives had sent me. Every month the *urki* harassed me by threatening to withhold my permit to leave the enclosure. What repeatedly saved me was the fact that criminals could not be allowed to run around outside the compound. Furthermore, there was no one else in the camp who was able to perform the work I had to do.

If they had taken my pass away, I would have had to return to felling trees in the taiga.

Following Ivan Ivanich's release in July 1940, I continued to work in the veterinary division. The old doctor, a kind, likable person, came from the Ukraine. He had been living in camps for a long time. The ten years to which he had been sentenced had long since passed by, but his sentence had been extended by another ten years. Why, he did not know. He had given up all hope of ever returning to his relatives in the Ukraine. Had he not been a veterinarian, he would not have lasted so long. Since none of the three veterinarians was familiar with the laboratory work, the treatment of the horses infected with brucellosis (eventually almost all of them) had to be limited to checking their temperatures at regular intervals. I had to learn all sorts of skills, such as how to approach a horse without getting kicked when I inserted the thermometer.

Our stay in the taiga suddenly came to an end. In August 1940 we learned that the camp was to be closed down and that we were all to be sent to other camps. Soon the transportation began. This time we did not march through the taiga on foot but were loaded onto boats that brought us back to Asinovka.

Shortly before our departure the men returned who had been sent to the more distant taiga camp. Kulikov was among them. I was frightened when I saw him; he was terribly emaciated and in dreadful condition. I pitied him so much that I immediately ran to Ushatin. Since he had the possibility of procuring food and was still receiving parcels, I thought he might do something to help Kulikov. But Ushatin angrily rejected my request: "For him? No. For him I won't raise a finger. He was the one who testified against us. Even in the court trial he called out, whenever anyone denied the charges against him, 'I was present when you discussed these things at the secret meeting!' And he pointed his finger at each and every one." That was sufficient. From that moment on, Kulikov no longer existed for me. Only now could I comprehend how he could have been so well informed about Pinin and others who had performed similar stool-pigeon services. Whether the others, like Pinin, were still free, I had no way of knowing. For Kulikov, at any rate, the betrayal had scarcely paid off, because to judge from his appearance it was doubtful that he would survive his fifteen-year sentence.

Now I was back in Asinovka again. I immediately got in touch with Mrs. Kirchner, and we once more lived in the same barracks. Several weeks passed before I was taken away from Asinovka. In the meantime I had to return to the sawmill to calculate the cubic meters of the loaded lumber.

At that time there was a constant coming and going at Asinovka. Daily transports of prisoners arrived from the remote taiga camps, and daily transports left by train. The camp was being cleared to make room for Jewish refugees from Poland who had fled before the advancing Germans. And they arrived daily in groups. They were not treated like prisoners, however, but were regarded as deportees and permitted to move about freely on the camp territory. In order to live, they had to perform the same tasks we did and live in the barracks we were evacuating, but the barbed wire enclosures were removed.

I left Asinovka with one of the last transports, and therefore I met some of the new arrivals, who were already working in the sawmill. I trained several of them to do the work I had done. The lucky ones among the newcomers were naturally those who could remain in Asinovka. Those who were sent to the more distant taiga camps were certainly not to be envied. Most adversely affected were the refugees from Polish cities who arrived in Asinovka with their families, including small children. They had never before had anything to do with agriculture or forestry. It was pitiful to see the wretchedness of these people, who had to live in barracks infested with bedbugs and do hard physical work to which they were not accustomed.

It was a policy of the camp administration to carry out constant regroupings of camp units. We had not understood the purpose of evacuating some of the camps until we were back in Asinovka again. The fact that the newcomers were Jewish refugees from Poland was a real cause for concern. At that time all kinds of reports about the persecution of Jews in the countries controlled by Hitler had penetrated to us, just as we had heard about the occupation of Belgium and Holland and the entry of German troops into Paris. All these reports had come to us from far distant places, and their significance was difficult for us to comprehend. But the discontinuance of this camp unit as such and the arrival of the refugees suddenly brought those events very near to us. We could not understand why the refugees were stuck into what had been our camp. What was the practical purpose of liquidating an existing and functioning camp in order to house people who were even more unsuited for such work than we were? Was it necessary to send these refugees—many of them families with small children—into the depths of the taiga? Would it not have been possible, with the same expenditure of money and energy, to provide temporary housing near cities, above all near industries in which these city people could have found suitable work for which they were trained? The transports back and forth were expensive—we rode the trains for three weeks from one end of the Soviet Union to the other—and that wasted money could have been used for the refugees. It was frightening to know that so many human beings would perish here whose lives could have been spared under other circumstances.

I never saw Ushatin or Kulikov again after leaving Asinovka.

The last transport included more than a thousand prisoners. At Asinovka we were loaded onto a long train of cattle cars that had delivered a large detachment of refugees. I had the good fortune of being with Mrs. Kirchner and of finding a place beside her on the upper tier of benches. The cattle cars were all stuffed so full that we lay beside each other like herrings and

could scarcely find room for our belongings. There were many
urki in our car. They had deliberately occupied all the places on
the lower bench because that gave them a great advantage: when
food and water were passed out, they kept most of it. Naturally
we had no idea to which camp we were being taken. But just
below the ceiling of the car there was a small peephole covered
with a grating, so we could at least see something outside. Again
we went by way of Tomsk and Novosibirsk. The train proceeded
very slowly. Sometimes it stood for hours on sidings.

On the way to Novosibirsk we assumed that we were to be
sent farther east or north. When we left Novosibirsk and crossed
the Ob River, however, I recognized at once that we were on the
way toward Omsk. Again we traveled through the West Siberian
lowland. How often I had passed this way: the first time in early
spring, when the snow had scarcely begun to thaw; later, through
the expanses of golden wheat fields. And finally it was autumnal
fields, with tractors plowing here and there, that our train traversed. Near the stations with the high grain elevators there were
congestions of trucks and horse-drawn wagons, all loaded with
grain, and we could hear the neighing of horses and the shouting
and cursing of truck and wagon drivers.

With what feelings Georgi and I had traveled this part of our
journey to Kuznetsk! What an impression this seemingly unend-
ing steppe had made upon me! Only a few years had passed since
then, yet how my life had changed in the meantime!

But even now I could not quite resist the impression that this
immeasurable vastness made upon me. On my previous journeys
the stretch from the Urals to Novosibirsk had required scarcely
more than a day and a half. This time we needed several days.
When the train had to wait at various stations, and we could hear
the calls of the drivers, what feelings overcame us! Sometimes
even the *urki* tired of their screaming, and the stillness of the
steppe prevailed in our car. Then we sang melancholy Russian
songs, or else one of the women related events from her life.

At least I was able to maintain my place in the upper corner of the car near the peephole! I stared out at the steppe and tried to determine where we were. Here and there in those vast expanses a peaceful village appeared, or a few birch trees rose up from the level steppe.

After crossing the Siberian plain we again came across the Urals, and then our train was on the Kirov-Leningrad line. We assumed that we were being taken to one of the Kotlas or Archangel camps, but we went directly to Cherepovets, where finally we could bathe and receive some warm food. Our stay in the local transit camp was very brief; then we proceeded to Karelia.

From Asinovka to Cherepovets our journey had lasted almost three weeks. The long freight train traveled very slowly. Sometimes we were shunted onto sidings where we remained for several days. Our car was terribly overcrowded, and we had to take care of our needs through a pipe with a seat on the top and an opening at the bottom as an outlet. As a result the constant stench was revolting, and it was lessened only a little by the draft of air through the car when the train was in motion. In addition there was the constant quarrel with the *urki* about the distribution of food and especially of the small amount of boiled water, the only liquid we received. Because of this interminable wrangling, several of the women had hysterical attacks or weeping spasms. The atmosphere would have been entirely unbearable if we—the few political prisoners, who had closed ranks on the upper tier of benches—had not attempted to establish some peace and quiet by relating long stories, to which everyone listened attentively. After the long journey many persons in the transport were sick; dysentery especially was rampant among us. In Cherepovets the seriously ill were hospitalized. In our car there were only a few such cases because most of us were relatively young and healthy women.

In Cherepovets we did not even stay overnight. We were again packed into the freight train, and off we went to Medvezh'yegorsk in Karelia.

9

The camp in Karelia was one of the oldest forced-labor camps in the Soviet Union. It had become well known in the 1930s through the frequent performances of Pogodin's stage play *The Aristocrats*.[1] The play tells about the reeducation of prisoners through work on the construction of the White Sea Canal. Now I was to experience the effectiveness of this "reeducation" in person.

The camp administration was located in Medvezh'yegorsk; individual camp units were scattered throughout all of Karelia. Our transport was divided in Medvezh'yegorsk. With a rather large contingent I was taken to Povenets, a camp located near Lake Onega, to which vast agricultural areas belonged. This was land that had been made arable by convicts. Canals and drainage ditches traversed the fields. Karelia is barren; it has many lakes

---

1. Nicolai Fedorovich Pogodin (1900–1962), a prominent playwright, publicist, and critic, was a traveling correspondent for *Pravda* from 1922 until 1932 and editor of *Teatr* from 1951 until 1960. He was twice awarded the Order of Lenin for his contributions to the dramaturgy of social realism. *The Aristocrats* was first performed in 1934.

and forests, but the ground is stony. To transform this ground bit by bit into arable soil required hard labor.

We were sent out to work in the harvest fields, where the crops were threatened by the early rainfall and snow in these northern regions. Gigantic potato, beet, and cabbage fields had to be harvested. The long train ride in cattle cars had quite exhausted us, but since we were permitted to cook or roast potatoes out in the fields, we somewhat regained our strength. This harvest work occupied us for three weeks, and we were all glad when it was completed, for the weather had already become very wet and cold. Mrs. Kirchner and I had remained together, but several days after the completion of the fieldwork she was assigned to the sewing room. I was sent to the camp located somewhat farther north on the opposite shore of the bay of the White Sea, where the city of Kem was located. We could see it in the distance.

Kem was a temporary stopping point for those prisoners who were being taken to the Solovets Islands. The camp's chief installation was a large factory in which clothing needed in other camps was produced. I worked in this factory for several days. Then I was sent to the nursery located beside the hospital.

Pregnant women from the various camp units were brought here for confinement. As soon as the children were born, they were placed in the nursery. In case the mothers were not freed in the meantime—which unfortunately was usually the case—the children were later put into an orphanage outside the camp. The mothers had to work, but during the first three months they could come to the nursery every three hours to nurse their children. As soon as the children no longer needed their mothers' milk, the mothers were sent on to other camp units. The doctors did endeavor to keep the mothers here for a year, however, for although the babies were cared for relatively well, the mothers' milk was the best protection for them in case of illness.

I can no longer recall exactly how many children we had. There may have been fifty, perhaps more. Another nurse and I were on duty together, and we had two assistants. One was a prisoner, and the other one was a girl from Kem.

A young doctor, who had just completed her studies at the medical college in Leningrad, arrived at about the same time I did, but not as a prisoner. She had been sent to serve as administrator of the nursery. She was very beautiful and made an extremely cultivated impression, but above all she was an especially good person. Although quite reserved, she never treated us as though we were merely wretched prisoners. I cannot recall her family name; at any rate, we called her Lydia Ivanovna. She was completely dedicated to her profession, and that was very advantageous for the children as well as for us; within the limited possibilities she did everything she could for the welfare of the children and for the maintenance and equipment of the nursery.

As grueling as it was, my work with the children, and, indeed, all my activities as a nurse, nevertheless had meaning and significance. The manner in which we behaved toward children and patients and the sense of responsibility with which we performed our duties were not matters of insignificance to them. My work with the infants made me think with a sad heart of my own children, but I also experienced a certain feeling of satisfaction that I could at least take good care of these children. It was delightful when they reacted a little to my words, showed their first smiles, and stretched out their little hands toward me. For the mothers who were "political" prisoners there was no prospect of being released soon. The majority of the mothers, however, were convicted "criminals," and so their children could not expect a good lot in life even in freedom. During this time the children became very dear to me. I observed how they developed, and rejoiced at their brightness. The more I came to love them, the more I was saddened at the thought of their fate.

After I had been in this camp for four weeks, I finally received some news about my boy Ruslan. As always, the letters from the relatives were meager, but after all, what could they write about?

They did not want to pour out their troubles to me. Furthermore I knew all too well how difficult life was for them. They even had to make contributions in kind for their cow, which yielded only a few liters of milk because of the poor fodder, and for the few chickens they were feeding. I also knew from experience how difficult it was to scrape together fodder for the cow in the wintertime.

The camp near Kem was very large, with both the factory and the workshops located inside the compound. Since work in the factory was regarded as easy, the younger and healthier women were not sent there. The sewing was done on electric machines, but there were also many other kinds of work to be done.

The number of men in Kem was limited. There were various specialists such as mechanics and locksmiths, and several men as well as the younger and healthier women were employed for freight handling and wood procurement. Most of these, however, were not regarded as political prisoners.

I lived in a barracks in which there were many wives of German colonists. Most of them came from the Ukraine—the region near Odessa—and from the Caucasus, where there had been rather large German villages. There were many aged women among them, sixty to seventy years or even older. In their long skirts and their kerchiefs they gave the impression of being tall and haggard, like archaic figures. They spoke dialects that scarcely differed from those of their forefathers, who had been brought to Russia by Catherine the Great or had sought refuge in this distant land for the sake of their religious beliefs. In their villages they had been pretty well isolated from the rest of the world, and for this reason they understood less than others what was happening around them. They had difficulty getting along here. Most of them knew scarcely any Russian, but this was probably a blessing, for the language of the camp would have been most offensive to them. Accustomed to hard work all their lives, they worked diligently here also and kept themselves neat and clean. They remained steadfast in their religious practice and kept solidly together. The fact that they were among people of their own kind may have sustained them.

These old women—those who were not widows—had been separated from their husbands and put into this camp. But what had happened to their husbands and to the younger people from their villages? It was not without good reason that I met Germans of all ages in all the other camps with which I became acquainted: women from the Volga colonies, from the Ukraine, and from farther south. Most of the old women in this camp probably had no prospect of joining their loved ones in freedom again, because none of them had been freed since the outbreak of the war. How many years remained for these old women? The ten-year sentences they had received were tantamount to death sentences for most of them.

In the barracks I had entered into very friendly relations with Berta. Berta came from Stuttgart. After World War I she had accompanied her husband—he had been surprised as a student in Germany by the outbreak of the war—to his home in the Ukraine. He had died several years before, and since then she had lived the modest life of widowhood. She had become disabled because of an arthritic knee, but this had not protected her from arrest. Over sixty years of age, she worked in the garment factory. She became very attached to me and looked after me with great kindness as far as possible. Naturally, I also did everything I could for her.

In most of the general camps there were loudspeakers for official news reports. With good luck, one could even get to see a newspaper now and then. Our curiosity, of course, was very great. We wanted to know what was happening in the country and especially in the rest of the world, though how we really interpreted the news was something we dared discuss with only a few individuals. At that time there were events enough to arouse our interest and our concern: France had been occupied, and

England was being bombed. In the Soviet Union fascism was being officially condemned—yet Stalin had made a treaty with Hitler and not with France and England. And everything that had happened and was still happening in the Soviet Union reminded me all too much of fascism. I could not forget how the arrogant behavior and new uniforms of the NKVD officers reminded me of the fascists, of whom I had had a little foretaste in Austria. All around us was violence! Everywhere people suffered because of it. How defenseless we were against it! In such an atmosphere we lived through the winter and the spring of 1940–41. The work in the nursery was strenuous, and sometimes I also had to help out in the dispensary and in the hospital.

It was probably about April or May in 1941 when our assistant from Kem returned to work following a two-week vacation. She was quite upset. When I asked her what had happened, she said helplessly that she would tell me if I would never speak to anyone else about it. She said that her fiancé had been home on furlough from military service somewhere on the western border. He had reported that the Germans were constantly abducting Russian personnel and that they were provoking and ridiculing them in the coarsest manner all along the border. His comrades, and especially the officers, were of the opinion that there would soon be war. When he took leave of her, he wept terribly because he was convinced that he would never see his loved ones again.

I was surprised, because this was the time of the German-Russian accord. But this had already given us quite a headache. The Soviet Union had annexed parts of Poland and had occupied the Baltic republics. It was conducting a foreign policy that contradicted all our principles, a policy that we had to reject on moral grounds. Of course, many important details of these events were not known to us, but it was difficult to find explanations for all that was happening. I simply could not imagine that Germany was still strong enough to provoke a war with the Soviet Union.

During the few days I worked in the garment factory, I had

met some Jews who had just come into the Soviet Union via Lvov, having fled from Austria, Czechoslovakia, and Poland before the advancing Germans. Among them there were several well-known Viennese merchants. From these persons I learned firsthand what had happened in those countries, how the occupation of their homelands had taken place, how the terror had intensified and the Jewish persecutions had begun. These Jews, who had hoped to find succor in the Soviet Union, had ended up as prisoners in a forced-labor camp. Most of them had even received sentences from the *troika*. There was no one here to whom I could unburden myself, and my few acquaintances—like Berta—were less able than I to find explanations to all of this. We had every reason to be deeply concerned. The Viennese in the camp had no illusions about Hitler's Germany; they were filled with despair and pessimism. And now, in addition, I had heard the young soldier's account of the Germans' behavior along the demarcation line.

Unfortunately, we got an answer to all these tormenting questions all too soon. Several weeks later, when I went on duty, I learned that the Germans had launched an attack against the Soviet Union. This explained everything. The soldier and the Russian army along the border proved to have been right. They had known what would happen if the well-equipped German war machine were to assault them, yet they had been prevented from taking appropriate countermeasures or even from speaking about such an eventuality.

News of the war struck the camp like a bolt of lightning. We feared that our situation could only worsen, and was it not bad enough already?

Shortly after the outbreak of the war our camp had to be evacuated. As we learned, enemy troops had broken into Kandalashka, which was 300 kilometers distant. We could occasionally hear the distant thunder of cannon, and some prisoners of war had been brought to a strictly isolated part of the camp. Scarcely a year had passed since I had had to endure a grueling transport, and now another one, still more difficult, was imminent for the entire camp. Again, no one knew what fate had in store for us.

Even with all prisoners assigned to the task of preparing to move, it took quite some time to procure the ships necessary for the transport of this extensive camp. Not only the hundreds of camp inmates but the entire movable stock—all the supplies, the dismantled machines from the factory and the offices, the camp papers and prisoners' records—had to be made ready for shipment.

To be sure, the work of terminating and totally evacuating one of the oldest camps in the Soviet Union was for us inmates not merely a change from camp routine; here and there it wakened all kinds of hope—but this did not mean that we so-called political prisoners did not fear something even worse ahead of us.

When our little fleet, which consisted of a motor ship and a series of barges, stood ready, it took several days to get the huge quantities of freight stowed and the hundreds of prisoners accommodated. The loading was accomplished directly from the camp, which was located on the bay of the White Sea, over the camp loading dock.

A special barge was made ready for the inventory and supplies from the hospital, the nursery, and the pharmacy. Below-decks this barge had room for floor-level beds, with the necessary bedding, for patients. Likewise belowdecks, but on two-tiered bunks, were accommodations for the weaker invalids and for the mothers with infants. Before departure the infants had fortunately been put in the personal care of the mothers and were thus fed exclusively with mothers' milk, since during the voyage there would be no possibility of procuring milk or other food suitable for babies. Within the limited possibilities, the mothers also received an increased food ration.

The entire inventory of the dispensary was stored on deck, where all materials were stacked. Between these stacks the personnel and those invalids for whom there was no room below-decks, as well as those who were in a somewhat better condition, had to establish ourselves. Among these invalids were most of the old German women with whom I had lived in the barracks, and to my great joy I discovered that Berta was with them. Here too the German women stuck together and endured all the vexations of this voyage with quiet resignation; scarcely any of them became seriously ill.

From Kem we sailed through the White Sea past the Solovets Islands to the White Sea Canal. The sight of these islands aroused considerable excitement in us, because Kem was the point of departure for the transfer of prisoners of a special category, who were kept on the islands in strict isolation and under very severe conditions.

Those of us who worked and slept on the barge of the medical division were fortunate, for the other prisoners were quartered belowdecks, kept under constant guard, rarely permitted on deck and then only in small groups. If prisoners became ill, they were brought to us. The ambulant patients came under guard, and they were usually brought singly or in groups of three at most. Whereas we had only a few bedridden patients to begin with, their number increased frighteningly during the voyage. What was worse, the nature of their ailments became increasingly more serious, and many died.

Although we did not meet any other ships before we reached the White Sea Canal, the voyage proceeded slowly. At night we had to lie to, usually without any lights. At several anchorages the canal showed signs of bomb damage. We also saw a plane that had been shot down near the canal, but we could not identify its nationality. Yet in spite of these obvious signs of war, we were not especially alarmed, possibly because we knew so little about the actual situation.

It took us six days to cross Lake Onega. At night we anchored close to shore without any lights. On the long voyage across the lake we had a most wonderful and unusual experience. Somewhere to port seaward we saw—so it appeared to us—fabulous spires and domes of old Russian churches towering up out of the lake. As we later learned, it was Kizhi Island. These domes and steeples were of a quite unusual kind. We all stood and gazed at them as though enchanted. What we saw there in this deserted forest solitude, as though floating on the water, seemed so unreal; and there was no one in our group who knew anything about this island. It seemed to us that we had encountered a fata morgana, so completely had this sight captured our senses.

Yet these were only moments that briefly diverted us from the despair of our situation. The moribund patients, the helpless old people, and the screaming infants brought us back again to the workaday routine, to our journey into the unknown. It was fortunate that the mothers took care of their children themselves, because we had enough to do to care for the sick, whose numbers steadily increased.

We left the White Sea Canal and entered the Mariinskii Canal System, which had been constructed during the time of Peter I. After the long voyage through solitude, we confronted a quite different scene. We came past inhabited places and smallish cities with a typically northern character. Nothing in these canals had been altered since the days of the czars. At times we had to be moved through locks with the help of horses. Now and then we were gaped at by people on the banks, but most of them seemed to have become accustomed to such sights.

After entering the canal system of the Sheksna, we met other ships carrying evacuees, which had come across Lake Ladoga from the Finnish border areas and from Leningrad. On this voyage we learned little about political events, although the war was already raging on all fronts. It was not until we came to Gor'kiy by way of the Rybinsk Dam that we learned of the siege of Leningrad. The ships we met were among the last to come from Leningrad with refugees. Several times we succeeded in exchanging a few words with the refugees, since their ships were allowed to pass whereas ours had to wait. I learned that among them there were fugitives from Finland, who could still find asylum in the Soviet Union. These were mostly opponents of the fascist regime who, in hazardous ways, had succeeded in escaping. Some of them were astonished at our flotilla because they could see so many guards with guns at the ready. They could not see, however, how many persons were actually belowdecks in our barges. The Soviet population had in recent years become accustomed to the passing of prisoner transports, but foreigners were clearly surprised. Whenever I succeeded in establishing a conversation with persons on such ships, I clearly revealed who we were and where we came from. I could not help thinking that the Finnish refugees would some day suffer the same fate as I had, and many others like me. How right this supposition was I learned later.

It was always impressive when we encountered ships. On the journey through the White Sea Canal we had not come upon any ships because we were probably among the last to be evacuated.

I was occupied on deck relatively often, helping with ambulatory patients and also taking care of patients who were bedded there. I also slept on deck. Since Berta was on our boat as an invalid, we prepared our sleeping places side by side on top of some bales and chests quite near the edge of the barge. Fortunately, it was summer, for we had nothing over us but the wide open sky. And despite the fact that I fell asleep quickly from sheer weariness, I always enjoyed the sight of the glittering stars and the shining moon. The most beautiful part of the voyage was the long crossing of Lake Onega. From the deck we had a clear view of the entire barge caravan. Several times at night we had anchored offshore. No lights anywhere, only the shimmer of the water and the sparkling of the stars, no barracks, no bedbugs! Yet even in such moments I could forget neither the patients suffering from diarrhea nor our impotence against death. As I indicated before, it was fortunate that the children were with their mothers and were nourished almost entirely on their mothers' milk. We tried to give the women everything we possibly could to eat (there was, of course, no milk; bread was the most important source of nourishment), so at least scarcely any children took sick on this journey.

Whenever I was on deck and saw the other barges ahead of me, I could not help thinking of the prisoners, who had to remain down in the hold. I was surprised that the people down there could remain relatively quiet. I could see how oppressive life in the hold was from the fact that we daily received new patients, many of whom died. But after all, who counted the dead?

When I think about it today, I cannot understand how just a few nurses and doctors coped with everything. I cannot recall how we managed the laundry, when blood and water ran from virtually all our patients. On one of the barges there was boiled water, and warm food was given to us daily, though it was mostly just thin gruel. There was water for washing, but no bath. Actually one could wash only one's hands and face. We had several very good medical orderlies, and the patients were washed to the extent that this was possible. The doctors, too, did everything they could. We had the pharmacy on board, but none of our medications were effective against dysentery.

Among the seriously ill who were brought to us from the barges were several Jewish students and refugees. They were young intellectuals, with good manners, who spoke an excellent German. Most of them had studied at German universities. They had been torn away from their families and for several months had had to perform difficult physical work in Karelia. They were already in such a weakened condition when they boarded the barges that they quickly succumbed to dysentery. Pale and emaciated, abandoned by all, they lay exhausted on their benches. Like all the others they excreted blood and water, and their languishing bodies were powerless against the sickness. There was no way for them to be saved; not a single one survived.

Almost every day I had to close the eyes of one or more dead patients. Many a one had clung to me and screamed for his or her mother, marriage partner, or father. Elsewhere, most of them would certainly have lived many years longer, but here there was nothing for them but death. The fact that those who died were mostly young persons made the matter even more terrible. Sometimes I was ashamed that I could bear this and go on living.

I recall that one day I had to sit down in the ambulatory area and suddenly wasn't certain whether I was awake or dreaming. I concentrated on identifying everything around me: the deck of the barge with the old and sick people who sat or lay around, dull and impassive; the mothers who brought their children up for fresh air; the piled-up objects; our entire caravan, which moved ahead slowly and sluggishly. All of this seemed so incredible. How did I ever get here? I closed my eyes and tried to become conscious of myself, to clarify to myself whether I really was still myself.

The doctor stepped toward me: "Nurse, what is it, don't you feel well?" I tried somehow to explain my thoughts and feelings to him. I can't recall what I said, but I remember his answer: "You philosophize too much. Whom does that help?"

The longer our journey continued, the greater our impatience became. No one had any idea where we were going. When we sailed from the Sheksna Canal into Lake Rybinsk, we at least knew that we were going to Gor'kiy, but we could not imagine where we might go from there. When we finally reached Gor'kiy, our barge with the sick people remained docked for some time. The other barges were evacuated as quickly as possible. We never learned where the prisoners were taken. I do not believe that I ever met one of them again.

The invalids—the Russian-German women and Berta—were taken away shortly before we were. I scarcely had time to say goodbye to Berta because I had to help load the most weakened women onto trucks. Berta wept, and we promised to do everything possible to stay in contact with each other, although we did not know what was to become of us. I never heard from Berta again. Probably she was taken to some camp unit for invalids, which for most of those women represented the final stage of their *via dolorosa,* their life path of suffering. Again I had lost human beings who were near and dear to me.

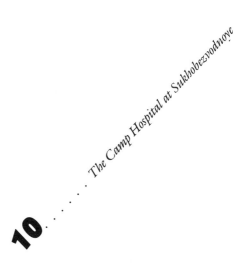

Finally the time came for us to depart as well. Our destination was the camp at Sukhobezvodnoye, situated 200 kilometers beyond Gor'kiy.

Our barge had moored at the bank opposite the city near the confluence of the Volga and the Oka. It was the end of September; already the days were occasionally quite cold, and sleeping on the deck became uncomfortable, yet I preferred this place to one in a camp barracks. Of Gor'kiy itself we got to see nothing but the contours of the city and the depressing suburb that lay adjacent to where we were moored. The confluence of the Volga and the Oka, however, had afforded us an impressive drama of nature.

We were transported from Gor'kiy in trucks. Since I was the last one to climb on after everything else had been stowed away, I could only squat there, hemmed in between crates and mothers. Tired, thoroughly shaken, and hungry, we reached our goal after a ride lasting for hours. I was directed to the central hospital of the camp, which also included a nursery. The individual divisions of the hospital consisted of rather well-built barracks. Sukhobezvodnoye was one of the oldest camps, and thus it was also relatively well organized and equipped.

Toward the end of our voyage, several infants had also become ill; now they were brought into the nursery, to which I was assigned. Strange to say, there were already sulfa drugs here for the children, which I had never even heard of. Now I saw how the children could be cured of diarrhea within a few days. If only we had had this medication during our trip! Then probably most of the patients who died would still have been alive.

Soon after our arrival, Lydia Ivanovna, who was so highly esteemed by everyone, again took charge of the nursery.

The director of the children's sanitarium was a splendid woman, a Georgian teacher. When she was arrested, her husband, who retained his freedom, had repudiated her. We two occupied a cubicle in the sanitarium barracks. The doctors and nurses with whom I had come from Kem also remained in this hospital. After a short while the children's sanitarium was transferred to an especially constructed building that lay near the camp entrance but outside the enclosure. With the help of the director we had everything organized and were cooperating well. But nothing in a camp is permanent.

The personnel who now worked with the children were less well trained, because we needed all the qualified personnel in the hospital: conditions in the camps had deteriorated greatly since the outbreak of the war, and the number of patients had increased. I too had to leave the children and was transferred to one of the wards for general medicine. In addition to the seriously ill from the camp, we constantly received new arrivals from the prisons and war areas. If conditions in the camps had deteriorated significantly, they were even worse in the prisons. Among the new prisoners were some who had come directly from the front or from places that the Soviet armies had reconquered from the Germans. Apparently, contingencies of the war did not permit sending the captives any farther; in any case their physical condition made additional transportation impossible. Thus they were brought to our camp, which was situated relatively close to the center. This produced new situations for us and new camp quotas.

Although we had received news reports through the loudspeaker and sometimes saw newspapers, we had known scarcely anything about the real course of the war, because all we got to hear or read were the official reports. But now we learned much about what was taking place. Among the many persons who had no possibility of fleeing when they were overrun by the Germans, there were some who had been willing to meet the Germans halfway. But once they were living under German occupation, many things happened to them that we would not have believed, had they not been reported to us by eyewitnesses. When we heard that young people from the occupied areas had been sent to work in Germany, we were all enraged. Finally the majority of us therefore came to have a hostile attitude toward the Germans.

Later, when these occupied territories had again been liberated from the Germans and the inhabitants had joyfully greeted their soldiers, many of them—and also many soldiers—had been sent to prison or to the camp. The soldiers related the terrible things that had happened at the front, especially at the beginning of hostilities. The surprise attack had been so overwhelming that the Russian soldiers had been unable to put up an effective defense. Casualties were high. The most dreadful part had been the air attacks, especially in open terrain. At least in the beginning, in areas without anti-aircraft defense and virtually no pursuit planes, the Germans had been able to fly quite low and to select their targets. Out in the open where there was no cover, the Russian forces had been mercilessly bombed and sometimes even strafed. What they said about the Germans' treatment of the people in the occupied areas seemed to me almost incredible.

The reports that Jews had to dig their own graves and were then shot surpassed the worst things I had imagined of the Nazis.

Yet again and again I heard from this and that person—especially from women—that not all German soldiers behaved like that; there had always been some who had behaved decently and had secretly given them food. Unfortunately, however, these were in the minority.

Some of my recollections of my activities as a nurse have become intermixed. It is not always easy for me to keep time and place straight, because the same conditions prevailed almost everywhere in the hospitals and wards. Except for acute attacks, the patients we cared for suffered chiefly from muscular atrophy. These were mostly hopeless cases, even though most of them were young men. The condition debilitated them so utterly that they were often more helpless than little children.

The difficult work that camp inmates had to perform all day long and the extreme weather conditions to which they were constantly exposed destroyed even the strongest of them. In the winter the severe cold tormented them, and in the heat of summer the mosquitoes plagued them. Nevertheless, most endeavored to fulfill their quotas because this meant the difference between receiving 900 or only 600 grams of bread per day. Even though the pay was a mere pittance, those who worked the hardest received the most, and before the war a person with money could always buy something. Furthermore, many had received parcels. But with the outbreak of the war, all this had come to an end. For many smokers the tobacco ration they received was so meager that they were prepared to exchange bread for tobacco. Among the prisoners there were always some who managed to get a tobacco ration, even though they smoked little or not at all; such persons took advantage of the situation and charged a high price in bread for their tobacco. Bread was the most valuable asset in the camp. It was now worth more than money.

There were two kinds of patients. Most of them were so emaciated that they were nothing but skin and bones. In such cases no long examination was necessary to determine the degree of their illness; they merely had to undress during the examination. The doctor examined the skin of their buttocks, and if it was flabby and shriveled, this fact sufficed completely for the diagnosis. The bloated patients who suffered from muscular atrophy and dropsy fared even worse. From time to time they were aspirated; several liters of water were drawn off each time. For a patient in this condition death was certain. I can't remember a single one whose life we were able to save. With such patients we had to see to it that they ingested as little water as possible; the food we had for them at that time was watery enough. Strangely enough, however, they always had the urge to drink. If possible, they even wanted to add water to their watery soup. The smokers fared worst of all. Even in this pitiful condition, some of them were so completely controlled by their addiction that they were prepared to give away their last bit of bread for tobacco. Since an effective treatment of patients suffering from muscular atrophy consisted in providing proper, highly nutritious food, of which there was precious little at that time, we had to see to it that they did not give away what little food they did receive. Most of the smokers were impervious to reasonable persuasion, and therefore, with the outbreak of the war, the death rate became much higher than before.

At this time I lived in the ward where I worked, sharing a little cubicle with another nurse and the female warden. Thus we were really surrounded by this misery day and night. The muscular atrophy cases usually passed away quietly toward morning. If we went to them early to take their temperatures, it often happened that a patient still reacted and could speak, only to die suddenly after breakfast, after he had swallowed the little piece of herring and the small amount of sugar that made up his ration.

We had an assistant who mostly took care of the paperwork. His name was Friedmann, and when we first saw each other, we realized that we had previously met somewhere. In fact, in the 1920s Friedmann had worked in the Soviet commercial agency in Vienna, where I too had been employed for a while. Friedmann, who was fluent in several languages, had last been with Intourist in Moscow before his arrest in 1937. He had a very pleasant personality. He had come here as a patient, and the doctors had kept him not only because of his poor health but also because he had proved to be very useful. He was a great optimist, or at least he pretended to be. He often said, "Patience, patience, in the end we will be conducted from the camp with a brass band!" Who in a situation like ours would not like to hear such words?

One day, when we had received a large contingent of seriously ill prisoners from the Moscow prisons and he was preparing medical histories during their admission to the hospital, Friedmann found an old acquaintance. Years before, they had been colleagues. If I am not mistaken, the patient, a Georgian, had at that time been manager of the Georgian Film Studio while Friedmann had been with the Russian studio Mosfilm. Then the Georgian for several years had been the director of the central office of the Gulag (*Gulag* stands for the Russian name meaning "chief administration of all correctional labor camps of the Soviet Union") and had been a member of the NKVD. As late as eight months before, he had been active in this function. Following the outbreak of the war, when Moscow had been threatened, the Gulag administration had been transferred to Kirov for a short while. Here, according to the patient, he had several times come into conflict with the party organizer of the institution because he had not been able to fill the latter's excessive demands for extra supplies of food. This had led to his arrest. Whether everything had actually happened in this manner or otherwise is not important; in any case, he had come to us in an almost hopeless condition. He was a large man who at one time had probably been very strong, but during the last eight months he had been starved to not much more than a skeleton. He was suffering from advanced muscular atrophy. Blood and water ran from him, but he was completely conscious. Although most of our patients up to the last moment did not believe that they would die, this man was fully aware of his dangerous condition. As long-time director of supplies for the camps, he knew exactly what rations the inmates received, and he also knew exactly how high the death rate was as a result of these rations. Our doctor naturally did everything he possibly could to help him, but what really would have been necessary, he was not able to do.

On the very day after the Georgian had been admitted, it happened that a commission arrived to inspect the hospital. It was the director of the Gulag in person who headed this inspection team. The patient had heard of this imminent inspection and had requested that his presence there be made known to the head of the Gulag in the hope that something might be done for him. The two men, after all, had been close friends until quite recently. As soon as the group came to our ward, our doctor and Friedmann called their attention to the patient. As they were proceeding through our ward, they even pointed directly at his bed; indeed, the patient even called out the leader's name. But the leader and his followers left the room without saying a word or so much as glancing in his direction. The patient realized then that his fate was sealed. His death was only a question of days. No matter what we did, it was impossible to check his dysentery.

When the patient saw that all was lost, he no longer refrained from confiding his deepest secrets to Friedmann. He told him that the number of prisoners in the forced-labor camps exceeded 12,000,000, and that the number of persons deported was 6,000,000—and these figures did not include the inmates of prisons. No one could have known these statistics more accurately than he, because only a short while earlier he had been in charge of supplying the camps every month and determining the rations for the inmates. In recent months their number had certainly not decreased, because provisions had been made for replacements and reinforcements.

During the fourth night the patient expired. Friedmann told me everything he had learned from him, and we were convinced that it was true. To be sure, we were horrified at these high numbers, but they seemed altogether possible to us. After all, as soon as I had learned that 5,000 individuals had passed through the Kuznetsk prison during the course of one year, it had become clear to me that five percent of the population of that city had been arrested—and the wave of arrests had lasted longer than one year.

Nothing could more vividly illustrate the condition of our patients than a scene I witnessed in the summer of 1942. It still nauseates me today when I think about it. Beside our ward, which was a large, extended barracks, there was a small wooden hut. One day this was torn down, and when the workers pulled the posts up out of the earth, several rats came crawling out. It was a warm, sunny day, and our patients—those who could still get about—were sitting in front of the barracks. When they caught sight of the rats, some of them ran there, seized the animals that were helplessly running about, tore them apart, and started biting into them. The other patients screamed in horror, and we quickly ran out to see what had happened. There stood the men, virtually reduced to skeletons, holding the bleeding rats in their hands and eating the raw flesh piece by piece.

In those years hunger was our truest and most constant companion, even though we did not all fare equally badly. It was somewhat easier for those persons who worked inside the compound. Even though the bread ration amounted to only 600 grams, we received warm, albeit poor, food three times daily. Those of us who had the necessary discipline to divide the bread ration into three parts and to eat one part with each of our meager meals could take the worst edge off our hunger. But for the men who had to perform heavy labor all day out in the cold and wet—or in the heat, as the case might be—and who received only two warm meals per day (although the total amount was the same as ours), 900 grams of bread was not enough. These men were always so hungry that they consumed their entire bread ration before noon and thus had to suffer hunger until the next morning. As long as it was possible to buy some additional food or to get parcels, they could hold out; some men endured such a life for many years. Yet it was precisely the youngest and strongest men who wore themselves out most quickly because they could not maintain their physical structure. For this reason there was a barracks for invalids in each camp. To be an invalid usually meant suffering not a disease but an advanced degree of muscular atrophy. For most men this condition signified the beginning of a slow death.

At the outbreak of the war the number of dying increased frighteningly. In those years we had nothing to do directly with the war, of course, but we felt its repercussions all the more. Several times at night we even got to see that the Germans were bombarding Gor'kiy; the sky glowed, and we could hear the muffled explosion of bombs. We knew that German units held positions near Kalinin, which was not very far distant from us. Not until 1942, when the situation in Moscow had changed and Kalinin had been liberated, did our anxiety concerning another evacuation cease, but the tense situation and the internal pressure in the camp continued unabated. At first a special news report was provided for the prisoners, and they were even called upon to volunteer for military service. I heard that several men had responded to the call, but no one from our camp was ever taken into the army.

When we arrived at Sukhobezvodnoye, several doctors there had just been arrested. The NKVD had also arrested several others and demanded that they incriminate the doctors. This caused a panic in the camp. Those who had been arrested were never seen or heard of again, and the opinion spread that they had been shot. In reality they had been sent to the solitary confinement building. Whoever has been in a camp knows what it meant to be put in solitary confinement; it was the worst thing that could happen to a prisoner. One of the hospital doctors, an interesting and energetic man of about forty, told me about these cases. He himself had spent several days in isolation, and from him I learned for the first time what was done there.

Quite aside from the fact that prisoners in the solitary confinement building were given food only once a day, the tortures to which they were subjected were much worse than in the prisons. When the doctor described to me the horror of the days he had spent there, I was deeply agitated. I understood at once the purpose of the NKVD units in the camps. The masses of inmates must be utterly intimidated. Naturally, not all doctors could be taken out of the hospitals, but the survivors had to be made absolutely tame. The fate of the confined doctors threatened us all. But since nothing remained hidden in a camp, I learned by chance who the man was who had been willing to testify against the doctors.

This man came into our ward one day as a patient. He had a very dangerous carbuncle on the upper lip and was in an extremely bad condition; at that time we did not yet have penicillin. Like all the rest of us, the doctors despised that man, yet they did everything humanly possible to save him, because we all took pity on him when his condition worsened. We did, after all, know the methods that were employed in the jails of the NKVD to transform human beings into traitors. Like everyone else, the man was terribly afraid of dying and begged the doctors to save him; but the means at our disposal were insufficient, all the more so since his weakened constitution could not combat the infection. He was in our ward for not more than three or four days, so quickly did death take him. We had to deal with carbuncles often enough in the camp; they were treated with the greatest caution. If they did not occur in the face or on the head, the danger was not so great, and the patient could be saved.

After the siege of Leningrad had been broken, we received an entire transport of Latvians. With the encirclement of Leningrad they had been jailed and apparently were one of the last contingents of prisoners from the three Baltic republics. Among them were former governmental administrators, officials, police, and activists of various parties—not only of organizations friendly to Hitler. There were many intellectuals, entrepreneurs, artisans, peasants, even laborers. Entire families had been arrested, torn apart, and sent abroad.

These Latvians, probably only the small remainder who had succeeded in surviving the blockade, were in terrible condition. All of them had come down with typhus fever. An entire barracks had been made ready for their arrival, and I was assigned to it as their nurse. The doctor there was the only free doctor in the camp, our beloved Lydia Ivanovna, who otherwise worked in the hospital.

When the patients arrived, we first of all carefully disinfected them. We cut off all their hair and provided them with a clean set of clothing. It does credit to our unit that in spite of the poor condition in which they arrived, not one of them died. But our doctor, Lydia Ivanovna, contracted typhus fever herself, and this was soon complicated by a severe attack of pneumonia. She was put into the office of our ward, and it was my duty to care for her. I slept in the same room and was relieved only now and then by the matron.

None of us was permitted to leave the ward until the danger of contagion was over. Thus it happened that the matron slept on my bed while I was busy elsewhere. How alarmed I was when I discovered a louse on my pillow. Now I believed that I had also caught typhus. As thoroughly as we had cleaned everything, we had trusted the matron to be responsible for her own cleanliness. After this incident I scarcely dared fall asleep and permitted no one else in the room. This precaution was worth the effort.

Although Lydia Ivanovna was our most serious patient, her life was saved.

Yet all these efforts turned out to be in vain. Early in the spring of 1943, I was working in a ward that lay near the exit. It was a Sunday, the sun shone, the snow glittered, and from the office I could see out over the gate, which was not so high as the enclosure. Lydia Ivanovna's room was located beside the kitchen of the orphanage. During the morning I saw her busily going back and forth. I pitied her because she was so young, and because she had to spend what should have been the most beautiful years of her life in the shadow of a camp, and because she was so lonesome on Sundays. She had a fiancé who, to the best of my knowledge, was somewhere at the front.

When I again had some things to do in the office about noon, I noticed that the women from the kitchen were excitedly crowding around the door of Lydia's room and that some men from the administration had joined them. What could have happened? I soon learned the crushing truth: Lydia Ivanovna had hanged herself in the doorway with a bath towel. She had had to pull her knees up as high as possible in order to suffocate. She had neatly put her room in order and prepared a farewell letter to her relatives with instructions about her affairs. She had spread out her ball dress and dancing shoes on the bed. A second letter, addressed to the NKVD, was also there, but of course no one dared touch it. It was only now that we learned that Lydia Ivanovna had been ordered to report to the NKVD at two o'clock that day. Had they wanted to arrest her because she had treated us so humanely? Or because she had made friends with an imprisoned female doctor? Had they demanded something from her that she could not reconcile with her conscience? Or was she so sickened from everything she had to experience here that she could simply not go on living?

The NKVD ordered an autopsy, and so the body was taken

to the morgue inside the compound. The examination was so thorough that they determined that she was still a virgin. Had she perhaps been suspected of having had an affair with a prisoner? When the body was removed from the morgue, the doctors, nurses, and the patients who were able to walk joined together to accompany the coffin to the camp gate. Quite unbidden, the thought came to me that she might have had a better death if she had died of typhus.

Certainly there were among the commanding officers of the camp, and especially among the guards, individuals here and there who behaved like human beings, but the system did not leave these human beings much elbow room. Each one knew all too well that tomorrow he himself could be a prisoner. Nor was there any possibility of their being relieved of this work; whoever was once assigned to the NKVD almost never escaped. The only possibility was suicide, and this sometimes happened, although not very often. The guard personnel was made up mostly of soldiers who had to do army service, since the regiments of the NKVD were a special branch of the army. Only the officers and the higher ranks of noncommissioned officers belonged to the cadres of the NKVD.

I remained in this hospital for almost two years and during this time found many friends, especially among the nurses with whom I worked. There was Maria Ivanovna. She came from Leningrad, was the wife of a professor, and was herself an academician. Her husband lived in banishment somewhere in Turkestan. She had left her twin boys in Leningrad with her sister, who also had children. For a long time she heard nothing about them. Not until the siege was broken did she receive a letter from her sister and learn that all the children, the twins as well as her nephews, had perished from hunger. Her sister apologized for having survived when the children had perished; she assured her that she had done everything possible to keep the children alive. Having had news about Ruslan only a few times, I too was very disturbed, because Borisoglebsk, where Georgi's brother lived, was not far from the Stalingrad front. News of the liberation of Stalingrad was the first great alleviation of worry for all of us in the camp; now we could hope for the first time that the situation at the fronts would change and that the war would thus come to an end.

The ward in which Maria Ivanovna worked soon became my place of refuge for the few hours during which I could leave my work place. Another nurse working there had also closely attached herself to me. With both of them I could speak frankly. They came from the old Russian intelligentsia, were educated, open-minded, unusually obliging, frank, and cordial.

During my first days in this hospital a man attracted my attention in passing. At once I had the feeling that he must have come from Germany or even from Austria. When shortly afterward I had to go to the dental clinic for treatment, I met this man there. His name was Fritz Duschner, and he was a dentist from Vienna. He had been brought with a transport to the Polish border by the Nazis. In this way Duschner, a Jew, had reached Lvov, from which he had fled to the Soviet Union following the entry of German troops. He told me that he had been arrested immediately after the occupation of Austria and sent to Dachau. On the basis of a foreign passport, however, he had regained his freedom; I believe he had planned to sail to Shanghai. But when he had been released from Dachau, his wife had fallen seriously ill and needed surgery. He had wanted to await the outcome of her operation but had been sent with a transport to Poland. As he learned later, both his children had been bound for Israel on a ship that had the misfortune of sinking because of an explosion. But about this he knew nothing at the time.

From Fritz Duschner I now learned what had happened in my homeland during recent years. His report, which was comfortless, disquieted me even more about the fate of my relatives. Full of care and worry, I thought about my sister and her child.

In this hospital I had another encounter that almost turned out to be my undoing. During my transport from Asinovka I had been in a cattle car with a woman named Lenz. I now learned that the manager of the bathhouse here was also named Lenz. Mrs. Lenz had told me on the train that her father, a well-known German revolutionary, had emigrated to the Soviet Union after Hitler's seizure of power. Erna—I believe that was her given name—had grown up in a milieu that was closely connected with the German labor movement. Her father, a left-wing Social Democrat who had disapproved of the policies of the Social Democratic party during World War I, had later joined the Communist party. Her husband—Erna had met him in her father's house—had been jailed as a Spartacist during the revolutionary struggles.[1] Like most emigrants who sought to escape Hitler in the Soviet Union, they had been arrested. When I met her, Erna had come from a remote taiga camp where there had been few women. She had worked there as a cook, but things had been difficult for her as a woman. She told me about the ambushes laid for her by the convicted criminals and about how glad she had been to be able to get away from there. In Karelia I had lost track of her. It was a surprise for me when I heard the name Lenz here and ascertained that this man was her husband. Now I could give him information about his wife. Since I had heard about Lenz even earlier, he seemed almost to be an old acquaintance. While living in Kuznetsk, I had taken a trip to Moscow and there met a German comrade who had stayed with me in Vienna for some time. Hermine Jonigkeit—that was her name—came from the Ruhr Basin and had studied at the KUNZ, the so-called West

1. A Spartacist was a member of the Spartacus League, which was founded by Karl Liebknecht and Rosa Luxemburg in 1917. An offshoot of the Social Democratic party, the Spartacus League was transformed into the Communist party of Germany in 1919.

University.[2] She had become a good friend of Lenz, who had given a lecture at the university on the history of the labor movement. Since Hermine as well as Erna had told me much about Lenz, I had complete trust in him. Whenever I went to the bathhouse, we would converse for quite a while. The West University had been closed down, because it was allegedly full of spies and traitors, and the majority of the students and teachers arrested. At that time I was still in freedom. The report of the closing had deeply disturbed me, because I suspected that the arrests would not remain limited to foreigners at the West University. With Lenz I was quite frank in expressing my thoughts. One day, however, I was very urgently warned by one of my friends. Lenz had threatened that if I ever again expressed such views in his presence, he would denounce me unsparingly to the head of the NKVD in charge of the hospital. I was terribly frightened, not only because of the danger to which I had exposed myself but also because Lenz was said to belong to the most hated and infamous clique in the camp: namely, the denouncers, the so-called *seksoti* or *stukachi,* which can be roughly translated as "knockers."[3]

The Lenz case confirmed for me once more what I had learned through my experience in the Kuznetsk prison, that it was often those who boasted most loudly of being Communists who felt the need of proving their fidelity to the cause by "unmasking" others. It was difficult to say whether they did this from conviction or out of fear for their own hides. If you were clever, you did not let such traitors notice that you knew what they were up to. And it was certainly better for your own protection to know who the stool pigeons were instead of being distrustful of everyone. But even so, deceptions occurred all too often.

2. KUNZ stands for "course for advanced training of command personnel."

3. *Seksot* is Soviet prison or camp slang for "secret collaborator" or "prisoner informant"; *stukach,* for "squealer" or "informer."

Quite unexpectedly my stay at the central hospital of the Sukhobezvodnoye came to a sudden end. On 7 July 1943 the five years to which I had been sentenced by the *troika* expired (the fact that I had been sentenced for only five years amazed the other inmates).

After the outbreak of the war, however, no political prisoners were released, even if their sentences had expired. Several amnesties had been granted in the meantime, but only criminals and *bytoviki* profited from them. Still, there were actually many among them who had been given up to ten years for stealing only a few potatoes or a few heads of cabbage. And during the war many others, usually young people, had been convicted and sent off to camp for being late to work (sometimes it was only a matter of fifteen minutes) or for not returning promptly from vacation—which was often unavoidable because of the great distances involved and the transportation difficulties that prevailed during the war.

Shortly before the end of my term I was summoned and told that I had to leave. When I asked where and why, I received the usual reply: a shrug of the shoulders. Since it was unusual for only one person to be called out, this had taken everyone by surprise. But the way in which I was addressed did not permit me to expect any good to come of it; there was no possibility of my being released, or they would have told me. Nevertheless, I was very excited: freedom was out of the question, but there was perhaps a possibility of banishment, and then I could have my son with me.

This time they were so considerate as to inform me a day in advance that I would have to be ready by the following afternoon. And so I had time to look up all my friends and take leave of them. What good friends I had had here! Nurses, men and women doctors, Friedmann, and above all, Fritz Duschner. Fritz was inconsolable, because he had no one else to talk to; he knew no Russian at all.

When I left, my closest friends accompanied me to the gate. There were bitter tears. Even the patients took leave of me with the greatest regrets. As a parting gift, Fritz Duschner squeezed into my hand a little piece of soap that he had scrounged from the quota. It was very useful to me during my journey. When I waved back the last time, I could see through the bars all those who had become so dear to me. The sad face of Fritz Duschner especially remained in my memory. I felt only too clearly that things would turn out badly for him.

Somewhat later I received several letters from friends among the nurses. They wrote that shortly after my departure Fritz Duschner had been sent to a camp unit that was engaged exclusively in agriculture. But Duschner was not up to such work, and he was soon brought back, deathly sick, to the hospital, where he died.

After the appeal for the restoration of Austrian independence had been made in the Soviet Union, all those who had formerly held Austrian citizenship (like Fritz Duschner) were informed that they would thenceforth be regarded as "internees." The Czech and Polish citizens who had come with Duschner from Lvov were, to the extent that they were young and healthy, transferred from the camp to the Czech and Polish armies in the Soviet Union.

I was again brought to the distribution area, and it soon became clear to me that only my place of work, not my condition, had been changed.

At the end of the distribution barracks a temporary infirmary, reserved for terminal cases, had been set up. The short time I spent there was probably the most trying of all my days in camps. The patients writhed with pain on the wooden benches; there were no medications. The doctor looked in briefly only in the morning. The rest of the day I was left alone to cope with the patients. One of them had advanced muscular atrophy, and blood and water ran from him. He did not have long to live, but he was young and his heart was strong, and this prolonged the agony of dying. There was no one there to help him except me. Again I was forced to think of how the men had to suffer. Perhaps Georgi had had a similar fate if, indeed, he had even gotten to a camp. Georgi had been a large, very strong man, but he had always been susceptible to infections. Perhaps he too had perished without help in such an infirmary. When nothing remains but a little pile of misery, it is difficult to know what sort of person a patient had once been. But none of them was willing to surrender to death. This patient wanted to write in order to request help from somewhere. I wonder whether all the letters he wrote with my help were actually posted. I doubt it, because one letter every three months was the most that we were permitted to mail.

Scarcely had he died when new transports arrived from Moscow. Fortunately, there were no seriously ill patients among them, but it took days to get them all registered and classified according to their condition of health. And so I got to know most of them. There were several especially congenial persons among them, including a stage director and an engineer. Most of them were intellectuals, highly cultured and well educated. Some were even members of the old Russian intelligentsia. They were happy to be able to move about after months of close imprisonment and to talk with a woman who could give them information about the camp. They thought that their arrests had been postponed because of the outbreak of the war, or that perhaps they had been overlooked or forgotten because of the massive wave of arrests before the war. All of them had been employed until they were arrested; there was still a great need for workers. The real reason for their arrests was the fact that the NKVD could not afford to be underemployed; if it were, the NKVD people would have had to go to the front. The prisoners from Moscow had no illusions about the future. Some actually thought it unnatural that they had not been arrested earlier.

The arrival of newcomers always saddened me, because I knew

what awaited them. Although they stayed here only a few days, we were soon on such good terms that we talked to each other like old acquaintances. I could get along well with Russians and found it easy to establish connections with them. Oddly enough, that is not always so easy for me now in Austria. But when people live in a situation that is totally lacking in human amenities, so that nothing remains except individuals as they actually are, it is easier for them to open their hearts to each other. It was difficult to take leave of these people when this transport had to continue on its way.

For me too the weeks of uncertainty at this transit depot came to an end. All that remained was the memory of a few dear persons of whom I never heard anything again.

In the contingent from Moscow there was a captain of a ship of the Bremerhaven Shipping Company which had been seized in the Persian Gulf before the war began. He had been handed over to the Soviet Union by Iran and had spent a long time in the Butirki prison in Moscow. Now he had been sent to this camp. He was an old, somewhat easygoing man, very friendly and obliging. He was very composed and still had all his belongings. He hoped to be sent to a camp where he would be able to do garden work. I do not know whether any regard was paid to his wishes, but I tried at any rate to explain to him what life in a camp was like.

A young German woman named Maria from the Odessa region, with her eight-month-old camp child, had been transferred here at about the same time I was. Maria was a young peasant woman who had left two children behind. She did not know any more than I did why she was now suddenly to be sent away. She had been sentenced to ten years in forced-labor camps.

The captain, who knew no Russian, had made friends with the German woman and her child and had given them some of his belongings. He insisted on giving me a sweater; I refused to accept it and urgently warned him that he would need his things and that he must take good care that they were not all stolen from him. In any event, I could draw the conclusion from his appearance and his behavior that until now he had been treated relatively well and simply could not imagine what awaited him. When he took leave of us before being transferred, I could attribute his optimism only to his belief in a quick German victory and his subsequent return home. Apparently he was not aware of what was actually happening, and he was absolutely inaccessible even to my unmistakable hints.

Although we had to reckon with our transfer at any time, it usually occurred suddenly and unexpectedly. Then we were expected to be ready to leave almost as soon as our names were called out.

With a group of men we were taken to the station. We were guarded very closely and strictly. How terrible it was for a woman with a small child to be marched around under such conditions. Among the men there must have been some hardened criminals, who frequently attempted to escape during such transports, because this time the precautions were especially rigorous. At the train we had to kneel as usual and wait for our names to be called. Beside nearly every prisoner stood a guard with leveled gun. We two women were among the first to enter the cattle car, and from the inside we were fortunately unable to see anything further.

The train took us to Kirov, some 250 to 300 kilometers distant. Again we had to spend several days in the filthy, crowded quarters of a transit depot. Maria and I, probably for the sake of the child, were taken outdoors every day until we were again marched to the station and crowded into a prisoner car. This car had come from the neutral part of Russia; it was filled with prisoners. From Kirov we were taken north on a branch line to the Kayskii region, located on the upper course of the Kama River.

Since I was together with Maria and her child for quite some time, I became rather well acquainted with this simple—I might even say primitive—Russian German from the Odessa region and could compare her with the old Russian-German women from Kem. In Maria the effect that camp life exerted on human beings was evident. She knew practically nothing about her two other children or her family. Since she was young and healthy, she had to perform hard physical work in the camps. The baby, born in a camp, had brought her temporary relief, for during the last months of pregnancy and as long as she was nursing, she had been released from the heavy work. In contrast to the old German women, whom even the worst terror had not been able to change, Maria easily adapted to life in the camps. Even though she spoke Russian very poorly, she was fluent in the camp argot, and nothing about her or her conversation distinguished her from the common camp mentality. She had retained little of the spirit of the German colonists, and it seemed certain that the years she still had to live in camps would destroy what little still remained. Perhaps she would have more camp children, who would never know their father and perhaps scarcely know their mother. What would remain of Maria when she again came to live in freedom?

These thoughts forced themselves upon me as I was experiencing all the difficulties that came from trying to take care of a small child in a Stolypin car, where there was scarcely enough water to drink, let alone for washing diapers. Why did a mother with a small child have to be sent around like this? What did it matter which camp she was in? Was there not an efficiently run nursery in Sukhobezvodnoye? Here there were guards who constantly observed us and even in the toilet kept a watchful eye on us. From other compartments the conversations of the men penetrated to us—their curses, bursts of fury, and a row with the guards, who had locked one of them in the cage. We heard his screams as the guards beat him. Besides this, there was the crying of this baby whose future was still more uncertain than that of its mother. I thought of all the small children I had cared for in the camps, and of their mothers, and then I recalled Masha.

After my transfer from Asinovka I had worked for several weeks at harvesting in Povenets. There I had heard a terrible scream one morning before we left for the fields. At this time there were more than a thousand persons assembled in the camp yard, and for that reason I was unable to discover the cause of the disturbance. I had only seen persons trying to subdue a small woman scarcely twenty years of age. She struggled with all her strength to resist when a long, bloody knife was forced out of her hands—the knife with which she had just killed a woman. The dead woman had seen the killer commit theft and had testified against her. To kill a traitor was one of the unwritten laws of the *urki*, and one to which they absolutely adhered; it was the cause of the numerous camp murders. Murder was also the best weapon of the *urki*. Because of fear of being killed, hardly anyone who happened to see a theft committed dared speak about it— not even the victim. I was told that this woman's name was Masha and that she was one of the most dangerous thieves; she had already been sentenced to ten years—the maximum penalty—for a previous murder. Her friend, who was the father of the child she was expecting, was also an especially dangerous criminal. The woman Masha had robbed was transferred to another camp immediately because Masha was threatening to kill her too. As is well known, in such situations the *urki* stick together—which cannot always be said of other prisoners.

When some time later I was working in the nursery at Kem, I learned one day that Masha, who had been in solitary confinement and had received an additional sentence for this murder, had given birth; several days later she and her child, accompanied by a guard, had come to us. The child was placed in the nursery, and she was told, as was customary, that she should report every three hours to nurse her child. At that time she was still in the solitary confinement building outside the camp enclosure. Although all prisoners were allowed to move about freely inside the compound, Masha was brought to us under guard; the woman she had robbed in Povenets was likewise in our camp, and it was feared that Masha would carry out her threat to kill her. This woman was soon taken away, and Masha came into the compound.

In our nursery the room where the mothers nursed their children was separated from our rooms by a door, and we handed the children out through a window. This was intended as a protection against infection, and the mothers had to disinfect their hands and breasts before nursing. Since the babies had their diapers changed shortly before nursing, it sometimes happened that one of them cried, either because the mother was not yet there or because we had not yet had time to get the child ready. Once when Masha had to wait, one of the children cried especially loudly. My colleague Nyanya and I were just handing the children out to the mothers who were already there when Masha came crawling through the window and rushed at us like a mad woman. She believed that it was her boy who was screaming so terribly and that we intentionally had not given him to her. When she saw that her boy was still lying in his crib, however, she was somewhat embarrassed. Since I had always treated her just like all the other mothers and now spoke to her calmly, explaining that we could not pass out all the children at the same time, she quieted down and left—this time through the door, which we opened for her.

It seemed as though a certain change had taken place in her because of the child. I noticed that she always treated the baby in a loving manner. She was working in the factory, and nothing happened there that would have verified her reputation of being a dangerous thief. One day she even applied for work in the nursery in order to be able to spend more time with her child. And indeed, Lydia Ivanovna, our doctor at the time, at my request arranged for Masha to work in the nursery as a floor cleaner. Thus things remained, not only in the nursery but also later on the ship. She was a loving mother to her child and did her work well.

While we were in Sukhobezvodnoye, she continued to behave well, and when Lydia Ivanovna returned to us, she saw to it that Masha was again employed in the nursery. Meanwhile, her son had become more than a year old. He was a lively, small, but very strong boy. With his broad, coarse face and his stubby little nose, he very much resembled his mother.

One day, however, Masha met another *urki* among the patients in the hospital, and suddenly she seemed transformed. She began to steal again, and her interest in her boy and in her work decreased noticeably. And so she was again removed from the hospital.

The boy was later placed in an orphanage outside the camp. I doubt if he ever again saw the mother he could not possibly have remembered.

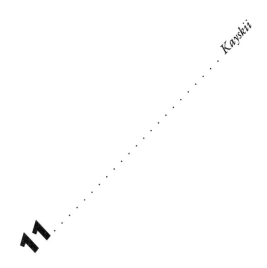

11

August 5, 1943, was a hot day. Maria, her child, and I were sitting in the prisoners' car. As usual, there was nothing to drink although we had been given salted herring to eat. Both of us were kept busy by the child, who had become very restless. From what I could see through the tiny peephole, we were traveling through wooded terrain, past wretched towns and villages of the northern regions. Again the train had brought me to the dreary taiga. It was early in the afternoon of the second day that we reached our destination: Volosnitsa in the district of Kayskii. That was the name of the last station on the rail line.

From this small, sooty station located in the middle of the taiga, the timber that was felled in the camp was transported into the central regions of the Soviet Union. It was brought here by means of a single-track line that extended into the widespread camp territory.

Following the usual unloading and transfer, we were taken to the nearby admissions camp. Now for the first time I had a close look at the men who had been in the same prison car with me. During the journey I had heard their conversations and their constant railing at the guards, who were not recruits this time; we had a regular convoy, which was characterized by extraordinary brutality toward the prisoners. After their long imprisonment and difficult transport, these prisoners looked completely exhausted. During the short walk to the camp there was not much talking, but I knew from their conversations on the train that there were among them both camp newcomers—mostly from the front—and men who were thoroughly familiar with camp conditions. Maria, her child, and I were the first to be admitted. I accompanied Maria as far as the clinic, to which she had been directed.

The camp seemed to be almost empty. Only a few persons were working in the compound. Several patients and invalids who could still walk were sitting outside in front of the ward. Upon our arrival they curiously surrounded us, asking the usual questions. But what did we have to relate? After all, we had just come from another camp. As soon as I knew that Maria and her child were taken care of, I went to the bathhouse, which was located at the opposite end of the compound (almost everything in a camp began with a bath, perhaps the only boon there was), but in the meantime they had already begun to process the men, and so I had to wait.

As we detrained, I had hoped to be led for at least a short distance through the forest, but even this modest wish was not fulfilled. Once again, barbed wire enclosed the world in which I was to live. As I walked back and forth, waiting for my turn to bathe, my mood became more depressed. We could not even see the surrounding taiga over the enclosure. I did not yet know which quarter of the camp would be my place of lodging, but whether this or some other—how did that affect my situation? I was suddenly overwhelmed by the total misery of this compound. Dusty, well-trodden paths connected a line of barracks to the canteen, the toilet, and the bathhouse. From the entrance gate the broad camp street led to the bathhouse. Along the side of the street the invalids had planted garden flowers, as though in mockery; these flowers made everything else look all the more disconsolate. Even the sun seemed to be gray in this area of the compound, even though there was scarcely a bit of cooling shade anywhere. What an accursed, puked-on bit of earth! Outside, the wide, uninhabited taiga extended in all directions, while here on a few square meters human beings had to live crammed closely together, tormented by unalleviated hunger, constant weariness, and countless bedbugs. From how many nations had these people come? The great majority would normally never have been imprisoned. At that time I felt the absolute absurdity, the utter inhumanity of the situation. Here, all that counted was the work category. Once again at the mercy of the arbitrariness of a camp, I stood on this befouled piece of earth, helplessly awaiting what was to come.

What all did not go through my head! My whole life passed by my mind's eye. I thought of my arrest and of everything that had happened afterward; I saw the abyss into which I was sliding more and more deeply. At that moment all these depressing thoughts and images dominated me with such intensity that I was overcome with deep despair, and my hopes, already so weak, seemed to perish utterly. But some spark of defiance must still have remained in my heart. How else could I have noticed the little daisy that had sprouted from this scarred and trampled earth? Instinctively I bent down and loosened the earth around it so that people could see it more readily and not crush it. Had I not just asked myself if there was any purpose in living any longer, since the chance of survival was again reduced and I had nothing but the worst to look forward to? Had this plain little flower, which had grown despite the thousands of footsteps that daily tramped by, become a symbol for me?

How we were being debased! But—had I debased myself? To be sure, I had occasionally been weak and indifferent. Yet whatever had happened, no matter what situation I had come into, I had never deliberately done anything that would have been harmful to others. I had always tried to do the right thing.

Was that not a great deal in a situation where egoism and the instinct of self-preservation had in many persons deteriorated into brutality? where good manners had lost their validity and social feelings had become a luxury? Was I really to perish thus anonymously?

Immersed in these thoughts I would probably soon have forgotten this little flower, had it not formed part of my introduction to a fine human being, such as existed in all camps. When it was finally my turn to step up to the sliding window, I found behind it a bearded man whom I had scarcely noticed until then. I had been struck in passing by some of the questions he asked newcomers, to whom he handed supplies for the bath, but of what interest were they to me in my situation? These conversations, after all, belonged to the world that surrounded me, and I had certainly learned enough about the sad fate of the prisoners during the transport here. Then a hand was extended toward me, and it gave me two little pieces of soap. How fortunate, since I always did my laundry while bathing! Two dark eyes looked at me warmly, and a voice spoke to me as though from another world, a world I thought had disappeared: "Where have you come from, girl with the sad eyes, to look for daisies here? Don't despair! In Camp Kayskii too there are human beings. One must accept it as a school—a very hard school, my child."

I did not immediately grasp the sense of what he said because this man's voice surprised and touched me so deeply. Many things that one scarcely notices in normal life become real gifts in the work camp, and these words had worked wonders. The man who spoke them was not nearly so old as he had seemed at first. As we told each other who we were and where we had come from, it was not what we said but how everything was said that enabled me to cross the threshold of the bathhouse a few minutes later with new courage and new strength. Something that had been completely buried in me came to life again, even if I was not yet entirely clear about the depth of this new feeling. With this day a new chapter had begun in my camp life.

There was still another event that made this day noteworthy. While I was still in the bathhouse, a voice over the public address system announced that Orel had been recaptured by Russian troops. At the time we did not know what the significance of this news report was, since we lacked a strategic overview of the battle in the Kursk Basin, but we were told that the retaking of Orel was just as significant as the victory at Leningrad. The end of the war, which we so earnestly desired and which alone could return us to freedom, thus advanced more and more into the realm of the possible.

Following the bath I learned that the new arrivals had not yet been assigned places in the barracks but would have to spend the night in the bathhouse. This was unpleasant news, because the only area that could be used for sleeping was the dressing room, which would be occupied the whole evening by the work brigades arriving to bathe. Further, was I really to sleep in the same room with those men whose conversations on the train had so horrified and often disgusted me?

But my new acquaintance—whose name, as I discovered, was Kita—freed me of my worries: he introduced me to the manager of the bathhouse, with whom he shared a small cubicle. And while I sat in the cubicle with these two friends, and it seemed as though our conversation would never come to an end, it had become evening. After the work brigades had consumed their evening meal, all of them whose turn it was to bathe on that day crowded before the sliding window, which had been built into the door and through which the men exchanged their dirty laundry for clean things. Talk became very loud; each one was in a hurry to exchange his laundry and receive the small bit of soap that would help him get rid of the sweat and dirt of the hard work week he had spent in the swampy taiga, which swarmed with mosquitoes.

During this pressing and crowding before the sliding window of the bathhouse, scarcely a decent word was spoken. In addition to the "mother" curses there was the unavoidable *Davay*. This word can be translated in various ways, most suitably perhaps as "Move it!" In the work camps this was one of the words most frequently used, by camp inmates as well as guards and NKVD officers. According to the situation, it could denote consent or else (and most frequently) express a threat. With this word one was called for interrogation in jail; in the work camp one was awakened with it, driven to work, hustled into the transit camp, plagued while eating, and chased away from the warming fire. *Davay* was basically the most important of the few words one needed in order to get along in the camps.

Kita, however, maintained a level of social intercourse found only seldom in forced-labor camps. He had to work without interruption and was addressed as *dyedushka* or *dyadushka*, which means something like "dear little grandfather" or "dear little uncle." "Do give me a little more soap; see how filthy I am!" "The underwear is too small, give me a larger set!" "The shorts are full of patches; don't you have another pair for me?"—these and similar complaints were made before his door. And I saw how calmly Kita tried, as far as possible, to treat each one justly and even to find a friendly word for this person and that. A small, pale lad complained that he had still not received any letters from home, and if the other inmates had not quickly hurried him away from the window, Kita would have talked to him for a long time. Some of the men called him "professor," and even those already too callous to be able to use decent language restrained themselves somewhat when Kita addressed them calmly and did not react to their cursing.

Since the name of Kita's friend has slipped my mind, I shall call him Viktor. In spite of the stiff knee he had acquired while felling timber in the taiga, this former army officer was still a man of imposing appearance. He could not walk without a cane, and he owed it to this disability that he had been assigned the administration of the bathhouse. In addition he was also the manager of the club, and under his direction the chorus and dramatic group had even performed operettas. His entire bearing seemed nonmilitary. Despite its gauntness, his face with its regular features was still handsome. He had a quiet, pleasant voice and made a very reassuring impression. Viktor had left his family in Taganrog. His daughter and his son had been carried off by the Germans. At that time he had heard nothing about his wife, to whom he had been happily married, and he was greatly concerned about her. Only later did he learn that she had been killed in a bombing attack.

It was the first time I had seen two so congenial human beings together in a work camp. I was received by them both as though I were a family member, and in the few hours that remained until bedtime we were able to exchange much information about ourselves. Kita even spoke some German, because he had studied for several years in Germany.

The problem still remained unsolved as to where I was to sleep. I could not sleep in the cubicle; if the guards were to make a check—as they frequently did—it could have cost both Kita and Viktor their positions. In this hot weather, however, Kita himself did not sleep in the cubicle; he and another friend, also a Georgian, climbed up into the attic above the bathhouse. Kita had introduced me to this friend, who had arrived in time to take part in our late-evening conversation. The Georgian worked in the railway workshop. He was a teacher by profession, but for reasons unknown to me had not been arrested as a political enemy; if he had been, he could not have been released during the war after completion of his sentence. This friend was fortunate not to have to spend the nights in the barracks and to be able to sleep in the attic during the summer, as Kita did. In order to spare me the terror of spending the night with the convicted criminals, Kita now suggested that I too sleep in the attic; in my desperate situation, this would be a means of escape.

Because of his stiff leg, Viktor could not climb up the ladder; besides, as manager of the bathhouse he had to remain in the cubicle. In the attic no one would see us because it could be reached only through a trapdoor. After we had climbed into the attic, we pulled up the ladder and closed the trapdoor. Fresh air streamed in through the opened dormer of the gable, which was not very high, and we could see a bit of the starry sky. Somewhere below us lay the camp. A piece of candle burned long enough for me to prepare my meager place to lie down. The resting places of the two men were on the broad loft beams. Kita lay on one to the side and his friend on the midbeam, but somewhat farther inward. I prepared my bed on the midbeam between them.

In spite of the sympathy I felt for Kita, I nevertheless had certain misgivings. Life in the work camps had taught me not a little. I am certain of one thing: although I longed more than ever before for the closeness of a dear companion, at that time I thought of everything else except the fact that I was a woman. Furthermore, following the last transport I was physically completely exhausted; I had hardly slept at all the previous night because of the uproar in the prisoners' car, and now had an overwhelming desire for rest and sleep.

But despite my weariness I could not fall asleep. During the day I had been assailed by too many things, and now the uncertainty about the course of the coming day kept nagging at me.

Kita's friend fell asleep immediately. His steady breathing was readily audible in the deep silence. I could not hear Kita's breathing. This made me uneasy, and I was filled with a strange tension. Long-suppressed emotions had surfaced today because we had talked not only about our views but also about our feelings, which had been so deeply wounded but not broken. It was at this precipice that we met. With no other human encounter in my whole life had I been so conscious of this, for I had never before met anyone like Kita, in whom I could so completely confide. All my longing, all my heartache, my suppressed will to live, and my vital force had come alive to the point of physical pain. Anywhere else I would have screamed, but here I lay still with bated breath.

I do not know how long I lay there. Kita may have had a similar experience, but in this camp we lived outside of human society and its norms and could reveal our innermost thoughts and feelings only seldom. Slowly Kita crawled toward me across the loft beam as though he wanted to see my face through the darkness. He put his arms around me and covered me with kisses. Silently and passively I indulged him; at that time I was incapable of doing more. But Kita was a much too sensitive person not to understand my situation. We spoke not a word, but he understood what gripped and paralyzed my body.

After Kita had left me, it was quite a while before exhaustion let me sink into sleep and freed me from my cares and worries for a few hours.

When I awoke, it was bright daylight. Only now could I see my strange domicile. Here one really seemed to be released from the wretchedness of the camp. There was nothing to be seen but the blue sky, and the camp noises that penetrated the loft were deadened. Only once in my long stay in work camps was it my privilege to spend a night in such a secure retreat.

When I climbed down the steep ladder, I again became aware of our deplorable situation: none of us could make a decision about a single day in our lives. To my surprise, however, I neither had to continue with the transport with which I had come nor immediately to join the work brigades, as was the custom. My assignment was quickly cleared up: I was to remain here to work as a nurse in the camp hospital. That evening, wearing a white smock, I was already on duty in the ward dispensary. I had been assigned a sleeping place in the women's barracks.

It was something quite unusual to be permitted to stay where one wished to be and to perform the kind of work that one regarded as an obligation. Here I was no longer a stranger. Kita was here. He was not merely admired by all and generally addressed as Konstantin Romanovich or Professor, but for me he was also a connecting link with the doctor, Maria Samoilovna, with whom I was to work, as well as with the apothecary, Maria

Alekseyevna. With both of them I got along equally well. In my Austrian home we might have said: "Man's extremity is God's opportunity." The road to Kayskii would probably have been too far for the good Lord, so I will hold to the Russian proverb: "The world is not entirely without good people."

That sentence, to be sure, did not apply to the administration of Camp Volosnitsa. They kept me here purely by chance, because they urgently needed a nurse and I had been classified in Akmolinsk as technical medical personnel; in general, camp administrators adhered to the specifications in the prisoners' records. I was primarily on night duty, since there was another nurse, the wife of a detachment officer, on duty from eight o'clock in the morning until two in the afternoon, not including Sundays, of course. I was on duty all the rest of the time. There were about forty beds, which were always occupied.

Maria Samoilovna Sadovskaya was not only director of the hospital and of the health service for Volosnitsa but also in charge of the medical care of the camp command officers—which was of benefit for our hospital. She was a very conscientious doctor, quiet, objective, and very energetic. She and her husband were from Poland; both had completed their university studies at Prague and had later come to the Soviet Union. In 1937 they had been arrested in Stalingrad; her husband had died in prison. Their child, a girl, had been placed in an orphanage, from which it had been taken by relatives living in an area occupied by the Soviet Union. From the very beginning her personal history provided substantial points of contact for both of us. It was through our work, however, that we came closest together. She needed someone dependable who could carry out her instructions precisely but who also could act responsibly and independently when she was needed elsewhere.

During the evening rush hour, when the work brigades returned from the taiga, I sometimes had to help out in the laboratory. In the morning I always remained in the ward until the doctor had made her rounds, helping with blood transfusions and major dressings of injuries. Therefore, I slept during the day in the barracks, and this was a real boon, since it was then quiet there and I was not bitten by bedbugs. I could also catch a few winks at night on the couch in the office; the orderly could always wake me if necessary.

The barracks in which the ward was located also housed the outpatient clinic, the pharmacy, a small dental clinic, and an office for the director; beside this office Maria Samoilovna had a small compartment for herself.

The pharmacist, Maria Alekseyevna, soon became my friend, since I had to see to the medication for the ward every day. She was a Ukrainian, a cheerful, rather poised human being and a close friend of Maria Samoilovna. She slept in the pharmacy and was therefore always at hand. The dentist, Elisabeth Mikhailovna, was a real gentlewoman, the wife of an industrialist from Riga and one of the first women students at the Petersburg Dental Institute. At first it had not been easy for Elisabeth Mikhailovna to do dental work in the barracks, but in time she had accustomed herself to it. She had scarcely begun to practice dentistry in freedom; shortly before the war, following the occupation of Latvia by the Russians, she and her husband and their three children, along with many other Latvians, had been sent from Riga to various camps (families never remained together in one camp). Their daughter and the younger son had not remained in camps but had been deported. Her husband had died shortly after commitment to a camp. The older son was in a camp, but she had had little information about him or the other children. She spoke German well, had traveled widely, and had seen and read much. Although she was no longer young, she was astonishingly good-looking and still attractive as a woman.

The supplies manager, Mikhail Simonovich, was an elderly, very correct gentleman who had held leading administrative positions during the time of the czars and had belonged to the old

Russian intelligentsia. Next to Kita, he was the most highly educated man in the camp. He lived in a little cubicle in the midst of his storeroom.

It is safe to say that such a group of co-workers were seldom found together in a single work camp. Yet for the care of the sick a certain selection of personnel had to be made; quite aside from the special qualifications needed for medical treatment, the question of reliability was paramount—all the more so when camp doctors also had to treat the officers of the camp guards. This task guaranteed a certain consistency, to the extent that anything could be constant under the prevailing circumstances.

When I had been assigned my sleeping place in the barracks, the woman directly under me on the lower tier was a young Georgian woman, who immediately greeted me most cordially. She was an engineer and worked in the railroad workshop. She was suffering from an advanced stage of tuberculosis and looked very bad. In her condition she could have been hospitalized, at least part of the time, but she preferred to go on working. On the basis of a decree issued during the war, it was possible to free incurably sick persons from the camps. Though this happened very rarely, to be sure, the doctors did succeed in having this engineer freed. But only a few months after her dismissal, Kita told me that he had had word from Georgia that she had died.

For me, quite unexpectedly, camp life had again attained a certain continuity. Above all, I could remain at Kayskii. After my meeting with Kita I would not even have dared to dream of that possibility. In the camps one could never know what the next day would bring.

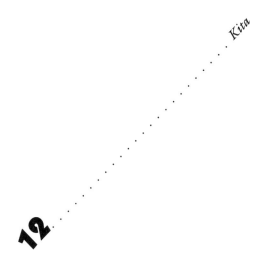

12

Since I had never had the opportunity to study at a university, I had the highest esteem for all the sciences and, especially, the humanities. During my years in forced-labor camps I became acquainted with several scholars who would be destroyed. Kita was the most significant one, not merely because he did not lose interest in his scientific work to the very end and continued his research under the most harrowing camp conditions, but also because he maintained his human dignity in all situations.

Kita—or Konstantin Romanovich Megrelidze, to use his full name—was born in 1900 in a Georgian village as the son of a priest. His father was still alive at the time when we first met, but he had not been active as a priest for a long time. Kita had attended secondary school in a Georgian provincial city, after which he had studied philosophy at the University of Tiflis. Following completion of his studies in 1923, he was sent to Germany for postdoctoral work; there he attended lectures by Husserl and Wertheimer.[1] Through critical analyses of their theories, he had arrived at his own concept of the bases of thought.

1. Edmund Husserl (1859–1938) was the founder of the philosophical movement known as phenomenology. He was concerned with the analysis of

In 1927 Kita returned to Georgia, where he taught at several academies. In 1932 he was summoned to the Institute for Linguistics and Philosophy of the Academy of Sciences in Leningrad, the administration of which at that time was in the hands of Marr.[2] There people were unpleasantly astonished because Kita was so individual and willful in his views. For this reason the first part of his major work, *Fundamental Problems of the Sociology of Thought*, which he had completed in 1934, was not published until 1937, and then only after long discussions and enforced abridgment. Even so, scarcely had the book appeared in print when Kita was arrested, subjected to long interrogations, and finally ordered to sign a statement implicating himself in espionage and high treason. When he heard this monstrous demand, Kita sprang up, seized his chair, and without a word hurled it at the examining magistrate. Thereupon he was thrown into jail, where he existed on bread and water and was forced to lie on a damp stone floor until he was transferred to the clinic with a severe case of pneumonia. Then he was suddenly and unexpectedly released.

Having been expelled from the Leningrad Academy of Sciences immediately upon his arrest, Kita went back to Tiflis, since he was still a member of the Georgian Academy of Sciences.

---

experienced reality, and believed in the ethical autonomy and the absolute philosophical self-responsibility of humankind. It seems likely that Kita studied with Husserl in Freiburg, where he held the chair of philosophy from 1916 until 1928. Max Wertheimer (1880–1943) was one of the founders of the Berlin school of gestalt psychology. He held professorships in Berlin (1918–28) and Frankfurt (1929–33) before emigrating to the United States, where he became a professor of psychology and philosophy at the New School for Social Research in New York.

2. Nicolai Jacovievich Marr (1865–1934) was a professor of Georgian and Armenian philology and a leading authority on Caucasian languages. His widely discussed Japhetic theory of language relationships was "refuted" by Stalin in his "Linguistic Letters."

When his wife, Zuza, returned to Leningrad to pack up their belongings, however, she was arrested. Thereupon Kita went to Leningrad, appeared before the NKVD, and demanded the release of his wife, who was needed by their seven-year-old daughter, Manana; if they absolutely had to arrest someone, he said, they should arrest him, not his child's mother. And, indeed, he was immediately incarcerated.

At that time such behavior was unique, for many persons turned their backs on arrested spouses to save their own skins, though this did not always prevent their own arrest. While in jail, Kita had brought about a meeting with his wife—another great exception. Kita knew that Zuza had been condemned to death and had spent many weeks in the death cell. Speaking in Georgian, she was able, despite the presence of the guard, to tell him quickly about a Finnish boy who had occupied the death cell with her. Despite the pleas of his mother, the naive lad had fled to the land of his dreams but had been apprehended as he was secretly crossing the border and condemned to death for espionage. The last human being who had spoken words of comfort to him was Zuza. The boy had been mercilessly put to death, and Zuza's sentence had been commuted. Although she was sentenced to ten years at forced labor in 1938, it was not until eighteen years later, in 1956, that she was able to return to Georgia from Yeniseysk in the far north.

Immediately after Kita's first arrest the entire first edition of his book was pulped and the plates destroyed. It was only by chance that his brother was able to rescue the manuscript. Thirty years after its first publication the book again appeared in print, and even at that late date it aroused great interest.

Whenever I now contemplate the pictures of Kita that appear in his book, I am struck by the fact that I never knew him as he looked in his earlier years. Life in forced-labor camps set its mark on people. Despite all individuality, it brought out certain common traits. Malnutrition, by which we were all affected to some

degree, left a certain imprint. Suffering and a sense of degradation were reflected in every face. Camp clothing also contributed
to the appearance that all inmates had in common.

Whoever got to know Kita well, however, paid no attention to
his appearance. In the camp, where people forgot how to speak
normally, the warmth of his voice and his correct, natural manner of speaking made people sit up and take notice and remember
their own dignity as human beings. How often did I see stupe-
fied inmates, accustomed to nothing but cursing, lift their heads
and stare in amazement at Kita, as though hardly daring to believe that anyone still existed who could speak to them like that.
It was for this reason that he was respected, and it was not by
chance that he was called "professor," even though intellectuals
were generally subjected to the coarsest mockery and contempt
in forced-labor camps.

Kita's sensitive nature and attentive human interest enabled
him to divine what was suppressed in others, to awaken their
slumbering spirits. So it was with me, too. Although our conversations at first had dealt merely with our experiences and
opinions, we soon found a common interest in literature, which
for Kita was not merely a personal hobby but the object of his
scientific research. He was so intimately acquainted with world
literature that he could quote freely not only from Russian but
also from English, German, and French works. Even in the camp
he could not get along without books. In addition to the works
he needed for his research, which he had had sent mostly from
Georgia, he succeeded again and again in getting hold of books.
His skill in doing so often amazed me.

He always had Rusthaveli's *The Knight in the Panther's Skin*
with him, a work composed in the Georgian language.[3] The lines

3. Shotha Rusthaveli (or Shota Rustaveli; c. 1172–1216), was the author of
the Georgian national epic, *The Knight in the Panther's Skin* (of which there

of the prologue that speak of "poetry as true wisdom" and of the "long narrative with concentrated plot," and the end of the epilogue, "When I, Rusthaveli, weeping, sang Tariel's fate," will always remain in my memory. "With what other tears," Kita commented at that time, "would we have to weep while describing our fate?" Kita also owned the collected works of Pushkin. Since I had a good reading knowledge of Russian, I knew these works well; but much that I had scarcely noticed in them became a real experience to me through Kita's interpretation.

As a young girl I had dreamed about becoming an author. I had written poems: "Up on the hill in the wind stood a lonely linden"—that was the beginning of my first poem; if I remember correctly, I had to make a copy of it for Kita. For a time I had tried to write seriously, but in the struggle for my daily bread I was in contact with people who had no appreciation for creative writing or even had a negative attitude toward it. Consequently, I lost my feeling of self-confidence. Then I became involved in politics, which fully preoccupied me. Kita was the first person who ever encouraged me to write.

The atmosphere I encountered in Volosnitsa was quite different from that at Sukhobezvodnoye. There, in the major hospital for the entire camp, operations had been performed and acute illnesses treated. Above all, prisoners were treated for muscular atrophy, for which there was really no cure. Thus we had constantly been surrounded by disease and death.

Volosnitsa was a transit camp as well as a forced-labor camp. In addition to the regular brigades that worked in the taiga, new prisoners arrived several times a week. Through them we received news about civilian life during wartime as well as from

---

are a prose and a verse translation in English). He also composed odes to Queen Tamara (c. 1160–1210). Some critics regard him as the creator of the Georgian literary language.

the battlefront. From time to time major transports, long trains of cattle cars crammed full of human beings, were unloaded at various points within the camp.

During the war a new category of prisoners had been created, the so-called *ukazniki*.[4] On the basis of a new special law, coming to work late—if only by ten or fifteen minutes—and similar minor offenses were punished with several years in forced-labor camps. Those affected were mostly young people, such as apprentices and women, who were both morally and physically harmed by the difficult camp work—if, indeed, they survived at all.

Prisoners who had been released were also processed in our camp. Since at that time there were several major amnesties for *bytoviki* and convicted criminals, sizable detachments of them occasionally passed through our camp—among them, many who were weak or sick and created additional work for us. Maria Samoilovna had so much to do outside the camp that I had to work even more in the ward and in the outpatient clinic. I did not have the pleasure of going to the bathhouse every day—my only place of refuge—for even a few minutes.

But as fully occupied as my everyday life was, the concern for my child never left me. Because of my transfer to this camp, months again passed before I received any information about Ruslan. It struck me that the short letters I did get made no mention of school, even though I had asked about it in every letter. Ruslan was seven years old and should be attending school. Had his relatives merely forgotten to write about it, or were there other reasons for their silence? Grigori had moved away from the village in which the Shcherbatovs had lived for so long; he and his family now lived on a kolkhoz closer to Borisoglebsk. As I

4. *Ukazniki* were lawyers who were familiar with imperial decrees (*ukases*). In Soviet prison slang the word designated prisoners who had been arrested and convicted under a *ukase*.

discovered later, he had moved not only because their daughter Nyura could find easier and better work there but also to escape the curse that weighed upon them because of Georgi's arrest. Borisoglebsk is a small city between Voronezh and Stalingrad. It was then not far from the front. I could tell from the letters how difficult life was becoming for them, and since they had no idea what my life was like, they could not understand my constant change of location or why I did nothing for my child.

At that time the need for wood greatly increased. Day and night we could hear the whistling of locomotives and the screeching of the freight cars as they were moved about. Although the camp lay in the middle of the taiga, there was not always enough wood to meet our needs during the cold season of the year. The work brigades could not even fill their quotas, and for that reason the healthier ones of us who worked within the compound occasionally had to go into the taiga to cut wood for fuel.

The taiga sucked up the strength of human beings just as the rotten logs that covered the forest floor absorbed the swamp water. Rotten vegetation and mosquitoes in the warm season of the year and the wet and cold of long, snow-filled winter months carried away more and more human lives; undernourishment and insufficient rest increased the number of victims—but the NKVD took care of supplying replacements. In Kayskii, as in all other forced-labor camps, there were also large potato and vegetable fields. For these there was no lack of labor, for the many invalids could take care of this kind of work. But despite the many thousands of tons that were harvested, the prisoners had to be happy to find a small piece of potato or a few bits of cabbage in their soup.

We knew that the soldiers fighting on the fronts suffered the most severe privations and that life was far from easy for the civilian population. But the dire need that prevailed in the camps was caused not by the war but by deliberate, arbitrary measures. That the country urgently required wood was something that we could understand. It was incomprehensible, however, that the wood was obtained at the cost of millions of human lives.

The purpose of medical treatment in the camps was generally the preservation of working capacity, the only standard according to which humans in work camps were evaluated. This factor established the limits of the doctor's activity. He could move only on a narrow ridge. If he were too conscientious, he would have had to free over half the prisoners from cutting wood—which the camp administration would never permit; at any time doctors, like all other prisoners, could be—and were—sent to fell trees in the taiga. If, on the other hand, doctors adhered too closely to the line of the administration, they incurred the hatred and contempt of the prisoners.

During my years in labor camps I worked with many doctors. Most of them tried with greater or lesser degrees of courage to do as much as they possibly could for the patients. They always had to proceed from the basic situation in a given camp and to take into consideration the prevailing conditions, for the leeway they had for their decisions depended on these factors. It was fortunate for the prisoners in Volosnitsa that Maria Samoilovna knew how to deal with the camp administration. She was cautious, certainly, but if someone became seriously ill, she did everything possible for him, even though most such patients were beyond our power to save.

Since the doctors usually only made rounds, it was the nurse who constantly had to remain with the patients, who was the good or evil spirit on the ward. It sometimes happened, of course, that a nurse had an eye for her own interests and regarded the patients entrusted to her as a necessary evil. Certainly, everyone in a camp sought to survive somehow and, as far as possible, to spare his or her own life. Furthermore, in the daily confrontation with human misery and death one could not help growing somewhat insensitive; otherwise, it would have been impossible to endure working with the patients. It had nothing to do with indifference; one merely learned to cope better with the daily horror and to treat human beings with the necessary forbearance. This was especially important in the case of patients with muscular atrophy, and these were the ones for whom we mostly had to care. In any event, our work demanded not only all our physical but also all our emotional and moral strength.

During the first years of confinement in prisons and camps our normal feelings and desires were overwhelmed by terror. We were, however, still relatively young persons and in the course of time came to realize that an end to our incarceration was not in sight and that we, like so many others, might well perish in a labor camp; this realization caused our natural feelings to burst forth. Whether the sexual factor was decisive, I do not know, for sexual activity as it existed in camps had an inhibitory effect on me. But the need for a truly close friend became stronger, the more one suffered from despair and desolation. To live constantly only on dreams and memories was not possible. In the camps, friendships and even love affairs developed again and again.

How happy I was when I entered the cramped, usually damp little room next to the bathhouse. There stood Kita in his wretched camp clothing, and I watched as the passionate smoker lit his little pipe of *makhorka* (there was no other kind of tobacco in the camp).[5] To do this he used two little stones on a cotton string (there were, of course, no matches). He struck these together so skillfully that he was able to light his pipe with only a few strokes.

The better I got to know Kita, the more I had to draw on my own inner resources in order to understand him. In Kita's presence I felt as I never have before or since. I could speak freely and clearly with him about matters that I otherwise never dared to mention. Therefore, it sometimes seems unreal to me now that I ever met and loved him.

5. Makhorka is a kind of coarse tobacco grown chiefly in the Ukraine.

It was precisely the combination of his intellect with a rare human warmth that constituted and projected his charm. The camp had in no way broken him; it even seemed to have strengthened him. He had more understanding for me than anyone else I ever knew. In those hours of being together—in the uncertainty of our future or even of the coming day, when we could not forget the mortification and the inhumaneness of our situation—we tried at least to be ourselves. And so those hours that I spent with Kita were some of the richest and deepest of my life.

It is difficult after all these years to revive memories of everything we discussed in his cramped quarters, where we were frequently disturbed by the noise of the bathing inmates. Even though I can still recall certain details almost verbatim, the mere repetition could never reproduce their essence. I remember especially one conversation in the early period of our acquaintance. Kita had gotten hold of Mayakovsky's poems, which were still rather unfamiliar to me. Viktor and Kita's Georgian friend were present. Kita rendered the poems without pathos but in such a way that not the finest nuance was lost. Finally he read the poem "On the Good Treatment of Horses." Kita's friends, intimately familiar with Mayakovsky, spoke about it. I listened in silence; it was difficult for me to say anything, even though this poetry already appealed to me at first hearing. It was not the poem itself that captivated me but the feeling at this moment that I really understood Kita for the first time.

Certainly, others also recited poetry. Among Russians this was nothing unusual, and among Georgians even less so. In almost every house the Georgians have their Rusthaveli, whom most of them know from memory. But Kita did not busy himself with the world of poetry and science merely from time to time; he actually lived in it. Whether he talked about Mayakovsky, Freud, or Hegel—everything was part of his view of life. The more often I was with him, the more deeply I felt the unity of his intellectual world. His surroundings could neither harm nor mislead him.

But something else in this conversation impressed me so deeply that I never forgot it. Kita, who usually spoke quietly and calmly in discussions, now tried with great animation to explain to us that precisely in forced-labor camps, despite physical and spiritual hunger, the individual condemned to loneliness could reach such depths of experience that he would be able to comprehend the essence of life and to lend it appropriate expression. Thereby the camp would become a genuine school for poets, and he repeated this with emphasis: "Yes, Kayskii, school for poets."

At first I was taken aback by these words. This hell in which we lived, where one could scarcely express one's thoughts—this hell Kita could call a school for poets! Still, the great attentiveness that he devoted to all kinds of creativity in the camp—his efforts to encourage all who seemed to have creative ability—could not fail to influence me.

I had already written several poems, which I showed to Kita. They pleased him, and I copied them into a small notebook that I always kept in a deep pocket in my dress. Unfortunately, it was stolen from me by a very skillful pickpocket who thought it was a purse. But now I ventured to take up a theme that I recorded in the form of a long narrative poem, not merely for the sake of camouflage but also because I did not yet think myself capable of writing prose.

I titled this poem *Der Meister*, "The Master." Kita followed my work with the greatest attentiveness. We discussed in detail the theme that, during the course of writing, swept me along more and more. For the conclusion, which eluded me for a long time, I finally found a previously unforeseen solution that especially pleased Kita: "It is the conclusion that makes the poem a valid piece of writing," he said. "If it had ended tritely, the entire poem would have been trivialized." Later, I revised it somewhat in both form and content; the revision was lost, but the original version remains to this very day a fond recollection.

Today, when I recall under what circumstances and in what a

short period of time I composed that poem, I can scarcely believe it, since it is now such a struggle to write a single page, which I must often rework. Only through Kita's understanding and his confidence in me did I lose my inhibitions and find the fitting mode of expression.

It was not Kita's nature to speak about the fact that he was continuing his research in the camp. That is why I did not learn about it until we had become close friends, and he knew that I would have an interest in and an appreciation for it. The shock of his death and my subsequent experiences made so many things that deeply interested me at that time sink into oblivion. As much as I endeavored later on to bring them to the surface, I did not succeed in picking up the thread again. It was not until several years ago, when I saw before me a copy of his work which had been published in Tiflis in 1965, that many a recollection again came to life.

The words that Kita—not by chance—underlined in the foreword seem so important to me that I should like to reproduce them here:

The old artificial boundaries, which, like the Chinese Wall, separate the sciences from one another, must be torn down. Going beyond the restricted purview of individual disciplines must become the motto of our research if we do not want to confine scientific thought to the narrow framework of formalism, which can only lead to sterility.

In this endeavor to comprehend every phenomenon in its multiplicity and complexity as a *whole,* Kita's criticism of all previous naturalistic, physiological, biological, psychological, and philosophical theories of thinking has its roots. Kita does not deny the validity of these theories; he does, however, criticize their one-sidedness, which leads to superficiality and impoverishment of the total picture and impedes the recognition of the true process.

Kita's application of the Marxian method, which precludes the development of dogmas, leads to a wealth of perceptions that are still stimulating today. Because he eschews all superficiality and simplification, he also interprets each philosophical theory differently than is customary in present-day pseudo-Marxian works. Kita's vigorous mode of thought, which gained him the hatred of the despots, his unique ability to analyze data and then not merely to derive numerous insignificant particulars from this analysis but rather to arrive at a synthesis of the whole—this was perhaps the inner resource that most effectively helped him to endure years of incarceration and to continue to work creatively.

In the environment in which we lived, we were almost never really alone, and we learned to communicate with few words and glances. When necessary, we wrote a few lines to each other. It is not at all easy to project myself back into the circumstances of that time, but these little notes, closely written, bring many details to life again.

I was always surprised at the attentiveness with which Kita listened to every line—yes, analyzed every word—of my poems. Since I had no other opportunity to express myself, and we seldom saw each other privately, I attributed great significance to my effusions. But today they would scarcely be understood.

In the winter of 1943–44 rations were worse than ever. To be sure, we had a separate kitchen for the patients, so that the food they received was at least better cooked and warm. But for weeks on end there was not a drop of oil, and for months there was no sugar at all, which, next to bread, was the most valuable form of nutrition for us. Thus the diet for the seriously ill was scarcely better than for others, and it was quite impossible to cure patients with advanced muscular atrophy. The mortality rate continued to increase.

As always, it was mostly the younger persons who were snatched away by death. I still cannot forget a young Moscow engineer who had been arrested at the front and whom we had all grown fond of. After months of felling trees he was brought to us in a hopeless condition. Since he had grown up without a father, his mother had meant everything to him, and he was greatly worried about her because he knew that he was dying. Before he died, he gave me her picture and asked me to look her up in case I ever got to Moscow.

When at night I walked through the dimly lighted ward, there was always at least one patient who lay there in fear of death and who called to me in order to hear a human voice one more time. No one wanted to die completely alone and forsaken.

In 1944, as the turn of the tide in the fighting became more certain and the Soviet army regained more and more territories, life in camp became appreciably more hectic. New prisoners were constantly arriving, especially convicted criminals, for as the war continued, the crime rate increased alarmingly. But there were also many victims of the war among those who had perforce remained under the German occupation. Most of them had waited longingly for their liberation, only to be thrown into prison and branded as political prisoners. In view of this situation our hopes, which had been tied to the advance of the Soviet army, were again dampened. It soon became obvious that a constant supply of reinforcements in the camps had been provided for. The forced-labor camps were and remained an essential part of the economy of the country and of the system.

About this time there were rumors that incurable patients and total invalids were to be released on the basis of medical certificates. Then one day Kita was summoned to the camp administration. Suddenly there was interest in his scientific research: some representative from the academy in Moscow or Tiflis came and interrogated him in detail. The possibility of his release was intimated. Kita was full of hope. He planned to care for my son; Ruslan could attend good schools in Tiflis and grow up with Kita's daughter Manana. I could not have wished for a better educator and friend for my child, especially since there was no longer any hope that Georgi was alive. But months passed by,

and Kita was not called, just as scarcely any of the political invalids and patients were released. And so we had to bury this
hope as well.

During this period I was receiving very few letters, and those
I did get were so scant that one could judge from their brevity
how difficult life in the village was. There was still nothing said
about Ruslan's school attendance. Not until much later did I
learn that Ruslan had broken his leg, had been hospitalized for a
long time, and did not begin school until he was eight and a half
years old.

The winter of 1943–44 slowly came to an end, and as always in
the north, spring was late in coming. The transition period was
difficult for everyone. The roads disappeared in mud and mire;
nevertheless the brigades had to go into the forest every day. An
epidemic of influenza broke out, and we were hard put to accommodate the sick. In addition we had to administer prophylactic
injections. We were even required to keep the patients in the ward
for several days after their fever had subsided—a most extraordinary order: for doing something like that previously, doctors had
been sent into the taiga to fell trees by way of punishment. The
death rate, however, was too high, and every prisoner halfway
capable of labor was needed for the work in the forest. Wood was
an important material for a war economy, and human material
was needed to obtain it. As soon as warmer and drier weather
arrived, we breathed a sigh of relief. The ward could again be
properly ventilated, and thorough cleaning became easier. All
the barracks were infested with bedbugs, and though there were
no insecticides, we could now at least thoroughly scrub the walls
and floors, douse the bedsteads with boiling water and kerosene,
and thus protect the patients at least somewhat from the ver-
min. Since the entire camp was infested, however, it would have
been impossible to rid the ward of bedbugs completely under
any circumstances.

Kita, too, had more work to do because of the spring dirt,

but he did not complain and was never angry or impolite. I did notice, however, that his beard seemed to grow whiter, and his camp garb dangled more loosely on him. He did not want to speak about this, and there was nothing we could do about it. I always marveled at the matter-of-factness with which he performed his duties. If he had had to live in the barracks like the others, matters would have been much more complicated for him. Because he never complained, I was unaware of his weariness.

It was at this time that Kita was working especially strenuously on his book, which was to be the second volume of his *Fundamental Problems of the Sociology of Thought*. How he rejoiced over every chapter that he completed! The closer he came to finishing it, the more we spoke about it in the brief moments in which we were together.

In addition to Viktor and his Georgian friend, another man who enjoyed visiting Kita had been the minister of agriculture in the last Latvian government.[6] He was one of a group of Latvians who were suddenly arrested in the camp and confined to the camp prison. All of them had already served a major part of their terms and had hoped to be freed when the war ended. These arrests released an outbreak of panic among the numerous Latvians and Estonians in our camp. Several months later this former minister of agriculture, greatly weakened physically, returned from the prison in Kirov with a new sentence: ten additional years of forced labor, with the strict stipulation that he was to be employed only for physical work. Formerly, he had been the manager of the barracks for invalids; now the certified agronomist was assigned to the pigsty of the camp kolkhoz, and

6. Latvia's last secretary of agriculture before World War II was Jānis Birznieks, who held that post from 1935 until 1940. In 1941 he was deported to Russia.

of course it was impossible to help him. The other Latvians who had been arrested had a similar experience: they returned to the camp with heavier sentences and in a much worse condition of health.

Among the Latvians interrogated at this time was Czeslav, who had been employed in the outpatient clinic as a doctor's assistant and with whom I had constantly been in contact. Whenever we had to cut wood for our camp, we always worked together, and he always came to me with all his worries. His wife and two children were living in banishment somewhere in Siberia. She wrote him despairing letters, but how could he help her? I can never forget how I once surprised Czeslav in the doctors' office as he stood before the map of Russia with tears in his eyes, searching for the place where his wife and children suffered hunger.

When he was arrested, he gave me a little note, which I still have: "My greeting; in remembrance; don't say no, but take these two things of mine. They are the most precious things I possess. Do not forget me! Have my words not been fulfilled? Czeslav." I can no longer recall what the two objects were that he gave me for safekeeping; I remember only that he had brought them along from his home in Latvia and that he always had them on his person. The final sentence of his note was an allusion to the fact that he had expected to be arrested and that we had always tried to talk him out of this conviction. We all feared for him. Maria Somoilovna and Maria Alekseyevna were as concerned as I was. But that time he was lucky. He returned to us several weeks later without being resentenced, and so I could return his keepsakes to him.

But the possibility now existed that any prisoner might be interrogated and resentenced within the camp. The agents of the NKVD (in the camp they were referred to as *Kum*, which means something like "godfather"), who had their spies in every nook and cranny, were mostly army officers who were dodging service at the front.[7] They sought to prove their indispensability in the camps and to that end daily hatched new conspiracies, with which they kept the prisoners in a constant state of terror.

In spring and fall the patients suffering from advanced tuberculosis were admitted to the hospital, where we had a special little room for them. Mostly they were terminal cases, young men who often had to endure agony for days. I recall especially well a young deaf-mute who had been hospitalized here once before. Since he could not be used for any other purpose, he was assigned to frisking other prisoners when they returned from work. For this reason he was detested by everyone. The other patients all had friends who came to the windows and sometimes brought flowers and berries along from the forest. No one visited this poor wretch. I believe that Maria Samoilovna and I were the only persons who had sympathy for him and treated him like a human being. As he lay dying, he did not want me to leave him alone. Whenever I had to be away for any length of time—and I did have other patients to care for!—he began to scream in his hollow voice and did not stop until I was again beside him. He died a slow and agonizing death; as the end approached, I dared scarcely leave his side.

One time when we had no other patients in this room, Maria Samoilovna assigned it to a young Russian poet for a while. He was not tuberculous but badly debilitated. He was supposed to regain his strength here. When we had time to listen, he read us some of his poems and showed us letters he had received from Pasternak and Kachalov, to whom he had sent his verse. Pasternak had replied that he found some passages in the poems very good and challenged the young poet not to give up writing under any circumstances—though he himself, Pasternak reported, had

7. *Kum,* which literally means "godparent to a king," is usually translated as "security chief" or "security operations officer."

not written anything for years. Kachalov, the well-known and popular actor who was friend and benefactor to many young poets, had also answered with appreciation. It was with heavy hearts that we had to dismiss the young poet. He was sent back to the taiga to fell trees, and we lost all trace of him.

We usually had our thin camp soup in the corridor of the hospital with the manager, Mikhail Simonovich, with whom I got along well. He was a dignified, somewhat eccentric old man who may once have been associated with the Social Revolutionists. In the corridor we had a loudspeaker, which we kept turned down as low as possible for the sake of the patients (we were not permitted to turn it off). Thus we were always bountifully supplied with the official news. Mikhail Simonovich had mastered the art of reading between the lines especially well; only now can I appreciate how well he kept me informed, thanks to his pithy, sarcastic comments.

He was highly educated. I was often astonished at his knowledge even of Austrian history and conditions; he sometimes put me to shame when I had only a faint knowledge of this or that detail. He had unconditional confidence in me. I was perhaps the only person with whom he could speak openly. When on duty, to be sure, there was sometimes a bit of friction between us because he rebuked us for not being economical enough with the laundry. On the other hand, we knew that no one could prevail on our behalf against the camp administration as well as this honorable old man.

Fortunately, his wife had not been arrested; she worked as a bookkeeper in Baku. They had no children. Her letters meant everything to him; whenever he did not hear from her for a rather long period of time, he became very uneasy. Yet he was the luckier one, because he received word from his wife more often than I did about my boy. After we were assigned to different camp units in the summer of 1945, I lost sight of him—as of so many others.

When the Georgian teacher with whom Kita was on close friendly terms was freed in the spring of 1944, he took along a little book into which Kita had copied all my poems and the first version of my *Meister*. How much better it would have been if Kita had entrusted his own work-in-progress to him, at least in the form of a sketch or rough outline. Unfortunately, Kita did not think of doing so at that time. He was convinced that ways and means would be found to publish it and thus preserve it.

Though he first wanted to complete his major work, Kita would have liked to deal with the subject of the camps. He could never get this thought out of his mind; it was a matter of great concern to him to make the concept "forced-labor camp" comprehensible to others. It was in this sense that he also viewed my writings. The more I thought about it, the better I understood him and his criticism of individual chapters of my *Meister*.

Everyone in the camp tried to cope with life there in his or her own way. Most of them had assumed some pose or other. Some tried to master their bitterness through cursing and obscenities. Others persevered in egoism, total indifference, and complete despair. Many fled into a dream world.

When I worked in the hospital, I often had no time for anything else than taking care of patients. But when I was still housed in the barracks, had no friends beside me, and lay sleepless at night among persons from whom one never heard a respectable word, I too sought refuge in a dream world. Yet even in these reveries I was unable to free myself from reality. Again and again I had to examine the difference between the world I had created in my dreams and the one that I was actually experiencing. Sometimes I imagined that a poet might write a drama of such power that its performance would make everyone conscious of the utter senselessness and cruelty of present Soviet policy. At the same moment I knew that such a drama could never be performed and that the likes of Stalin would never be convinced by it. Yet such wishful thinking helped me to endure the horror of the camps.

My *Meister* also contained some of these notions. The poem was an attempt to create a character, a human being, who, in contrast to the power-greedy politicians, was a man of significant achievement. Today my *Meister* reveals how far I was from comprehending all the complex interrelationships of that time, and how thoroughly I was still afflicted with my earlier concepts. No matter how great the foresight that some persons then had, there was no one who could then have applied the standards of today.

I frequently read to Kita and other friends from this poem. And thus my *Meister* had not been composed in vain since it provided pleasure for so many.

In the spring of 1944 Viktor had succeeded in organizing a group from among the prisoners to perform an operetta. Among Russians, singers and dancers could always be found. Except for the November celebration in Akmolinsk, I had never before experienced a performance in a camp. Almost everywhere the "club rooms," where there were any, stood empty. Actually, they existed only in the older camps as ornaments in a stage setting, left over from the days when the government still pretended that the purpose of the forced-labor camps was to "reeducate" the prisoners.

During the presentation I sat between Kita and Maria Samoilovna and can well remember that we discussed the opera *Prince Igor*. I greatly admired the performance of the group, but I marveled even more at the patience and self-restraint of Viktor, who not only had quite enough to do as manager of the bathhouse but was worried greatly about his family, who were living under German occupation and from whom he had no news. In the camp, Viktor was an admirer of Maria Alekseyevna, who came from the same region as he. Before my arrival they had been very close friends, but then Maria Alekseyevna had become attached to someone else. It had been difficult for Viktor to get over this.

In spite of the difference in their characters Maria Alekseyevna and Maria Samoilovna were good friends. Maria Samoilovna, a responsible physician, was a sober, objective, and reserved person, whereas Maria Alekseyevna was of a pronounced cheerful and sensuous nature. During the long winter, when the camp had quieted down somewhat and Maria Samoilovna was getting her medical reports together, Maria Alekseyevna and I frequently took short walks through the camp to catch a bit of fresh air. Sometimes she came along with me for a few minutes to visit Kita and Viktor. How quickly the cold and rainy spring had merged with the short summer. The first anniversary of my meeting with Kita, 5 August 1944, arrived. On this day Kita wrote me a letter, the only one that bears a date. In the posthumous edition of the first volume of his work, which appeared in 1965, the year of his death is erroneously given as 1943. This letter is important because it verifies the existence of the second volume, which was written by Kita in the camp and was almost completed at that time. The letter reads in part:

5 August 1943–44

For today's gift I can choose only the most cordial and precious. The most precious thing I possess is only my world of ideas, although it is of no practical use. My book, which is virtually complete, belongs to you. . . . I have never dedicated my scientific ideas to anyone, and all my publications have appeared without dedication. I did not consider it necessary. . . .

Now, however, I think differently—and now all my thoughts belong only to you, my dearest one. And if an evil fate should part us forever, I tell you that you will receive this book, and on the first page you will find the following printed line:

Dedicated to my unforgettable friend.
Wherever you are, you will get to read it.

Probably I had not suspected until that moment that Kita's feelings for me could be so deep that he would dedicate to me the volume that he regarded as a major part of his life's work.

Yet not only then but in my entire life the most traumatic

experience was the separation from my children, and the only thing I still dared to hope—as improbable as it might seem at this moment—was a return to my Austrian home together with my son Ruslan. Never in my life, neither before nor afterward, had I been capable of such feelings as I felt for Kita; nevertheless, I had to write in my answer:

Your dedication has deeply moved me, but let us leave this question to the future. What you have done is sufficient. What is yet to be is something we cannot decide today. Our future lies in the clouds. Whatever may be, let us keep this year in fond memory. In you I found not only the best friend I ever had; through you I found the way to myself.

This reply has also been preserved; I doubt that I could have re-created the text of these two letters from memory, because it is so difficult for me today to put myself into my mental and emotional state of that time.

Kita finished his volume shortly after this and neatly copied it into a thick, bound notebook. In the few quiet moments at our disposal we planned to read through it together, chapter by chapter. But we could peruse only the first chapter. It related to themes of his first book, which I did not yet know. Kita tried to explain it to me, and when in 1967 I obtained a copy of his first book, many things suddenly became clear to me.

The summer of 1944 passed, but this year there was an exceptionally beautiful and warm September, so that several times we were able to sit on the wooden stairs in front of the hospital with Kita. It was always for just a few minutes before ten o'clock, because that was bedtime.

That is the way it was on 20 September, on a clear, moonlit night. We sat together for scarcely a quarter of an hour. Kita was especially excited; although I cannot recall exactly what we talked about, I do remember that it was a very stimulating conversation. Yet Kita, who had been unusually lively and hearty, in conclusion said abruptly: "May God protect you! It would have been too beautiful. May God protect you! It was not to be."

Afterward, as usual, I had much to do, but I could not stop thinking about those words. At two-thirty the night watchman, who was stationed in front of the outpatient clinic, came running to say that there was a patient there. I followed the man immediately, for if anyone came to the clinic at that late hour, it had to be something serious.

I was alarmed when I saw Kita. He looked pale and pitiful. He told me he had felt so cold in his cubicle that he had lain down in the sauna. There he had suddenly had a seizure. I put him on the couch in the clinic and sent the watchman for the doctor on duty, who slept in a small compartment close by. The doctor came at once, felt Kita's pulse, and ordered me to prepare a pantapon injection. While I was filling the syringe, Kita reached for my hand and said, "That is much too weak for me." I calmed him although I felt that he was in a very serious condition. He asked me to call Maria Samoilovna. I had intended to do this anyway but did not know how long it would take her to get to the clinic; that is why I had just called the doctor on duty. I asked Kita to remain lying quietly and was about to go to waken Maria Samoilovna. Then suddenly a spasm shook his body, and I knew immediately that he was dead.

I seized Kita's hand, and there was still warmth there, but his eyes were extinguished and his mouth could say nothing more. At this moment I knew I would never again meet a human being like Kita and that I would never again be able to love anyone as I had loved him.

How miserable he must have felt, and he had told no one, not even me. He had known how serious his condition was when he said, "That is much too weak for me." But I had comprehended nothing, neither his departing utterance in the evening nor his final words. As serious as his condition had seemed to me, I had not dreamed that he would die. And so I now stood there, poorer even than when I had first come to Volosnitsa and a strange man had handed me two little pieces of soap. Was there any purpose in going on living? Never had this question confronted me so unconditionally as at this moment. Yet I had to go on living for the sake of my son. I thought of Kita's wife and daughter. Poor Zuza! Poor Manana!

I had to go. I had patients to attend to. Tears ran down my cheeks, and I could not stop them.

The patients did not dare to speak to me. But one thing I was able to do. Before morning came, I ran to Kita's cubicle, hastily gathered Zuza's last letters, Manana's pictures, my letters, and Kita's book manuscript, and hid everything.

After my work in the clinic there was nothing else for me to do but to return to the barracks and lie down on my plank bench. Maria Samoilovna had asked me in the morning why I had not sent for her; but I had not been able to do so; everything had happened too quickly. Toward noon she came to me in the barracks, where I lay as if petrified. An autopsy had been performed on Kita; his sudden death had made this necessary. It brought me no comfort when she said, "Kita's death was unavoidable. The walls of his heart were as thin as tissue paper. They had to tear."

Kita had concealed his real condition only to keep from alarming me. He had not even sought help from Maria Samoilovna, whom he trusted completely. How serious had his condition been when we had met just a few hours before? In the darkness, to be sure, I had not been able to see his face clearly, and I had suspected and understood nothing. So I had to lie in the barracks with my impotent pain and wait until it was again time to begin my work in the ward.

How many human beings had I seen die in the last few years, and yet I had never become callous in the face of death. Among them were some who probably would have died even in freedom.

There were also convicted criminals among them, although not so many, because the convicts knew how to establish themselves and attain all the prerogatives. In order to spare themselves, they drove others to work and took the last piece of bread from the weak. Those who died were mostly the younger and the more valuable ones, to whose deaths I could never resign myself.

Kita's sudden death evoked sympathy throughout the entire camp. The "professor" had been a legendary figure; he had, after all, been part of the permanent personnel of the camp, which otherwise was characterized by a constant coming and going. Now the prisoners learned that he, who had always had to be there for the sake of others, had himself been a very sick man. Because of this high respect it was possible to have a simple wooden coffin made for Kita, to dress him in clean clothing, and to lay some flowers in his coffin. Maria Samoilovna and Maria Alekseyevna helped me. I gave the gravedigger my bread ration for the day so that he would bury Kita's coffin by itself. Ordinarily there were only mass graves into which the bodies were tossed.

When the body was taken out before morning muster, I accompanied it as far as the gate and waited until the guard had let the wagon pass. Then I had to return to my work. The gravedigger assured me that he had buried Kita's coffin beneath the highest spruce tree standing there. Since there were no grave markers in this cemetery, he thought that would be the best way to help us find Kita's grave.

Kita was forty-four years old when he died. In freedom, too, he would probably not have lived to be very old, but in no case would he have had to die so early. If the book he wrote in camp had been published, its original ideas would certainly have aroused the same sensation as his book of 1937. Even today I must marvel how, cramped in the cubicle of the bathhouse, caught between steam and the stench of dirty laundry, with poor light and incessant noise, he had continued his work without granting himself even a little bit of rest. This would surely have undermined the health of even a robust man used to hard physical work.

I had to save his book! For the time being I kept it hidden in the office of the hospital without telling anyone about it. This seemed to be the safest place in the camp.

13

Life in the camp went on as usual. What did my personal pain mean in this general misery around us! Autumn and winter merely increased the disconsolateness. The only things that brought a little hope into our lives were the victories of the Soviet armies. In the spring of 1945, after our rations had been worse than ever, there was suddenly an improvement, presumably because the death rate had increased so terribly. After months without sugar, the sugar ration was restored. The gruel became much better; indeed, it was the best gruel we had ever had in the camps. Apparently it came from American shipments, because the Russians seldom used wheat for gruel. Also, the drop of oil that we were supposed to get was again put on the gruel.

I had had no news about my son for a long time. In my anxiety I wrote to the administration of the "Red October" kolkhoz near Borisoglebsk, where Grigori worked. My relatives resented my doing this, because they had moved to that place so that no one would know that they were harboring a child of arrestees. Now they were burdened anew because of my letter. Their letters, to be sure, continued to be meager, but things seemed to be in order as far as Ruslan was concerned. The thought of my child was the only thing that motivated me in those days. Otherwise, I alternated between the barracks and the hospital like an automaton.

At the same time, difficulties also began to develop in my work. I had always cooperated splendidly with Maria Samoilovna, and she had also had complete confidence in me. But now she needed to devote more time to her duties outside the camp, so the second doctor had to look after some of her duties in the hospital. He was a German from the Latvian Courland, but even the Latvians did not like him. As the physician for the invalid barracks, he had seldom had to serve on night duty for the outpatient clinic. Now he came to our ward rather frequently during the day.

I had formerly not been able to endure him because of his condescending manner, and after Kita's death I resented his indifference. As a doctor he must have been able to see how serious Kita's condition was, but he had merely felt his pulse without examining him, had prescribed the injection, and had immediately left the clinic; I had had to call him back as soon as I saw how badly things were going with Kita. Kita had not been able to endure him either, and to this very day I have regretted that I did not call Maria Samoilovna immediately, although this would have changed nothing in the situation. It was especially difficult for me to work with this Dr. Kraus (I believe that was his name), because he rated human beings according to their rank and wealth, and only those at the top gained his recognition. In his German arrogance he looked down his nose at other nationalities, especially smaller ones. He also despised me because of my relationship to Kita. In respect to me he regarded himself as the protector of the good German tradition.

With his increased presence, the atmosphere in the hospital completely changed. It was most fortunate that Maria Samoilovna retained the supervision of the hospital and made the decisions regarding admissions and dismissals. Yet she was a close friend of Dr. Kraus and listened to his advice in many matters.

Dr. Kraus wanted to vex me, but I remained stubborn and minced no words. I rebelled against him because I knew that I performed my duties responsibly and with greater sympathy and understanding for the patients than he was capable of. In the camps the essential medicaments needed to provide real help for the patients were often lacking. For this reason our attitude and conduct toward the patients was of the utmost importance.

Dr. Kraus complained to Maria Samoilovna about me, and things finally came to such a pass that she called me to account. That hurt me because I held her in high esteem, but I could not resist telling her all my thoughts. Suddenly all the rancor I had against this person erupted. It was certainly unwise of me to let myself be overwhelmed by my feelings, because Dr. Kraus was her friend. She was, after all, not merely a doctor but also a woman. Consequently, there followed difficult days for me, which I could endure only in the hope that everything would soon come to an end and that I would see my child again. After all this, I was not able to do any writing. I was burned out.

By then it had become known that the Volosnitsa camp was to be abolished, since it was no longer advantageous to cut timber in this region. I do not know whether Dr. Kraus restrained himself more or whether I became more indifferent to whatever hurt me, but everything continued its usual course. Mikhail Simonovich understood me much better. He did not care for this arrogant Dr. Kraus either, but since he had little direct contact with him, he ignored him as far as possible.

Then May arrived and with it the end of the war. How we rejoiced about this in the camp! It was on a Sunday that we received the news, when everyone was in the barracks; we celebrated and were perhaps somewhat nicer to one another. But amidst all this joy I thought about Kita more than ever—Kita, who would not have the opportunity of experiencing the day he and I had so ardently longed for. We had been so firmly convinced that a victorious end of the war would give the country more democracy and finally bring freedom to the prisoners who had long since served out their terms—possibly even amnesty for the other political prisoners. For the time being, however, there were no such liberations. These did not begin until the early summer of 1946, and then they proceeded very slowly.

In the summer of 1945 the Volosnitsa camp was liquidated, and our unit was moved into the deeper regions of the taiga. I was the first and only one to be sent to the camp for invalids not too far distant, where I was to serve as a nurse. By way of exception I was notified a day in advance; for once I had ample time to make ready and say goodbye to all my friends. Most recently I had been on especially good terms with the dentist, Elisabeth Mikhailovna. I sometimes sought refuge in her quarters, since there were many points of common interest between us for conversation. She also liked to hear me read from my *Meister* and some of my other poetry. There really was so little reading material available.

But now I had to decide what to do with Kita's manuscript. I had not yet succeeded in getting in touch with one of his Georgian friends who would have taken care of his book. Should I take it with me? That was too risky. During transportation we were always examined so thoroughly that it would scarcely have been possible to hide the bulky notebook. After lengthy consideration I decided to confide in Maria Alekseyevna and ask her to hide it in the pharmacy. Because of the position that Maria Samoilovna occupied, it might be possible for one or the other to get the manuscript into safekeeping during their removal to new quarters. After some hesitation, Maria Alekseyevna took the book and promised to take care of it. We were, after all, counting on early liberation and thus on the possibility of finding ways and means of somehow getting Kita's work to Georgia. Of course, I was assailed again and again by doubts as to whether I had done the right thing, but my further experiences confirmed that I really had had no alternative.

The invalid camp signified only a brief sojourn for me. Before autumn arrived, this camp too was liquidated, and the invalids, of whom there were many throughout Kayskii, were brought together in a single camp unit in the depths of the taiga. Both doctors were from Latvia, as were many of the prisoners—mostly older ones who had become invalids in the camps.

All those who could manage to get around had to work. Only a few could be sent into the forest, but there was a lot of farm work, and a large apiary was a part of the camp. Inside the compound there was also plenty to do. I was assigned to a barracks in which only the sick and those unable to work were housed. Since this camp was specifically designated for invalids, everything was even more primitive and wretched than in the forced-labor camps. Our barracks consisted of a single room. I had to live in a small compartment among the patients and was surrounded by their laments and moans day and night. Here lay the slowly dying, the decrepit, and the crippled. Some had been crippled or partially paralyzed by strokes while living in camps. As the only nurse, I was on duty day and night, and in addition I was burdened with my own cares and sorrows. My situation seemed more disconsolate than ever, despite the fact that I was the only person beside the doctor who could still bring some warmth and hope into the lives of these banished and abandoned human beings. In Volosnitsa we had at least had constant contact with the world outside; here, however, we were almost completely isolated. Even the single-rail, narrow-gauge camp railroad that connected units of the camp lay far from our compound.

I met several patients whom I had treated at the hospital in Volosnitsa. Among them was a rather young man from Prague,

who maintained that he had been the secretary of Eduard Beneš.[1]
When Hitler occupied Czechoslovakia, he had fled across Poland
to the Soviet Union, where he was arrested. Later he was transferred from the camp to a prison in Moscow; from there he was
returned, quite exhausted, and had been in the hospital for some
time. This young man, whose name completely escapes me, was
very handsome and greatly admired by the few women in the
camp. From him I learned a great deal about what had happened
in Europe during the years preceding his arrest. Certainly he had
not been incarcerated without reason. It was clear that he simply
knew too much.

The physician with whom I worked closely as well as the
nurses on duty here were not very old. Since the doctor wanted
to improve his German, he and I usually spoke German together.
His wife and children were living in banishment somewhere in
Siberia, and he sent her what little money he received, but her despairing letters greatly oppressed him. The second doctor, with
whom I did not work directly, was very well read and spoke German well. There was also a Latvian woman who worked there as
a nurse. I made friends with these Latvians as well as with others
who were there as patients, among them a professor of Russian
with whom I studied Russian grammar. With these persons I
could speak more or less openly.

Nevertheless, I was in the worst possible frame of mind.
Through this transfer I had again lost all contact with my child.
I was isolated from everything and did not know whether those
prisoners who, like me, had already served their terms were
finally being released. And then before autumn had really come,
this camp unit too was disbanded. All the inmates were transported away, and for a few weeks I was assigned to the camp

1. Eduard Beneš (1881–1948), student and disciple of Tomáš Masaryk, was
twice president of Czechoslovakia (1935–38 and 1945–48).

sovkhos,[2] where I worked at stocking the storerooms with field produce. Had it not been for the hope that all this would soon have to end, and had it not been for concern about my son, I do not know whether I would have been able to endure all this.

Now the cold time of year arrived, and soon there was snow. It may well have been the beginning of November when I was again summoned and quickly had to pack my things. A thaw occurred precisely on this day, on which, following a march on foot and a train ride into the unknown, I arrived at a camp unit located next to the hospital of Volosnitsa. During the journey on the single-rail camp railroad we had seen a train of German prisoners of war at a station. I had spoken to them through the car window, thinking that they were already being transported to their homes. But this was not the case. They had been brought here from somewhere or other, and they had complete confidence that they would soon be released. It turned out, however, that they were taken to a nearby camp unit and, like all the rest who had hoped for freedom, would not so quickly be sent home. They still had to fell many trees in the taiga before they could begin their way back. There were surely not a few among them whose bodies would fertilize the taiga.

Again the gates of a camp compound had closed behind me. After the formalities of the transfer—I had been brought here completely alone—I was assigned a place in the barracks. The room in which my bench stood was only for women who worked inside the compound. Although we slept on two-tiered benches, these had spaces between them, which made a neat—yes, one could even say a friendly—impression. A dear old lady was in charge of this room.

As a nurse I had to report immediately to the ward where I

2. *Sovkhozes* were state farms. Whereas a kolkhoz was formed by merging privately owned farms confiscated by the government, a *sovkhoz* was formed by extending agriculture into areas that had formerly been range lands.

was to work. What a surprise for me to find a flowerbed in front of the hospital—a flowerbed in which the most beautiful pansies, fresh and untouched, peeked up through the melting snow. In the office a luxuriantly blooming fuchsia stood on the table, and flowers were blooming at the windows of the two wards. There were even several rose bushes among them. I soon learned that it was Berta, the pharmacist, who had created the blooming splendor. A German from the Caucasus, she was a friendly, still vigorous woman in her mid-sixties. Although the pharmacy was located at some distance from the hospital, she came over to us whenever she had a few minutes in order to tend her flowers and plants. In the hospital there were two nurses, who had to be on duty alternately.

The atmosphere in this camp unit reminded me somewhat of Volosnitsa; located near the railroad station, it fulfilled the same function in regard to new admissions from the Stolypin prisoner cars. The processing of released prisoners was carried out at that time directly by the headquarters of the camp, but it was still only *bytoviki* and convicted criminals who were being released.

The stream of arriving prisoners did not lessen, but there were different categories in the prisoner cars. More and more frequently there were those who had come from German internment camps or from the previously occupied areas. Soldiers and officers who had been freed from German captivity felt fortunate to be home—but first they were subjected to the torment of special camps, in which they were usually condemned to at least ten years of forced labor. I recall especially well a rather young Moscow engineer who as an officer had been taken into German captivity. He had succeeded in ridding himself of his officer's insignia, because officers not infrequently were shot to death as "commissars" by Nazis. In the prison camp he had suffered such hunger that he had searched for food in garbage cans. After his return home he had been interrogated for three months and finally condemned to ten years of forced labor. He was quite sick and dispirited when he came to us at the hospital. He never again wished to write to his wife, a dear and lovely person. Who, after all, could believe that he was not conscious of some guilt or other?

We had hoped for liberation, for a reduction of the political pressure, and now we incessantly experienced the very opposite. I was especially shaken when I found among the new arrivals a man from Baden, near Vienna. He told me he had been arrested for offering to sell wine to Soviet soldiers. Whatever the reason, I was frightened by the fact that the Soviets felt free to condemn Austrian citizens and even to deport them instead of turning them over to the local courts. I had been dreaming about a return to my home, but what was happening there?

Finally I again received news about my boy and learned that he was attending school, though life in the village in which he lived still seemed to be very difficult. We already knew that there was severe hunger especially in the northern and central regions of the Soviet Union: not only had there been bad harvests, but the war had laid waste huge areas that had to be supplied and restored. In general the war had exhausted so many resources. Also, following the brief improvement we had experienced in the spring of 1945, the customary wretchedness again prevailed in camp. Yet we did receive our bread ration. I cannot recall a single day during my years in camps on which we did not receive our bread ration. With iron discipline I divided the 600 grams into three parts. When I was on night duty, I tried to eat the third piece as late as possible so that the hunger before morning would not last so long. But for those who had to work in the taiga, even the somewhat larger bread rations did not suffice. Therefore, the death rate did not come down, just as the number who became invalids did not decrease.

An elderly doctor from Poland had charge of the outpatient clinic and of admissions. He was also consulted in borderline cases. The infirmary doctor was a young Russian. He shared a small wooden hut beside the infirmary barracks with the general manager and spent as little time as possible in the infirmary. While quite young he had been arrested with several other students at a Leningrad institute because of an alleged attempt to form a counterrevolutionary group, even though he had never meddled in politics. Since such an injustice had been committed against him, he at least wanted to get even somehow or other. He passed the time as best he could and did scarcely any work. It was depressing indeed to be a witness to how such young persons coped with life in the camp. How few possibilities there were to live as a human being! Our doctor was at least in the fortunate position of not being compelled to perform hard physical labor every day.

My days were filled with hard work. This was actually fortunate for me, because it kept me so dead tired that I was able to sleep. In Berta, who sometimes sat with me in the office in the evening, I had again found someone with whom I could speak about everything. She had two German books. One was *Friedemann Bach* by Brachvogel; it was the description by a German from Prague of a walking tour through the Austrian Alps. I can't recall the title of the other, but the content of these two books remains firmly fixed in my memory even today. We had read them over and over again with such close attention. There was nothing else. At her wish, however, we often paged through my *Meister*. For all my friends who knew German, the man in the poem became a figure that accompanied us through the desolateness of our days.

Thus the long winter passed. In the first days of spring our camp made preparations for a large prisoner transport. Several barracks were vacated for them. The detachment arrived during the night, and early in the morning I had to administer inoculations to prevent an epidemic of dysentery. In the graying morning light I went along the benches, startling these weary, exhausted persons from their sleep. They scarcely knew what had happened to them. During recent weeks they had endured so many strange and frightening experiences that they could no longer believe in something good. They came from the areas of the western Ukraine and Carpatho-Russia annexed by the Soviet Union. After years of war and German occupation, these people had hoped for a return to normal life—and now they were here. They had suddenly been taken away from their homes and put into prison. Most of them had been condemned to ten years at forced labor. The majority were younger persons, mainly peasants and craftsmen. There were also some healthy, unassuming peasant girls; it hurt me to think of what awaited them. After several days of quarantine they were taken to various units of the Kayskii camp and sent to work mostly in the taiga.

One episode connected with this detachment affected the entire camp. A peasant, the father of one of the girls, came to visit his only daughter a few months after her deportation. He had been told that she was merely being mobilized for work and would be treated well. The peasant had sold his only cow to pay for his trip here, and only after long discussion did he receive permission to visit her. He soon discovered under what conditions his daughter had to live here, and that this was a prison camp. Those who are acquainted with camp conditions can imagine what later became of his daughter.

A second transport, which may have arrived during the winter of 1945–46, horrified all the camp inmates. It too was a detachment from the liberated regions annexed to the Soviet Union, but these were persons who had been employed by Germans during the occupation. Among them was a former railroad station agent who during the journey had made an attempt to flee, together with several other railroaders. Since the long freight train filled with prisoners moved very slowly, they had broken up the planks of a car floor and had attempted to slip under the train. They had been detected, however, and recaptured. As soon as they were brought to the camp, they were shot to death and their bodies left lying in the snow before the camp gate for days as a deterrent.

It may seem incomprehensible that no possibility was found to escape from the camps. There were always some who attempted it, but I do not know of a single case in which the fugitive succeeded. Convicted criminals had the best chances, since they were prepared to commit any outrage to secure food and clothing, and they also had the possibility of disappearing into the underworld. Nevertheless, in the depths of the taiga and the desolate areas of the northern and eastern regions of the Soviet Union, flight was an almost hopeless undertaking from the very beginning. The fugitive would have no weapon and no food. He would have to walk for days before he came to an inhabited region. No one would dare give food or shelter to a man in camp garb. Without identity papers he could neither work nor exist. For the criminals all this would have been no problem. They would have taken everything by force; but they too knew that they could not possibly make it to an inhabited region. It was for this reason that they resisted being deported to remote, desolate regions. They knew that flight could be undertaken only from inhabited regions or the vicinity of fairly large cities.

In the Kayskii camp I was aware of two attempts at escape. Once it was a Latvian, who had not taken the wide Russian expanses into account. While working in the taiga he succeeded in slipping away, but after two or three days he was tracked down by the dogs of the search party, bitten, shot, and terribly beaten; nothing remained of him but a miserable bundle. He stayed in the infirmary only until we had attended to his wounds, after which he was at once put into the camp prison. I do not believe that he left it alive.

The second escape attempt took place in February 1946 and kept the entire camp in suspense. Two very dangerous criminals, who were put into the camp prison because of a crime committed within the camp, succeeded initially in the most fantastic way.

They broke out of the center of the camp, where the camp administration with its well-constructed living quarters was located. This was not easy. It sounds almost like a joke, but they actually spent the first night in the house of the camp commander, under his matrimonial bed. Then they procured NKVD uniforms, for all roads stood open to those who wore these uniforms. The house of the commander was surrounded by a fence and under constant guard; nevertheless, while the sentry was making his rounds, they managed to climb over the fence. The camp commander himself was not at home that night. One of his uniforms, which had been hanging over a chair, was missing in the morning. When his wife discovered that the two inmates had spent the night under her bed, she was badly frightened. Every night for over a week the two broke into the stores and canteens of camp personnel and supplied themselves with food. And yet they did not succeed in breaking through the ring of barriers surrounding the camp and in making their way to the Kirov railway; they were captured still within the camp compound. Nevertheless, I am convinced that they were treated better than the poor Latvian, who had been classified as a political prisoner.

Not until the summer of 1946 did we hear that political prisoners whose period of detention had expired were to be released. But, of course, it would not be a real liberation, because they could return neither to large cities nor to the central regions of Russia. Especially severe were the limitations imposed on Soviet Germans, who could settle only in precisely determined, far distant areas, where they were subjected to special supervision and registration.

More than ever I now lived between hope and despair. Only work, which demanded all my strength, sustained me, and every evening weariness let me sink into a heavy sleep, interwoven with chaotic dreams. Sometimes I awoke at night, paralyzed by terror, and it took a while before I gradually regained my contact with reality. But my trials were far from over. I had kept all my papers and writings in the office, which seemed to me to be the securest place.

The young doctor with whom I worked was a real windbag. He became involved with criminal convicts, who somehow had obtained valuables such as rings and watches from the nearby camp of the German prisoners of war; from them our doctor, who made money by selling alcohol to the criminals, also acquired various valuables. This was discovered by the *Kum* of the NKVD, however, who wanted to get as much of this loot as possible for himself. Therefore, he had nothing more urgent to do than to organize a search of the infirmary.

The office was thoroughly searched. The doctor had been shrewd enough to find a secure place for his plunder; neither in the infirmary nor in his cubicle could the NKVD agent find anything. But in the office he discovered all my writings, which he naturally confiscated. All my assurances that these were merely harmless poems—for the most part, copies of poems—were to no avail. I knew that it did not matter so much what I had written as how it was interpreted—or to state it more exactly, what could be read into my writings. My release was imminent, but if new legal proceedings were initiated against me, as had happened to so many others, I could remain in camps for ten years longer. That would be the end of me. I would never again see my child and my home.

In my boundless despair I went running to Berta, the only person to whom I could confide my fears, since she was acquainted with my writings. Berta immediately set my mind at rest. She told me not to be afraid: the *Kum* would not immediately take the papers to his superiors; he would first want to be certain of what they contained, since they were all written in German. She said she would find means of getting through to him.

Of all the officers of the camp administration, the ones who were most hated and feared were the agents of the NKVD. I had had the good fortune of not having had anything to do with them directly. This *Kum,* who seemed to be a jovial and merry sort of person, was especially corrupt. He exploited every possible opportunity in the camp for his own purposes. The tailors, shoemakers, and cabinetmakers all had to work for him personally. Like most officers of the camp administration, he was also very fond of alcohol, and often enough he had Berta give him some from the stores in the pharmacy. The advantage was that it didn't cost him anything. Berta knew when the *Kum* would come to the pharmacy again. She would naturally say nothing directly about the writings—the fact that we had often read from them could have made matters worse—but she knew that he could not read them and needed someone to translate for him, and there were not many here who knew German. Fortunately for me, Berta was the one he called in order to have them translated.

Berta was a wise woman, who "had gone through all fires, waters, and copper pipes," as a Russian proverb says which we often quoted in the camp. She had the necessary boldness and cleverness to deal with this sort of person. At that time she had served almost her entire sentence of ten years in forced-labor camps, and the fact that she had charge of the pharmacy was also a form of security, since she could be replaced only by someone who knew something about drugs and medicines. As a very proper person, she also possessed the necessary reserve.

Nevertheless, about two weeks passed before my fate was decided. I suffered through days of the most anxious fear and expectation. One day the *Kum* summoned me. Since he had the worst possible reputation in regard to women, I went to his office with unpleasant feelings. But everything proceeded well. To be sure, he spoke to me in an especially sugary manner, but I had, after all, become somewhat hardened in dealings with such people. I behaved as correctly as possible but left him with the impression that I recognized and valued his appreciation of my writings. I had indeed escaped a great danger. (Fate willed that I should have one later encounter with him. As I was leaving the office of the central administration, quite staggered at the news of my so-called "release," I bumped into this *Kum* in the doorway. At that moment I was in such a state of emotional turmoil that I scarcely noticed this meeting. Shortly afterward, however, I learned that he had just then been apprehended and that he was sentenced to five years at forced labor. Someone had denounced him for his dealings, especially because of those valuables that he had appropriated from the German prisoners of war. His "friends" in the camp administration certainly must have been envious of him; otherwise they would not have abandoned him.)

After this adventure I knew for certain that it would have been impossible for me to save Kita's work. Still, I suffered pangs of conscience for having exposed Maria Alekseyevna to such dangers, although I had to remind myself that at the time I had given her the manuscript, there was no cause to think of danger. The pharmacy served not only the camp but also the free population of the surrounding area. Yet how quickly such situations could change in a camp, all the more so when the Volosnitsa camp was discontinued and we could not know how the regroupings would be carried out. For this reason I was in a constant state of uneasiness about Kita's manuscript.

At this time we heard repeatedly of releases from camp, but I learned from comments and conversations that most prisoners were not optimistic. They knew the conditions on the outside better than I did. Those who were forbidden to return to where their families lived but had to take up residence in strange regions were in a bad way. They could not always find work, without which it was impossible to get food-ration cards or lodging. All anyone received upon leaving a camp was a certificate of dismissal, not a certificate of employment. We might be released, but we could not get rid of the brand that had been stamped upon us. In the prevailing atmosphere of the time, former inmates were avoided everywhere because the others already had sufficient reason to be afraid. None of this could depress me, however, because I thought that I could not be worse off anywhere than here, and in freedom I would at least be with my child.

So the summer passed. More and more transports came from the regions the Soviets had occupied and from those they had recaptured. Among the newcomers was an engineer from Telefunken who had been instrumental in the development of television.[3] The firm had been evacuated from Berlin to Czechoslovakia, and the Soviets had apprehended him in the workshop just as he was, in his lab coat. He was a small, elderly man in very poor health.

In the vicinity of the camp there was a dairy farm, and so we sometimes received a distribution of milk for our most seriously ill patients. The manager of the dairy—a former camp prisoner and herself seriously tuberculous—brought us as much as she could possibly spare. Unfortunately, she soon succumbed to her illness, and shortly before my departure from the camp I received the sad assignment of taking her five-year-old daughter to an orphanage that was located in a distant village.

This milk was a blessing for us. I always tried to apportion it as fairly as possible among the weakest patients. Thus Schubert, the engineer, who was quite exhausted after long imprisonment in Moscow, sometimes received some of this meagerly rationed milk. Schubert's wife lived in that part of Berlin now occupied by the Soviets, and he asked me, if I were freed, to notify her of his whereabouts. When I was finally summoned in the fall of 1946 for what I thought would be my liberation, I gave Schubert, who had no personal belongings, my fur cap, because his camp garb was completely worn out.

When I was in Moscow in July 1948, before my departure for Austria, I gave Schubert's name to a Soviet officer who was entrusted with the task of identifying important specialists in the

3. Telefunken was an important branch of the radio and television industry founded in 1903 in Berlin.

camps. Soon afterward I learned in Vienna that this officer, a former Austrian, had suddenly been recalled from Moscow. He was said to have succumbed to a mysterious heart attack. Then I became skeptical as to whether anything had been done for Schubert. Immediately upon my arrival in Vienna, I sent Schubert's wife his camp address, and she certainly made an effort to do something for her husband. This, or my intervention in Moscow, may have been the reason why his situation worsened. Schubert did not get back to Germany until after Stalin's death. When he finally returned to his firm—which had moved to West Germany, as had his wife—he wrote to me that shortly after my departure from Moscow he had been transferred from Kayskii to the far north, where conditions had been much worse. The fur cap had been stolen from him while he was still in Kayskii.

With every transport—usually two or three per week—seriously ill patients were admitted to the infirmary, and so we knew that the victory of the Soviet Union had brought no essential changes. The prisoners merely hoped to be united again somehow with whatever members of their families still survived. We women wished above all to find our children.

More than a year had passed since the end of the war. What had changed? More and more prisoners arrived, and the number who died did not decrease. How many more patients—each with his individual fate—must I still come to know, only to have them vanish from sight? For how many more would I still have to close their eyes? We could expect less and less from liberation, and yet we longed for it with every fiber of our beings.

Finally the day arrived on which I was summoned to the camp administration. It was the end of September 1946. As usual, such matters proceeded slowly. For days I had to wait in the termination camp. Everything I heard there was more than bleak, for many could not return to their home regions or to those places where their families and relatives lived. Some first of all would have to set out in search of their children. Others, who really did not know where they should go, preferred to stay in the vicinity of the camp rather than to venture into a strange region where they had no security. Here they could at least find some kind of work and a place to sleep, and, most important, they were certain of their food-ration cards. I became convinced that I would not be permitted in the region where my child was, but I had at any rate decided to choose a place as close as possible to where Grigori was living.

In the club of the central camp I met Viktor once again. He still had more than a year to serve, and he was very depressed. His wife was dead, and he still had no information about his children. He himself, who had become a cripple, did not know where to turn, for he would not be permitted to go back to his home in Krasnodar. We spoke together for a long time and reminisced about Kita. We took leave of each other as good friends.

Everything that I had learned during these past few days was much worse than anything I could have imagined. When I was finally summoned, the first information I received was that I had been classified among the "special deportees." Thus I was to suffer the fate of all Soviet Germans, despite the fact that I had been an Austrian citizen until 1936. The worst blow of all, however, was the fact that I could not yet leave the region of Kayskii. I was assigned to the *sovkhoz* of the camp to help with the harvest.

When I learned this, I collapsed. I suddenly had a high fever and had to be taken to the hospital immediately. I had previously had severe headaches, which now became much worse. It was the beginning of a serious middle ear infection. During the eight years I had spent in camps, I had never really been sick before. Yet in spite of my high fever, I was permitted to stay in the hospital for only a few days. I was, after all, no longer a prisoner and therefore had no right to treatment in the camp.

Instead, I had to report to my place of work, the *sovkhoz*. How I survived the difficult journey with my baggage I cannot remember. The barbed wire enclosure had been removed from the *sovkhoz,* but we had to live in the same barracks and under the same conditions as before. To be sure, we were now paid for our work, but with this money we had to buy the same rations that had formerly been given to us. We had to get up just as early as in the camps and had to march to work. For me this was impossible. I was delirious for a whole night, and in the morning I was taken to the doctor, who had me transferred as quickly as possible to the central camp hospital. The only thing I can recall is that two nurses had to lead me to the doctor because I had so entirely lost my sense of equilibrium that I could not walk. It seemed to me that all hope was gone, but once again my good luck prevailed.

In the central hospital there was an aural surgeon, Dr. Pollak, a Hungarian, who had studied for several years in Vienna. He had formerly been a physician in the Kremlin and had been sentenced to fifteen years. To the great fortune of many persons, he had been assigned to this camp. It was he who made the correct diagnosis and shortly afterward performed a trepanation. He literally saved my life at the last minute.

I was in a state of complete collapse. Spiritually and physically exhausted, I lay for several weeks in the surgical wing of the hospital. Since there was no room in the wards, my bed stood in a corner of the corridor. Gradually I began to realize that I had to go on living. When my condition had improved somewhat, I was permitted to work in the therapeutic department. I was still classified as a convalescent and continued to sleep in the hospital. As far as possible, doctors and nurses looked after me.

During this time I met a Viennese woman who had worked in the hospital shortly before she was released. She was married to a Bulgarian who had studied in Vienna. After the German invasion of Bulgaria, they had fled to the Soviet Union, where, of course, they had been arrested. Her husband had been set free soon after the end of the war on the initiative of the Bulgarians, and he did everything he could to find his wife and bring about her release. When she left, she promised to try to find Austrian friends in Moscow who might be persuaded to use their influence on my behalf. I did not place much faith in her promise, but I hoped that at least she would send me names and addresses of persons to whom I could appeal.

Although the doctors were very considerate of my health, they finally had to yield to the pressure of the camp administration and dismiss me from the hospital. It so happened about that time that a nurse was needed for the infirmary of the camp administration. An infirmary employee, who lived in one of the barracks, shared her room with me. Beside the barracks there was a shed in which this woman kept a goat. Thus I could buy some milk every day.

In the infirmary I worked with a doctor who, as a former prisoner, felt as much out of place as I did. We were surrounded by mistrust, and even though not all the patients treated us like former prisoners, we could not forget that most of these patients were NKVD officers or their dependents. For me the situation had only one advantage: I could write as often as I wished. But I received letters no more frequently than before.

The first thing I did when I had a free day was to look up Maria Samoilovna and Maria Alekseyevna. As I had learned, they had also been released but had remained at the camp, where they were again working together. Now, however, they lived outside the compound enclosure. Maria Samoilovna was living with her daughter, whom her relatives had taken from the orphanage to stay with them and had now returned to her.

Although the primary purpose of my visit was to find out about Kita's manuscript, I had been looking forward with pleasure to seeing these women again, for they were two of the persons who had been most precious to me here in Kayskii. Maria Samoilovna was not at home, and Maria Alekseyevna was more embarrassed than surprised at my visit: "The book, well, the book simply disappeared from the pharmacy." That was a blow to me, but I had no right to reproach Maria Alekseyevna. I knew all too well what dangers she was exposed to. She was compelled to remain here for the time being because she could not return to her home, just as Maria Samoilovna was not permitted to go to her relatives. They had stayed in the hope that in time the situation would change and these prohibitions would be rescinded.

Still, I was terribly hurt to learn this, and I was deeply offended at Maria Alekseyevna's attitude. She did not even invite me in, and her embarrassment led me to doubt whether she was telling the truth. What else could I do but leave?

Sometimes I thought that Maria Alekseyevna might have found an opportunity to pass the manuscript to a Georgian who was released around this time and that she did not tell me so as not to endanger him. The Georgians always helped and supported each other, and in that case the manuscript would certainly have reached Kita's family. That the book could simply have disappeared from the pharmacy in Volosnitsa, as she told me, seemed highly unlikely, because she had always lived in the pharmacy and certainly kept it well hidden. If anyone had had the opportunity of removing anything from the pharmacy, many other things would have been of better use in the camp. Only persons who knew about the book could have been interested in acquiring it.

What seemed most likely to me was this: when Maria Alekseyevna decided to remain in Kayskii following her release, she destroyed the manuscript in order not to be burdened with it any longer. Yet I was not able to believe this either because she had greatly admired Kita and knew much about his scientific publications as well as about the manuscript. In order not to jeopardize herself, she had perhaps had no other alternative but to turn the manuscript over to the camp administration. After all, it had been well known that Kita was working on this book, because shortly before his death someone from Moscow had come to the camp to discuss the work with him.

Again poorer by one hope and burdened with doubts and

self-reproach—I still do not know to this very day whether I did the right thing in letting the manuscript out of my hands— I now had to go on living. Now I was a "free" person in the camp area. I had a more or less regulated work period and lived in the well-built residential area of the camp administration, in which there was even a theater. Among the prisoners there were many prominent artists—for example, the prima donna of the Estonian opera—who were all used for the purpose of offering the camp administrators metropolitan entertainment. I never set foot in this theater, but I did hear about the harassment and the humiliation to which these artists were subjected, even though they enjoyed certain privileges in comparison with other prisoners.

All this time I was in a condition of greatest tension, since I had to be very careful while at work. Even with my landlady, a simple, lovable soul, I could scarcely talk about matters that troubled me.

My stay in this privileged infirmary was of short duration, however. After just a few weeks, one of the leading NKVD agents of the camp was admitted as a patient. He noticed to his horror that there was a German-speaking foreigner employed in the infirmary. For the sake of vigilance I was transferred to the central camp hospital, which I had recently left as a patient. I was not offended by this, for here I was at least among my own kind. In the barracks (naturally outside the enclosure) I was assigned a place in a room already occupied by two women who had likewise recently been released. One of my roommates was a German acquaintance, whose release had taken place much like mine. She was more fortunate than I, however: she had a Latvian friend who was also to be set free soon, and the two planned to get married. The other woman was the pharmacist of the hospital, who had also chosen to remain here following her release in the hope that the stringent regulations would be relaxed and that she would be able to return to her family (these regulations were not changed until after Stalin's death).

As the last person to be assigned to this room, I did not even have a bed; I had to prepare a sleeping place with a straw sack on the floor. I really felt as though I were an annoyance, because the other two women had settled in tolerably well, and I made things a bit uncomfortable for them. But unfortunately, there was no other place available.

At the hospital I was enlisted for a task that was really very difficult for me. I had to serve as anesthetist in surgery, and this was something I had never done before. Furthermore, I did not tolerate the odor of ether very well. There were terrible injuries that had to be bandaged, and the dressing material was very scarce; we washed the bandages and used them again and again. And since we had no modern remedies for wounds, treatment required a long time. The patients suffered inexpressibly. We mostly had to deal with serious accidental injuries to workers in the taiga, with severe frostbite, and with scurvy.

Shortly after I began working in the hospital, I received a letter from my Austrian friends in Moscow. I had already given up hope that the Viennese woman married to the Bulgarian had kept her promise, but she really had taken pains on my behalf. The letter had wandered about in the camp for a long time before it finally reached me. I was beside myself with joy. This letter was the first real ray of hope in my more than desperate condition. My friends wrote unmistakably about the possibility of my return to my home. They had enclosed the necessary forms, and I began at once to fill them out. Naturally, I had already written to Grigori that perhaps I would soon come to get Ruslan if it should not be possible for me to live in their vicinity; I would have brought him here if I could have found lodging for both of us. But now I hoped soon to return to Vienna with my son.

Meanwhile, May 1947 had come. The camp administration

had assigned each of us a small plot of ground so that we might grow some potatoes and vegetables. This was done in the Soviet Union more than ever during the war years—there certainly was enough land for that purpose—and this measure made it possible for many to survive these difficult years.

At the beginning of June, just as I was about to begin planting potatoes, I was summoned to the administration and given permission to leave the camp area. I could travel by way of Moscow and pick up my son, but it was specified that I might live only in those areas designated for the Soviet Germans; even the request from Moscow had not changed this limitation. Therefore I chose as my place of residence the city of Buguruslan, some 200 kilometers from Kuybyshev. An acquaintance of mine, a Volga German, had already moved there, and of all the areas where I was permitted to live, it was closest to Moscow. I was given travel money, I had saved a little money, and I received my bread ration for a week.

The beginning of June was the time of spring floods, during which all roads became impassable. But the single-track camp train came near the hospital and the settlement in which I had lived. I took leave of my acquaintances and was envied by all. Dr. Pollak gave me the address of his wife in Moscow and asked me to look her up.

Berta, with whom I had once shared a room, accompanied me. We rode to the railroad station in Volosnitsa, where I had arrived four years previously. Now it seemed to me that I finally had to keep a promise I had made to myself: to find the place where Kita was said to be buried. Yet when we arrived at the station, hundreds of persons were waiting for the train, and I was informed that I still had to undergo a camp search here. Again I was forced to experience how helplessly the individual is delivered up to the mercy of despotism.

Perhaps it was assumed that I had some of Kita's writings in my possession. In reality, the NKVD agents exploited the possibility of selecting and stealing what seemed valuable from the possessions of the released prisoners. Thus they took underwear and bedclothing from the liberated prisoners in order to replace what they had stolen from the camps. In any case, they searched me thoroughly, ransacked all my belongings, and even stole a bedcover I still had from Austria as well as all the underwear and bedclothes that I had used and carefully taken care of all these years (in all this time I had received only one dress). All my protests and protestations were of no avail.

Berta was so horrified at the manner in which this was done that she returned to the camp at once and did not await my departure. I too was stunned at the shameless procedure that had been carried out in plain view of everyone. I had been treated like a thief even though all the things were my original possessions or fairly well-preserved, legal camp issue. Fortunately, I was not subjected to a close frisking, because as a precaution I had concealed all written material on my person; after all, they could not dismiss me completely naked.

Now that Berta was gone, however, I had no one to look after my remaining possessions. I was lucky enough to procure a ticket for the following day, and since I could not risk missing the train—I had no way of knowing whether I would be issued another ticket—I had to abandon my plan to look for Kita's grave site. I wanted to get to my child as soon as possible.

The train was overcrowded, but I managed to squeeze in. Among the passengers there were several who recognized me and spoke to me now and then, but I could not remember them. In general, the camp atmosphere still prevailed here in the language of the conversations. I scarcely listened, because my thoughts were completely elsewhere. I pictured to myself my reunion with Ruslan and our return to my home in Austria. How suddenly my situation had changed after all I had had to endure in recent weeks! All that I had hardly even dared to dream about had suddenly come into the realm of possibility.

Through the window I could now look at regions I had formerly caught only glimpses of through a barred peephole. We were again on the way to Kirov and then covered the stretch back to Gor'kiy, which I had traveled on the way from Sukhobezvodnoye. In Gor'kiy we had to wait several hours for the train to Moscow. I looked around in the city, walked along the bank of the Volga, and from there peered at the place where our barge had landed in the autumn of 1941. I thought of everyone who in all those years had been close to me and with whom I had endured such difficulties. Where were they all? What still lay before them? How many of them had already died?

One thing was clear to me: I would not really be free until I could again return to my home. Everything was still uncertain. But one thing at least seemed sure—that I would soon be able to press my son to my heart.

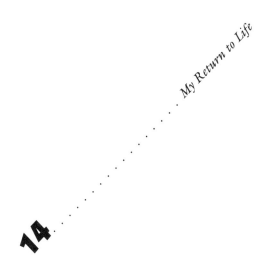

The train from Gor'kiy to Moscow left toward evening. Although the calendar said June, the weather was very cold as I forced myself into the overcrowded train. I was tired and yet full of suspense when I arrived in Moscow the following day. The Austrian friends, whom I looked up immediately, were astonished at my half-civilized appearance, but all who left the camps did so in rags and tatters. During all the years I had preserved my light coat, a skirt, and a blouse; and even though I had no real footwear, I was still halfway properly dressed. That I was nothing but skin and bones did not seem so extraordinary at a time when there were scarcely any well-fed people.

Again I had to fill out forms. My friends advised me to go to the Austrian embassy in order to expedite my return home. I took their advice and set off. My Austrian passport had expired in 1936, and it would have been difficult to have it extended under the circumstances of those times because of my earlier political activities. For political reasons I could not have returned to Austria at that time, and so I had acquired Soviet citizenship. The Soviet authorities had forced me to take this step by granting me only short-term residence permission and through other kinds of pressure. I explained all this to the people in the embassy, but they could do nothing to expedite my return. I left with a heavy heart.

My friends gave me some money and some food and also the advice to take up residence in a city not far from Moscow. But I could not make up my mind to do this. I was without documents—everything had been taken away from me when I was arrested—except for my certificate of discharge from the camp, and this certificate identified me as a special deportee with residence confined to Buguruslan. Even though I would have preferred to remain closer to Moscow, where I could have tried to help hasten my return home, what guarantee could anyone give me that I would not be penalized even more severely if I did not obey the orders of the NKVD? It was clear to me that the camp had alerted the NKVD in Buguruslan of my scheduled arrival. If I did not go there promptly, a search would be made for me.

My friends were also afraid that Grigori would not let me have my child, but they had nevertheless applied for permission for Ruslan to leave the country as well. I did not share their misgivings. I knew Grigori and Natasha, and I was certain that they could not bring themselves to deny me my son or to oppose his departure from the country.

Moscow was of no further interest to me. I settled matters as quickly as possible so I could get to my child as soon as possible. I had bought my ticket to include the stretch from Moscow to Borisoglebsk, because at that time one had to wait around for days at the stations in order to get tickets. I wanted to take a present along for Ruslan, but there was practically nothing to buy in Moscow. Finally in a secondhand bookshop I found Kipling's *Jungle Book* in a very beautiful edition.

I kept my word to Dr. Pollak and looked up his wife. She was also a physician and invited me to stay with her, although she already shared her room with another family. Her only son, who had contracted a serious spinal paralysis, was at that time in a sanitarium. I told her about her husband and explained to her what steps she needed to take in order to visit him. As the wife of a man sentenced to fifteen years in forced-labor camps, she did not have an easy life. When I took leave of her, I promised to stay overnight at her place when I returned with Ruslan. For the emigration permits I needed a photograph of my boy, and I could have him photographed only in Moscow.

My impatience was so great that I cannot recall anything about my train trip to Borisoglebsk, which was probably close to 500 kilometers from Moscow. It was afternoon when I arrived in Borisoglebsk. The weather there was already significantly warmer. It was a mild, sunny spring day. I left my baggage at the station, slung a pack over my shoulder (as we were accustomed to do in the camps), and set out. The "Red October" kolkhoz was several kilometers from Borisoglebsk. Through a small forest, past meadows turning green, I came into the village with a light stride. People looked at me in astonishment when I asked where Grigori lived. I knocked impatiently, but before there was even an answer, I had already opened the door. There stood Natasha, somewhat older and much thinner. She did not recognize me at first; it was only when I threw my arms around her that she realized who I was. Somewhere out of a corner of the spacious room came a pale, thin boy who looked at me with large, blue eyes— my boy, my Ruslan! But for him I was a strange woman. He had scarcely known me; it was only from letters and hearsay that he knew anything about his mother.

Now the moment had arrived that I had longed for all these years and anticipated in my dreams. I did not know what he had been told, what he imagined I was like, or whether he even reckoned with the possibility that I would return. He had never received any word from his father and certainly had little hope that he would ever show up.

Ruslan was a sensitive boy. He was unprepared for what pressed in upon him: my great joy and excitement. He did not know exactly how to behave toward me. In part it was shyness, and then again curiosity, yet all this did not suffice to bring him out of his shell. How different was reality from all the dreams and hopes I had cherished for years, but—it was reality, with all the joy of reunion and all the worries about what was still to come. I remembered a poem I had composed in the depths of the taiga, in the veterinary laboratory:

> And should I return to you as an old woman, my son,
> you will recognize me by my voice—
> And should my eyes go blind
> I will recognize you by your footstep,
> And by the trembling of my hands
> You will feel my concern for you—

Somewhat later Grigori came home, and I felt that he as well as Natasha behaved toward me as they formerly had. We spoke about Georgi, from whom they had never received a line, nor had they heard anything about him. After all these years none of us could believe that he was still alive. It would have been impossible for him not to have found a way to give us some sign of life.

I had to relate some of my experiences. They had not been able to understand why I had changed my address so frequently and why I had done nothing for Ruslan. They had not been able to imagine that I had had to travel so much from one camp to the other. They told me that they had been angry with me for writing to the kolkhoz, because they did not want anyone there to know about Georgi, and still less about me. For Ruslan's sake they had not wanted that, for fear that he too would have to suffer. They had been afraid that Ruslan might be taken away from them.

I had suspected the entire time that things were difficult for them. As long as they had lived in their native village, they had gotten along tolerably well. But when they had moved away, the war had just broken out, and with that, real destitution had begun for them. Yet as much as they regretted it—especially Grigori—they understood at once that I had to take Ruslan with me.

I could not stay very long with Grigori and Natasha because people here were truly suffering from hunger. I had brought some bread and groats along, because I did not want to consume any of the little food that they had. So I merely took Ruslan's few belongings and washed and patched them. I had also prepared a few things for him in my baggage.

Grigori was already very old and exhausted from toil. Both he and his wife had just turned sixty-three, and they had a difficult life behind them. Grigori still worked on the kolkhoz, and Natasha also worked there from time to time. They understood my situation all too well, however, and with heavy hearts they let me leave. I also knew that it would really be easier for them if I left than if I remained. The only thing they really owned was the cow, and even though she gave only a little milk—for poor harvests had left scarcely any fodder for the cows—nevertheless it had been this little bit of milk that had kept my Ruslan alive.

On the fourth day I took leave of these dear and close people. For them it was a painful separation from Ruslan. Grigori especially had become attached to him, for he had had no child of his own, and now he was losing his brother's son, whom he had reared and who was now quite a big and intelligent boy. Natasha went along to the railroad station and stayed with us until we had successfully struggled for our ticket. When we said goodbye, it was goodbye forever, although we did not know that at the time.

Again I was in Moscow, this time to complete all the formalities for Ruslan's emigration. There I really saw for the first time how weak and emaciated he was; we were invited for a meal by friends, and as simple as the meal was, Ruslan got terrible stomach pains from the meat and had to vomit. He was simply not accustomed to normal food. I was greatly worried, but his distress passed, and the rest of the food we got to eat in Moscow was not substantial enough to damage his weakened stomach. I went to the Moscow zoo with Ruslan. We again spent the night with Mrs. Pollak, and she and the family staying with her were very kind to Ruslan. Among the books belonging to Mrs. Pollak's son was Mark Twain's *The Prince and the Pauper*. Ruslan pounced upon it and at once became engrossed in it. He also enjoyed *The Jungle Book*, which I had bought for him.

Ruslan wished by all means to visit the Lenin mausoleum, so we went there and took our place in line. When we finally got to the entrance, however, I was told to check the little suitcase in which I kept all the valuables I possessed—above all, my notes and writings from the camps and Kita's letters. I had to let Ruslan go in by himself; rather than allow the suitcase to leave my hands, I preferred to forgo viewing the mausoleum.

Our stay in Moscow may have contributed somewhat to the fact that Ruslan became accustomed to me. I myself, however, was too full of concern and anxiety to be able to pay him the necessary attention; I hardly knew where we would stay and how we would live. Since I could not expect our gracious hostess to keep us one day longer than necessary, we had to leave Moscow several days later. We spent a whole day at the railroad station before I was able to get tickets. Finally, heavyhearted, we set out for an unfamiliar destination. My friends had again given me some money and food, and so we had supplies at least for the journey and for a few days more.

The trip to Buguruslan took more than one day. We crossed the Volga, not on the Trans-Siberian line but on the stretch from Kuybyshev in the direction of Ufa. Ruslan had been looking forward with great expectation to the bridge across the Volga. Until now he had not traveled much by train.

It was a Sunday afternoon when we arrived in Buguruslan. I at once looked up my Volga German acquaintance, for whom I had brought a letter from her good friend Berta. She was living

in a village situated a few kilometers from Buguruslan. She lived
with her sister, who, as a Volga German, had been mobilized
during the whole war for work service. With a large group of
such women she had worked in the oil fields, where she had to
perform the most difficult physical tasks. The two sisters spent
the summer with a peasant; the rest of the year they lived in a barracks with the other women. The peasant's house—or rather, his
cottage—consisted of a single room, but it had a fairly large loft
in which the sisters slept. They were quite dismayed at my visit;
everything they had to report about conditions here was far from
encouraging. There were large numbers of deported Germans;
those who were not housed in barracks roomed as subtenants.

Ruslan and I were put up for the night in a makeshift manner, but I set out the same evening to seek lodging among
peasants in the vicinity. After considerable searching I found a
Mordvinian who had a cottage with two rooms where Ruslan
and I could make a bed on the floor of the second room. This
house was incredibly filthy; the one in which my acquaintances
lived was scrupulously clean.

On the advice of my acquaintances I went that very same evening to see the doctor, who was also a deported German. The
doctors in Kayskii had written an excellent letter of recommendation for me so that I might perhaps find work as a nurse. But
this doctor was frightened. I understood at once that he would
not help me; everyone was afraid to do something for others
if he had the great good fortune of being able to work in his
professional field. All deported Germans were under constant
surveillance; they had to report to the NKVD once each month,
and the work they were assigned was also decided by the NKVD.
And so I went to the NKVD the following day. To all appearances
I was already expected. When I asked the agent to procure work
for me in a hospital if possible, he merely laughed mockingly.
The only work for me, he said, was physical labor, and that only
in the *sovkhoz* of the oil administration. When I asked him about

lodging for myself and my son, he merely shook his head. And so, in order to get food-ration cards, I had to accept work in the *sovkhoz.*

Provided with a work permit, I immediately applied for the food-ration card. For Ruslan I had received confirmation from the kolkhoz in Borisoglebsk that he had had a food-ration card as a pupil there. In good faith I left this confirmation with the official. When I returned several days later, as directed, to pick up the cards, the official to whom I had given Ruslan's confirmation denied having received it and gave me only a card for myself. With this I could get 600 grams of bread daily but not the 400 grams to which Ruslan was entitled. It was not until many weeks later, after Grigori had sent me a second confirmation, that Ruslan's food-ration card was issued.

What a life that was for both of us! I had to get up at five o'clock—after having slept little because of the bedbugs—in order to reach the local train that I rode to the *sovkhoz.* I could also take this train to return, but what I earned did not suffice to pay for a round trip. And so I learned something I never did before or since—fare dodging: that is, I moved constantly from one car to the other in order to evade the conductor. From seven o'clock in the morning until five in the afternoon, with a one-hour lunch break, I had to perform the most difficult tasks. There was only one advantage to this job: at noon one could get warm potato or vegetable soup for very little money.

Ruslan had to walk the ten kilometers every day so that I could share my soup with him; otherwise he would have had nothing warm to eat, nothing but a piece of bread. In the peasant's cottage where we lived I could not even cook anything, since the Russian oven was not heated until after I had left in the morning. Even the modest soup ration was not easy to get. The book-keeper of the *sovkhoz,* a Volga German, daily collected the money, distributed the coupons, and made certain that no one received a second bowl. But each time I implored her earnestly to sell me a bowl for Ruslan too. The boy was emaciated and had to remain alone all day with only a piece of bread to eat; what was one bowl of soup for both of us? According to the mood she was in, and with indescribable condescension, she sometimes sold me a coupon for the second bowl of soup. Of all the humiliation I had to endure during those years, this was the worst. Had it not been for my child, I would never have begged. As difficult as the work was for me, I performed it honestly and should not have found it necessary to beg. And the soup was not a gift; we paid for it. What little money I received was well earned.

Our situation could be endured no longer. When I succeeded in getting a place in the barracks of the Volga Germans, although the barracks consisted only of a single large sleeping room, a kitchen, and a laundry room, we were overjoyed to be able to live there. Here cleanliness prevailed, and the women were more or less nice to each other and especially to Ruslan. Here he was not alone all day. Even though we had only one bed, it was nevertheless a bed. And there was also a little chest beside it, and in the middle of the room were tables and benches. Most important, however, was the fact that there were no bedbugs. From here it was not so far to my work, and it would also not be so far for Ruslan to go to school.

But suddenly I fell ill and had to be taken to the hospital. I had come down with famine edema: my feet were terribly swollen, and I could scarcely walk. My boy was alone again. And so he came to the window of the hospital every day at noon, and I shared my lunch with him so that he would at least get something warm into his stomach.

I was not permitted to lie in the hospital very long. As soon as the swelling had subsided, I was ordered back to my old job. Whenever I had to report to the NKVD—that was once each month—I demanded to be assigned to some other kind of work.

In Buguruslan as well as in other schools in the vicinity, German teachers were needed. But the NKVD agent to whom I reported consistently rejected my proposals.

It was deeply moving to see how these Volga German women and other deportees had been compelled to live here all these years. In their heavy boots and rough men's work clothing, their faces roughened by wind and cold and their hands coarse and calloused, they were barely distinguishable from the men who worked in the mines or at road building. Many of these deportees were completely separated from their families; the men who were still alive were in forced-labor camps and the children were widely scattered. Because most of those sent here had been too young to be married, they had passed the most beautiful years of their lives between hard physical work and the barracks. During the year I was forced to spend here—it was already 1947–48—nothing had changed in their lives. Living here differed little from being in a forced-labor camp, though they could at least move about freely within the region of Buguruslan, and they did not have to live among criminals.

There were scarcely any arguments here, and there was no cursing. We all helped each other. Ruslan and I were happy to be able to live in the barracks after several weeks with the Mordvinian farmer, even though his family had been very friendly to us. Now, however, we could cook, and in the winter it was warm because natural gas was used for heating.

I had hoped to be here for only a few months, or at least that the emigration formalities would be taken care of before winter. But as autumn approached, though reports from Moscow were full of hope, nothing concrete happened. Ruslan again went to school. I had the bread-ration card for him now, and some money was sent to me from Moscow. In addition, there were already some potatoes and vegetables. But my work became more and more unbearable. When the harvest began and we had to work outside in the cold and damp, I had such a severe attack of sciatica that I could scarcely move. Again I was admitted to the hospital. But there was a young Russian physician on duty there who was eager to prove her worth and was ruthless in regard to deportees. After only a few days she dismissed me as cured, and so I had to go out into the fields again with my back twisted from severe pain.

For a while I was assigned to the threshing floor, where there were several Tatars among the workers. My pronunciation of Russian attracted their attention, and they always referred to me only as the *zhidovka* (damned Jewess). They arranged it so that I usually had to carry the heaviest sacks, although I had long suffered from an umbilical hernia. I began to protest this work with every means possible, but no one paid any attention to me. All this time I had to look on as the others stole grain. In spite of my hunger I did not yield to that temptation, because I did not want to run any kind of risk. Fortunately, this work soon came to an end. Winter came, and we now worked mostly in the cellars, sorting potatoes so that they would not rot. Then I also pocketed a few every day. We wore heavy clothing, and I always kept them so well concealed that they were never detected, even though we were all searched as we left work.

The nearer the spring of 1948 approached, the more impatient I became. I wrote desperate letters to Moscow. From Vienna I even received a food parcel and again some money, but that was not what was needed. Somehow or other Ruslan and I could now survive. I had received a *pood* of grain in payment for my work, and bread rationing had now been discontinued—though one had to line up early to be sure of getting a two-pound loaf; otherwise, it could be sold out, and then there was none until the next day.

When spring finally came, I decided to give up my work. My sciatica was worse than ever, all my joints ached, and my umbilical hernia caused me more and more trouble. I did not want to become a helpless cripple. So I returned to what I had done so often in the camps: I took up knitting and sewing for people. This way I earned almost as much as I had in the *sovkhoz*. I took payment in food and other provisions, and thus we could scrape by. Ruslan went to school, which he enjoyed very much, even though he had some difficulty in adapting in the beginning. Buguruslan was quite an industrial city; children of various nationalities lived there. For Ruslan everything was new. He was a serious, quiet boy who did his homework carefully, and he enjoyed reading as much as he could. Whenever I possibly could, I tried to obtain books for him.

The women in the barracks were very fond of Ruslan, and even though he could not understand their peculiar German dialects, the women all knew enough Russian so that they could exchange a few words. Rusland spoke only Russian, but I tried to teach him some German.

When we had arrived at Buguruslan, I had at once written to Kuznetsk to request a birth certificate for Ruslan. I had had all my documents with me when I was arrested, including his birth certificate, which, like everything else, was never returned to me. I could not possibly go back to Vienna with a child for whom I did not own a single document. Yet months passed, and I received no reply. In my desperation I wrote to the state attorney, but again I received neither an answer nor a copy of the birth certificate. I was not allowed to leave Buguruslan. How strictly this rule was adhered to can be seen from the fact that the NKVD official to whom I reported each month was dismissed from his position because two deportees had gone to visit relatives without permission. He had even been ordered to find them. The new NKVD agent was not so stupid as the one he replaced but all the more severe.

I simply did not know what to do. I wrote increasingly desperate letters to Moscow but got only reassurances in reply. It was already May when a telegram finally arrived: my emigration papers were ready, and I was to come to Moscow. What mockery—how could I go to Moscow when I would have been stopped at the station? Under no circumstances would anyone issue me a ticket. I ran to the post office at once and sent off a detailed telegram giving a comprehensive description of my situation and asking to be granted permission through the NKVD to come to Moscow.

Again several weeks passed. It was already 20 June 1948. I was so exhausted that I had scarcely been able to sleep at night; I finally had permission to return to my home, and I was unable to leave this place. I had no papers to show. The school year had just ended. I asked the educational authorities for a certificate for Ruslan, who had now completed the fourth level. Since there were no official forms on hand, the certificate had to be written on plain paper.

I decided to go to the district office again, through which I had requested a copy of Ruslan's birth certificate. Just a few days before, there had been nothing there. Our barracks district was located rather far from the center of the city, but after wandering about for a long time in my feeling of despair, I found the office. A miracle had happened: the birth certificate had arrived! My letter to the state attorney had helped after all. On the way home I had to pass the building of the NKVD. A young officer was standing outside the door. I did not know him, but he called to me: "Your permission to go to Moscow has arrived." My knees trembled. After another night of despair, miracles had happened.

I followed the officer into his office immediately. Finally I held in my hand this important document, which had been issued in Moscow. Then, while Ruslan was still at the school commencement celebration, I went to the office of the commander in control of our barracks; here too I had to report my change of residence. The commander's eyes opened wide when I presented the documents to him. He had never seen anything like that before. But everything was in order, and I at once received the necessary document verifying my permission to leave Buguruslan.

I had already told the few women who lived in the barracks that I was being permitted to leave, and the news had spread like wildfire. When Ruslan came home from school, he and I went to the bathhouse nearby, then came back and packed our belongings. I took only what was necessary for the journey and shared everything else among my friends. When we took leave of the women, they could still not quite believe that I was going home.

At six o'clock we were already sitting in the station, even though the train did not leave until nine. It was early the next morning when the local train arrived at Kuybyshev. We had had hardly any sleep because the train was so crowded. The station at Kuybyshev was stuffed full of people who, with bag and baggage, were trying to get their hands on tickets. Days might pass before I could get a ticket, because there was only one train daily to Moscow. With iron discipline I had saved enough money for the fare, but beyond that I had next to nothing. Now I went to the stationmaster and showed him my permission to go to Moscow, issued by the NKVD. Perhaps the man took pity on me, because I received a ticket with a seat reservation for the train that was to leave within a few hours (on main-line trains, seat reservations were required).

I sat in the station with Ruslan and was conscious of nothing else. It was exactly one year since we had come to Buguruslan. What a long and anxious year that had been! Ruslan could not possibly understand what this journey meant for me. He knew nothing except what he had previously seen and experienced. For him, even I was still a bit strange, different from the other people he had known up to that time.

For my part, I had little connection with anything that had made up his life. What he had experienced with me during the past year was new and unaccustomed and very sad. He could not imagine what he had to look forward to. He was surely pleased that we were returning to Moscow and that we would then undertake a long journey, about which he was simply curious. But of course he was still somewhat homesick for what he had left behind in Borisoglebsk. He missed Grigori especially. It may have pleased him to have a mother of his own, but during the past year I had been under such emotional stress that I was scarcely able to attend to my son, although I probably did more to provide for him than anyone else ever had. I was a harassed person, struggling against unheard-of adversity. It had incessantly been a matter of life and death in the literal sense of those words.

According to the terms of my notification, my return home was in the hands of the Red Cross in Moscow. I had hoped to arrange my trip in such a way that I could get to Borisoglebsk once more, which could only be done via Moscow; I had thought I might be able to take a train from there. But only those who know what was happening on all the railroad lines in the Soviet Union at that time can understand what an undertaking that would have been. The only document I had was permission to go *to* Moscow. To get permission to take the train *from* Moscow was out of the question. I could do nothing but write to Grigori that we were in Moscow and would soon be leaving for my home. As I learned later, Grigori and Natasha actually came to Moscow to see us off, but we had already left.

In Moscow, following the bath and disinfection, we went to the Red Cross immediately. I cannot say that we were received in a friendly manner. First of all I was asked under what charges I had been sentenced to serve in a forced-labor camp. Thus from the outset I was consigned to the place allotted to everyone who had had the misfortune of landing in the clutches of the NKVD. When I replied that I had been a detained family member, the woman became somewhat friendlier. She functioned as the head of the Red Cross on the order of the Central Committee of the Communist Party of the Soviet Union. Again I had to fill out endless forms. Then we were both directed to a hotel. What luxury!

I had to share the hotel room with six other women; Ruslan, already too old to stay with me, was quartered with the men one floor below. The men received the boy in a friendly manner, and so we quickly adjusted to this situation. I had also been given some money, and bread was not rationed; in Moscow all kinds of bread were for sale. There was sausage, too, which was really quite expensive, but we were able to buy a little, and we could get hot tea in the hotel. With the money I had received, I even managed to buy a decent pair of trousers for Ruslan.

Almost none of my Austrian friends were there any longer, but a woman whom I had met earlier had remained in Moscow to attend to Austrian affairs, and she treated me very well. Through her I received a shirt and a pair of good shoes for Ruslan, and from the Red Cross I got a dress and a pair of shoes—which pinched terribly, since my feet were no longer accustomed to good footwear. But now we looked a bit more civilized. I was not the only Austrian woman in the hotel. There were several others who had suffered fates similar to mine and were now being permitted to return home.

As I noticed very soon, among the temporary guests in our room there was also a woman who lived there permanently—a Russian, alleged to be from Sverdlovsk. I quickly discovered what her function was and was careful not to become involved in discussions that might in any way be compromising.

The NKVD headquarters in Buguruslan had given me an address and a telephone number to call from the building in which I had to register immediately after my arrival in Moscow. I did this the day after I arrived, and I was told where and when I had to report to the NKVD. It was clear to me that this was one of the highest agencies of the NKVD, and with a pounding heart I went there at the appointed time with Ruslan.

We sat for a while in a very elegantly furnished waiting room until I was summoned. Ruslan had to remain in the waiting room. I was received by a handsome man in the uniform of a high officer of the NKVD. I can no longer recall all the questions he asked me, but I asked him immediately about Georgi. The officer's answer was curt; he informed me that he knew nothing about Georgi and therefore could tell me nothing. Then I asked about the possibility of rehabilitation for Georgi and me. He energetically rejected such a possibility. Thus mercy was shown in permitting me to emigrate, but justice was not granted!

I had my little suitcase with me, which for understandable reasons I never left out of my sight. The officer asked me if I had any documents pertaining to the camps or to my deportation. I said I did not, but then I recalled that I still had the letter of recommendation that the doctors at Kayskii had issued to me before my departure. I was prudent enough to say nothing about my own writings or Kita's notes, but I showed him the letter, on which I had noted some train schedules and Viennese addresses. He found nothing objectionable in the document—which he did not return. How had I been able to enter the lion's den with the most important treasures that I possessed? On the other hand, where would I have been able to leave them?

Finally, the NKVD officer got around to his real reason for summoning me. I must clearly understand, he emphasized, that I must never and nowhere talk about what had happened to me. In my position I certainly had to promise this, all the more so since I was returning to a country that was occupied by the Soviets and since I could not begin to imagine how my future life would turn out there. I had only one thought: to get away as quickly as possible, for after everything I had experienced, I was afraid that something else might happen to prevent my departure from Russia.

Ruslan, who found Moscow very interesting, had no way of knowing what was going on in my mind. I had discovered that I was suffering from agoraphobia, a condition that persisted for a while even in Vienna. Had I not lived for almost ten years behind barbed wire in dense forests, or else under the close supervision of guards with their guns pointed at me? As soon as I came to a street intersection, or whenever I did not know what was behind me, I became uncertain, and sometimes I was overcome by something like vertigo.

I called on Mrs. Pollak once more. I wanted to know if she had visited her husband and if she knew what had become of some of my friends and acquaintances in Kayskii. Mrs. Pollak had actually been in Kayskii. For her husband nothing had changed, and as far as she knew, this held true also for the others, except for those who had served their terms. But she was very angry with me for not letting her know that her husband had a girlfriend in the camp. Naturally, "good friends" had told her about it. I tried to explain to Mrs. Pollak how things must be for a man in the prime of life just to vegetate without knowing what would happen to him from one day to the next. I told her that such friendships usually had nothing to do with one's own family and explained how fragile they were. But she really could not quite understand, and it saddened me that this matter cast a shadow over our good relationship.

By chance I recently discovered that Dr. Pollak has been back with his family and living in Budapest for several years.

Ruslan and I spent over two weeks in Moscow, frequently running to the Red Cross to check on our departure date. We had been photographed for our passports shortly after our arrival. I still have one of the pictures. Although we had already recovered somewhat from our hunger years, at that time we still looked rather haggard.

Finally, on July 7, 1948, an automobile called for us at the hotel at daybreak. We were handed our passports and driven to the airport. We flew in an American Dakota plane, which apparently came from the wartime deliveries. Most of the passengers were officers of the Soviet occupation forces; I was still surrounded by the military. Among the few civilians was Mrs. Bischof, the wife of the Austrian ambassador, with whom I carried on a casual conversation. How pleasant it was to hear words in the language of my homeland! In these surroundings Ruslan and I must have made a really wretched impression—though actually, we were scarcely even noticed. I had bought Ruslan a sketchbook and some coloring pencils, and he drew pictures full of fantasy. Some were drawings of the white clouds we could see from the airplane; others were of things he remembered. He enjoyed the flight in such a large, beautiful plane with all his childish heart and was full of suspense in anticipation of what was still to come. Unfortunately, we left the sketchbook in the plane when we landed.

At Lvov we made an intermediate landing, where we were served a warm lunch. Around the airport there were still signs of the war. Of the city itself we saw nothing. I was really not in the mood to take in all the details of this flight. I had to ask myself over and over again if it was not all a dream. But in the afternoon we actually did land at the Vöslau airport. I was in my home country again with my child.

After my return to Vienna it was not always possible to avoid mentioning among close friends various things that had happened to me in Russia. But scarcely anyone could comprehend what I had experienced; no one would have believed me if I had told the unvarnished truth. Much still had to happen, years had to pass before all that had occurred in the Soviet Union became comprehensible to people elsewhere. I too needed time to put my experiences in the proper perspective.

In no way did I feel morally obligated to remain silent, for those who have committed such grave injustices have the least right to exact a promise of silence from those they have wronged so grievously.

Spring 1967

Dearest, precious Zuza!

How fortunate that I have finally found you! How I have always wished to hear from you, to know that you are alive. Now that it has finally happened, I scarcely know what to say to you. I am that friend who was close to Kita during the last days of his life, and everything that has to do with Kita is precious to me even today. Only those who have endured what we had to suffer can understand what it meant to have a real friend in that terrible time, especially if that friend was Kita. You know who he was and what he was, and therefore you are and will always remain close to me even though I should never see you. But I do want to see you and Manana, and as soon as possible.

I have been able to preserve all the little notes and letters that Kita wrote to me during those days, but unfortunately not the most important thing he wrote—his second book. He completed it just before he died and had just begun to acquaint me with its contents. His death, which came so suddenly and unexpectedly, touched me so deeply that my mind was paralyzed. Many things were buried, so that it is difficult for me to retrieve and to express his ideas.

It seems to me, dear Zuza, that it would be better for us to discuss all these matters in person, or else that you write and inform me what you would especially like to know. At the moment I am still too overwhelmed at the thought of having found you. Throughout all these years I have been able to save one of your last letters to Kita despite all baggage and body searches. How often I have read it! Even if Kita had told me nothing about you, I would have to feel attracted to you because of this letter, and so all of this has become part of my own severely tried and tested life. Therefore I want to return to you the content of this letter, the words of which have probably long since disappeared from your memory.

Will you and Manana accept my heartiest greetings and good wishes. I want you to know that you are among the dearest and closest human beings to me.

Hilda

Enclosed, your letter:

My dear!

Your letter, which you intended to write on the day after you sent the postcard, has not arrived. And I could scarcely read the dry and brief postcard—as though it were not written by you—because it was so worn and faded when it arrived.

My dear Don Quixote! You have developed the very bad habit of asking questions but not writing anything about yourself. And so I know nothing about your activities. I do not know whether you are still in the bathhouse or whether you work somewhere else. I don't know if you are writing legends for your girls or essays on the Greek drama. Although I have not been able to read any of these essays, it makes me terribly happy to think that you are still obsessed by your old fascination for abstract ideas and theoretical problems. It would have saddened me if you had changed in this regard, but I believe that you are incorrigible and will never be like the philistines who wax enthusiastic discussing gastronomical questions.

It has been a long time since I received any letters from home, and from you I have only an uninformative postcard. I am well, but the lack of news from all of you—this is the only thing that can bring me to the verge of despair.

But do not worry about me. I am now working as a nurse. In this new role I am not exactly making great progress, but it helps me to keep going, to make life a little easier for others, and to dream of a reunion with my daughter and with you, my boy.

It is difficult for me to write to you when I have no news from you. I would so much like to talk to you, because writing is somehow difficult for me.

About four months ago I received a touching note from Manana. She always reports to me solemnly that she is on the honor roll and will soon appear in a concert. I am afraid that our relatives put too much emphasis on good grades and that she is not being reared strictly enough. But it is fortunate that she is surrounded with so much love and care. I hope that you will have the opportunity of seeing her before I do, and to give her the necessary attention, to protect her awakening thoughts from common, vulgar, and evil influences that threaten her in the environment in which she is growing up. Thinking of the atmosphere in which our child is living always causes me pain and sorrow for her youth as well as bitterness about the fact that we cannot give our child everything that was possible in Leningrad. Worst of all are banality, provincial manners, affectedness, and a superficial attitude toward work. Smugness and dilettantism and finally a lack of genuine and deep interest or knowledge. All the qualities you dislike, but which our daughter will inevitably acquire if she is deprived of your influence for very long. And I do not know what I wish for more—for you to be in freedom or for you to have our child with you. It seems to me that you can protect her mind and heart much better than I from the blatant affectation that pervades the environment in which she is growing up. How late does wisdom develop, and how wonderful when it is found in such a young creature as our daughter. I am not speaking of the wisdom of experience or the wisdom of the heart, which must be cultivated.

My dear friend, my dear gray-haired boy, write to me more often so that at least your letters will bring me a part of you. If you knew how much I long for you. The longer I live and the better I get to understand people, the closer and dearer you are to me.

Do not worry about me. I am getting along well, am healthy, neither sick nor forlorn. More gray hair and wrinkles, fewer illusions and teeth. This does not frighten me, however, if only we could see each other again. Write to me; I am waiting for your letters. I love you, think about you, and kiss you a thousand and one times.

Your Zuza

P.S. Greet your friend who writes poems as well as all others whose companionship brings you joy and adds beauty to your life in any way. I am looking forward to your letters.

Address on the envelope of the letter:
Kirov District, Kayskii Area
Post Office Volosnitsa
P/3321/1 Megrelidze K. R.

Stamp on the back of the envelope:
Inspected by the military censor 14175

Tiflis, 1967

Dear, dear Hilda!

Your letter made an overwhelming impression upon us. How great was our excitement; it was pain and joy at the same time. For Manana no less—perhaps even more—than for me.

How fortunate that we have found one another—or rather, that you have sought and found us, that you are alive and with your son, that you have such a warm interest in everything that is connected with Kita, and that you cherish his memory. This all seems like a miracle. I do not know when we shall meet, but I do know that you are one of the nearest and dearest persons for all of us, that is, for Manana, for me, and for my sister who reared Manana—yes, was more of a mother to her than I was. . . .

I returned, old and sick, in 1956. I worked, did translations of Georgian literature into Russian. Of my friends and relatives I found only a few. . . . Life is difficult for us here; it has not spoiled us with success and good fortune.

We were able to publish Kita's work in a limited edition, but only after long delays and with abridgments. Yet Kita's work lives. The publication of this book is also a chapter in our lives.

I hope that we will succeed in finding his last book. If we do, it will be thanks to you, my dearest Hilda.

I am now confined to the hospital because my heart is acting up. I have been lying here now for six weeks and am scheduled for some repair work in a few days. That is why I am writing in such a confused manner. Your letter was brought to me here.

I am firmly convinced that you and I will meet sometime. But who knows when that will be? Therefore I beg you to write us everything you know about Kita. I do not know what happened, why he died so suddenly. Had he been ill? Three persons have told me about him, but each one had a different story, so that we do not know the truth.

Kita wrote so many nice things about you. For this reason I have such a deep affection for and great gratitude to you, because through your friendship you enhanced and through your sympathy you warmed the evening of his life. He greatly valued your friendship. Kita had great difficulty in making friendships; I am certain that he would have been very lonely without you. Thank you, my dearest, for all you did for him and for preserving his memory during all these difficult years.

The little blue notebook containing the poems is here. I do not know how it got to us. Apparently someone from the camp gave it to my mother. Manana has preserved this little booklet like a holy relic.

I am looking forward with impatience to your letter, dearest Hilda, and with still greater impatience to meeting you, so that I can embrace you and so that we can talk about everything. Once again thank you for everything.

With warm kisses, Zuza Megrelidze-Kartsewadze.

In the summer of 1968 I went to Kapitsunda on the Black Sea in the vicinity of Sochi. Here Zuza and I met. I spent two days in Tiflis, where I became acquainted with Manana. She takes after her father in many ways.

In 1971 Zuza planned to come to Vienna for a visit. Before she could do so, however, she succumbed to a heart attack. When I met her in 1968 the traces of the fifteen years she had spent in the snow and cold of the far north, far from her southern home, were etched only too distinctly in her face.

Now she is no more and cannot read these recollections, to which she looked forward so eagerly.